THE STAGE IS SET

MILDRED ADAMS

Those who planned the Conference on Tensions in Development in the Western Hemisphere won extra values when they set it in Brazil's Salvador, Bahia. Other conferences called by the Council on World Tensions in earlier years have met in familiar centers —Chicago, Geneva, Oxford—but the knotted problems of the Western Hemisphere are best discussed where they exist most abundantly. In Brazil, these are the painful stuff of daily life.

In Salvador, a small and beautiful old city off the main air routes and free from too eager a press, these problems could be faced and discussed with frankness by men of many nations. The city itself sets the stage. Once the capital of the Portuguese empire in America, it is a microcosm of the extremes that beset the continent. Salvador is now the center of Brazil's new petro-gas industry; it is also the gateway to Brazil's turbulent northeast, and the portal through which refugees from famine flee to the better-fed southern cities. Salvador has its share of slums and slum dwellers. It also has a university which is strained by other kinds of tension, those of the young and growing who are hungry for knowledge to help them decide whether to accept the established but unstable order, or to move to change it.

Into this setting the Conference brought men, and a few women, from every continent except Australia, speaking English, Spanish, Portuguese, French or German. Their fields of knowledge included political and economic affairs, finance and education, industry, commerce, agriculture, labor, the church and the army. Among the seventy participants, two had been Presidents of Latin American republics, a number occupied important posts in national governments or international organisms, five held the rank of Ambassador; these, however, like all other participants, were invited as individuals in their private capacities as experts with special experience in various problems of development. Several were department heads from Bahia University, the center of Conference hospitality.

What absorbed the conferees was the tense and tangled stuff of modern life, the political, economic and social problems that directly concern the Western Hemisphere and that stir the rest of the world to anxiety. In order that all would be mindful of the fact that development is a global problem, shared in many ways by all peoples, six participants from different sections of the world were invited to open the Conference by presenting viewpoints on tensions in accelerating economic and social development.

B. K. Nehru of India commenced by observing that "Perhaps the most important distinguishing feature of the times in which we live is the determination of two billion people to move themselves rapidly from past ages of history into the twentieth century. History has known of migrations, big and small, over space; never before has migration taken place on so colossal a scale over time. . . . international tensions caused by this great migration are felt in both the political and the economic fields. . . . Although one great cause of international political tension, colonialism, is disappearing from our midst . . . international economic relations leave much to be desired." Within countries, "societies which for centuries have remained unchanged tend naturally to develop a static system of power relationships. There is usually a small élite . . . together with a vast mass of underprivileged citizenry whose voice has negligible influence. . . . Development needs the energy of the entire population and its harnessing requires a revolutionary change in the power relationships. . . . In the economic field a system of distribution in which the many produce and only a few consume must be changed." This static system can no longer contain the "headlong rush into modernity"; the changes needed to meet the changing world are as inevitable as they may be explosive.

From a nearer continent, Godfrey Amachree of Nigeria spoke of "cultural, ethnic and religious affinities between the peoples of Africa and those of some of the Latin American countries." Though the Negro came to the Western Hemisphere "in rather unfortunate circumstances," many of the ex-slaves who returned to Nigeria took back trades such as masonry, carpentry, bricklaying, cabinet making, and tailoring. They played an important part in the social and economic life of Lagos. They provided the masons and carpenters who were responsible for the construction of cathedrals and churches, not only in Lagos but also in Dahomey and the Gold Coast.

Yet, "the emancipation of the Negro slave in the West does not appear to have materially altered the status of his descendants everywhere. . . . I understand that here in Brazil the descendants of the emancipated slaves enjoy the full rights of citizens. If this is true, we may wish to discover how Brazil has overcome the problem.

"Two other sources of tensions, especially in the underdeveloped countries, are corruption and subversion. In the wake of the flow of foreign capital there is often the despicable practice by some unscrupulous foreigners of corrupting highly placed government and other officials."

Then follows "the reluctance of well-meaning foreign investors to be associated with countries having corrupt governments. The tensions caused by corruption can be detrimental to a country, not only in disrupting its stability but also in driving away badly needed foreign capital for development.

"On the matter of subversion, foreign aid is fraught with political considerations. Aid which is conditioned on the acceptance by a government of a foreign political system is no aid, it is a bribe.

"Where a government is stable enough to resist foreign political pressure it usually discovers that some of its citizens are employed by foreign powers as agitators and agents of subversion. Many underdeveloped countries are confronted by this problem.

"What is the solution to these problems? Admittedly, part of it lies with the integrity of the leaders of the underdeveloped countries. Also, foreign investors and countries giving aid can, to a large measure, help stamp out these evils. There can be no bribery if there are no bribe-givers."

In between Asia and Africa, the gentle voice of Hazem Nuseibeh of Jordan also spoke of cultural values and "the increasing awareness concerning the interrelationship of development and technology, on the one hand, and of social philosophy and organization on the other. We thought earlier that the Arab world need only take those mechanical and scientific techniques which would enable it to operate the economy upon a higher level of energy and efficiency; its cultural values need not be unduly disturbed in the process. We have travelled a long way from this oversimplified and innocent approach."

He warned that "the problems of want and the desire for betterment are among the greatest forces in our lives today. They concern each and every community, as well as the comity of nations." At the same time he declared: "While I fully understand those in my part of the world who state that democratic freedoms are largely meaningless without economic emancipation, I do hope that we would show an equal appreciation of the fact that economic progress would be too high a price to pay if it should lead to a loss of political freedoms.

"In the Arab world, a catastrophic break in social continuity occurred during the past several centuries, with the result that not only do we import new technology but also new ideas which, in many instances, tend to intensify the dislocations of a rapidly changing civilization."

José A. Mayobre of Venezuela saw the contemporary world in general, and Latin America in particular, suffering from three sources of tensions: (1) "The breakdown of the colonial system" which has left Latin America with an out-dated social structure that kept the Latins from participating in the nineteenth century industrial revolution; (2) "The growing disparity between the income of a minority of rich countries and that of a majority of poor countries," a disparity which in Latin America is crucial; (3) "The conflict between an ideology based on private enterprise and one founded on regimentation and political and economic centralization." From this conflict the Latin Americans have escaped until recently, but the "presence in the hemisphere of a country organized on extreme socialist lines has made some people think that the solution to economic underdevelopment and political inferiority lies in the violent revolution that leads to a centralized state. The intensification of the ideological battle has brought a sharpening of tension in the political fields both internally and internationally. . . . However, not all is darkness in the Latin American scene. We are now an experimental station for an unprecedented international fight against poverty and underdevelopment. The Alliance for Progress is a valuable step forward in the removal of obstacles to economic and social progress," although "some doubts and worries have emerged as to what has been achieved so far . . . The answers produced here may provide useful lessons not only for the American hemisphere but also for those other underdeveloped countries that are so rightly observing our work."

An expert voice from the UN was that of Paul Hoffman, who expressed his certainty that the goals of the UN Development Decade and the Alliance for Progress can be reached if "all nations work together in concert. Each nation must, of course, develop its own program and have primary responsibility for carrying it forward. But it must not expect to achieve its goals at the expense of its neighbors. Only by cooperating with other nations in its region or hemisphere can it succeed. Similarly no regional or hemispheric plan can be carried out in isolation; all nations must go forward as partners. . . . May I add that no country is so poor that it cannot help another country, and no country is so rich that it cannot benefit from an expanding world economy . . . Donor nations should not think of assistance as charity. There are compelling political reasons and sound business reasons for extending aid. From the standpoint of maintaining peace in the world foreign aid expenditures are second only to expenditures for defense. While external aid has a vital role to play, the main impetus toward economic growth and social betterment must come from within the country itself. . . ." He also pointed out that before development can be properly financed "the increased financing nesessary for adequate pre-investment work should be made available at once. There is no dearth of capital for sound development schemes—but to attract investment we must define more specifically the natural resource and production possibilities of modernizing countries. We must also step up the training of technicians—an essential part of a pre-investment program." All sources of external assistance have their part to play and some of them are complementary, but "there is a very pressing need to establish criteria for determining the best channel through which aid should be provided, and we should use the channel that will produce the most effective results at the lowest cost. I believe that if this test is used, governments will channel an increasing amount of their assistance through the United Nations. . . .

"Over and above the compelling political reasons and the sound business justifications for making a success of the United Nations Development Decade and the Alliance for Progress lie profound moral reasons that none of us can afford to ignore. Secretary-General U Thant has put it this way:

Can our imagination match our abundance only when the ugly, destructive risks of war are at work? Is the only challenge that of fear —in weapons, in outer space, in international rivalry? Is there no way in which the great constructive and peaceful purposes of man can so grip our heart and conscience that the spending needed to end starvation, to prevent the death of little children, to shelter the homeless and clothe the naked comes to have first priority in the purposes of the human race?"

To the variety of comments coming from such different points of view, Milton Katz of Harvard added the shrewd and pertinent observation "that despite all the advances of science, it still requires nine months to produce a baby, and babies are still unable to read, write, talk, walk or feed themselves. Roughly two decades of growth and training are required to transform a baby into a man or woman educated to the level represented by the first university degree, and additional years are usually necessary to develop and refine him" into a valuable professional expert. It takes time, yet today's people are in a hurry. "The mood of insistent and demanding restlessness breeds popular indifference, disdain or hostility toward the kind and duration of effort required to produce the qualified men and women who are needed for development." The result is frustration and tensions, which "bear profoundly upon contemporary international relations."

Against the background of these disparate points of view the Conference moved to its week of debates on tensions between and within countries and the basic preconditions for development. In order to establish a common background of knowledge against which debate would be engaged, technical papers had been prepared; these form the substance of this volume. In the course of the debate the general subjects of the Conference fell into three principal areas of interest—Latin America in the Western Hemisphere, concerned with tensions between nations; internal tensions and preconditions for economic and social development; and the relationship of Latin America to the European Common Market.

The discussions were informal, off-the-record, always illuminating and sometimes exciting. They formed, however, only the most visible of the Conference values. Hours of personal experience and responsible thought lay behind them, long private conversations were larded between them. The casual words exchanged around a breakfast table or over a late drink proved sometimes as valuable as the thoughtfully measured speech.

As in other conferences held elsewhere by this Council, the essence of the Salvador interchange was, on a very high level, an exercise in mutual education. If prejudices were aired and frustrations uncovered, the Conference members were the gainers. It was openly agreed that a meeting of this kind benefits most when speakers are allowed to give tongue to worries which can only be formulated in a friendly and favorable atmosphere.

The general Conference topic, Tensions in Development in the Western Hemisphere, was prickly in itself, and pregnant with controversy and misunderstanding which emerged more sharply in discussion than in background papers. International tensions ran most vigorously north and south, between Latin America and the United States. Disagreements between Canada and the United States were mentioned, but old and familiar border disputes between various southern countries lay unremarked for the day.

The degree of bitterness revealed in the longitudinal give-and-take shocked many participants who had known in theory that relations between the two American continents were not happy, but had not been prepared to see them approaching the fever point. Yet the explosive moments had their values, if only in revealing danger points and in convincing the listeners that the situation must somehow be eased.

However, because there were Africans and Asians, Europeans and Canadians at the same table with Latin Americans and North Americans the issues did not appear so exclusively as a north-south conflict of interests. It was important for Latin Americans to discover that some African and Asian leaders did not fully share their views and were, in some respects, closer to the points of view of the Americans and the Europeans.

The mutual interest of the Latin Americans and Western Europeans in their changing relationships, the impact of the European Common Market and potential aid from Europe helped to put old conflicts into a new perspective. When and if Latin America can escape from its feeling of undue dependence on the United States and experience a greater degree of aid and understanding from Europe it will be more at peace with itself as well as with its northern neighbor.

The amount of information on modern problems in Latin America, and the depth of scholarly analysis with which these were handled is apparent in the papers published here. It would, of course, be impossible to expect seventy people from such diverse backgrounds to agree on anything more disputable than the warmth of the Brazilian sun or the beauty of the bordering beaches; no such agreement was sought, nor was there any attempt formally to adopt recommendations or resolutions based on the opinion of a majority. The important ideas and conclusions which emerged in the discussions, however, are summarized in the concluding chapter of this book.

There were cross-currents and overlappings in debate as the crowding immediacy of the subject would not be denied. The most repeated of these were the values or evils of nationalization and of inflation, the pressures of rapidly multiplying populations, the desirabilities of closer association between Latin American countries, and the role of the Alliance for Progress. This latter development was considered with caution by all three groups, and warnings were frequent that a structural change of the type foreseen at Punta del Este and the new kind of hemisphere cooperation it involves cannot be achieved overnight. What has already been done, or begun, should in no way be underestimated.

Finally, the question was raised as to whether the institutional development of the Western Hemisphere, in terms of both the creation of common markets and free trade areas, and of the Alliance for Progress, was not tending to set up a closed political and economic system in the New World, thus leading to a weakening if not a severing of traditional ties with Europe. The very idea of such severance roused vigorous denial within other groups, and the sessions closed with a clear indication that what Latin America desires above all is to be considered an active, responsible and respected part of the world economy. Only in a multilateral world can tensions between south and north substantially subside.

The inevitability of this multilateral world was stressed by Albert De Smaele of Belgium, who said: "Development is becoming less and less of an internal problem, localized or regional. Internal and external problems have become intertwined, they flow into each other. Reabsorbed into large continental units, countries will soon see their foreign policy carried on at a continental level. These regional or continental units in turn will have to recognize that they carry global responsibilities. At that point, global cooperation will require intellectual and material resources on the same scale as the attempts made by each of the continental groupings to solve its internal problems. While allowing each region to adopt the structures which suit its particular development, this cooperation will really and effectively thrust all regions into the great current of international exchanges.

"Shall we know how to make this leap? The question is political. It is a matter of whether the peoples, eager for peace, will succeed in giving themselves governments capable of assuring them of peace.

"What are the signs of the times—the encouragement or fear to be drawn from world events of the last twenty years? We call it a period of cold war because of the opposition between two great political and economic regimes, but even during this period we have been able to accomplish the immense revolution of decolonization. Hardly fifty years ago events such as Korea, Suez, the Congo, Algeria, Berlin or Laos would have triggered a general war. The antagonists deserve credit for having stopped short of general conflict and the United Nations deserves credit for its contribution toward persuading them to do so. All of this must be considered as encouraging; but the hour has come when nations must do more than postpone war until a later date."

THE ESSENCE OF THE PROBLEM

LESTER B. PEARSON

*Leader of the
Liberal Party, Canada*

Tensions are inevitable and not all are bad. Indeed, progress without tensions is unachievable, and tranquillity, on the same basis, is undesirable.

Equally impractical and contrary to all the lessons of history are neatly packaged formulae offered as instant cures for undesirable international tensions. Those who press them on us do little good for the cause of peace or progress. They would merely take our minds off the complex day-by-day problems, which can be adjusted only with effort and which must be lived with until the adjustment can eventually lead to a solution. This process of adjustment to the requirements of democratic development, or of good neighborhood, can never be easy or simple. There are no patent medicines to cure our troubles by a few doses, though there are many to conceal their symptoms.

We are a long way from achieving the idyllic state of world brotherhood. Meanwhile, there will be conflict, competition, and tensions—even between men of good will. It is not their elimination, but their control and challenge that we have been seeking.

In this search, we must begin with the fact that relations within and between states are changing more rapidly than at any time in history. They will continue to change and the pace will not slacken. We cannot stop this process, even if we wished to. The tensions that inevitably result from such rapid change are not all the work of wicked men, though wicked men—the tyrants and totalitarians—can, and do, exploit them.

In our hemisphere—particularly in the Latin American part of it—the ardent champions of nationalism, or of change, of equality, or of social justice, often increase these tensions because they feel more strongly than less passionate people. It is futile to ask them to be quiet in the name of peace and order. Those who denounce such people as tension-makers are quite right. Yet the denouncers have often themselves created, by their insistence on an established order, on tranquillity based on inequality and injustice, those very tensions which they denounce.

Tensions, then, are neither good nor bad in themselves. Moreover, when they become neurotic and menacing, their removal cannot any longer be brought about by the kind of force and fighting that could be effective, if only in a temporary sense, even a century ago. The atom and outer space have changed all this.

There is only one thing to do. Liquidate, or render harmless, dangerous tensions by pressing toward a world of peace, with freedom, justice, and a decent life for all. We must seek the establishment, and the general acceptance, of processes for political adjustment of disputes and for the upgrading of life, as absolutely essential for the easing of tensions without violence.

The complexities of international relations, economic and political, in this hemisphere are obvious. They will be unraveled only if the best minds in all our countries work together for this purpose; if we give up the futile pleasure of scoring points, rejecting attitudes of critical superiority on the one hand or critical suspicion on the other.

This will require a great and sustained effort. We of the industrially developed countries, the comfortable countries, have some reason to fear that we may not be equal to the test. Similarly, a feeling of frustration and impatience grips governments and people in the less developed countries who are determined to catch up, but who are often unable to match their desires with their efforts.

In the face of the agonizing complexities of such a situation, the temptation is strong to self-deception and wishful thinking, to feverish and aimless movement as an escape from harsh perplexities. By increasing our speed in the familiar political and economic grooves, by shouting the same old slogans, we seek to reassure ourselves that things will continue more or less as they have been, though we are aware that this is now impossible. We know that we must make fateful decisions. Yet we are often quick to denounce each other's views of what those decisions should be, if only to conceal our inability to make the right ones ourselves. Indeed, we sometimes doubt whether anyone really knows how we should act to be saved. We cling to a mystical belief that our democratic system, in spite of its limitations for emergency action, will show us the way and give us the means. Yet we are troubled by doubts that we will not have the sense of purpose, sacrifice, and self-discipline which is essential to the effective operation of democracy and which alone will enable us to take the hard and speedy action necessary for progress, security, and even survival.

There is no assurance today of survival, let alone security and progress. This is because of the two great gaps in our world, the two great chasms in which, if they are not bridged or closed, humanity will be lost.

The one is the gap between moral and material progress, between man's scientific genius that split the atom and conquered outer space and the idiocy of his social and political behavior in the face of these revolutionary changes.

The other gap is that between the poor and the rich, between the developed and the developing countries. We can be lost in this gap, too, because the tensions it creates could result in the explosions that destroy.

At least we now recognize this second gap, and its implications. Moreover, our nations are pledged to do something about it. This is one pledge we should keep. It attaches to all nations, rich or poor, developed or underdeveloped, whatever their circumstances. The obligation, of course, must be discharged in different ways. No nation, however, owes anything to any other nation which does not discharge the obligation it owes to itself.

In this hemisphere there are great extremes of wealth and poverty, of development and underdevelopment. This applies within and between nations. These are two aspects of the same problem—and the domestic is as important as the international. It is inadmissible, for instance, that the annual per capita national income of a Latin American country should be less than $200, while that in the United States is over $2,000. It is also disturbing to compare, inside a state, the magnificence and the cost of a new factory with the primitiveness of a new primary school; to learn of the amount of electric power available for the factory, and that there is not enough of that power in the school to run the film strips that are important in education.

Disparities of this kind, within or between nations, are dangerous. Where they exist, there will be tensions arising out of insecurity, instability, impatience. Their justification and their continuance, irrespective of their origins and causes, are no longer to be tolerated by civilized men or nations. However, we may take comfort from the fact that, for the first time in history (and this is often forgotten), the richer and industrially developed countries—most importantly the United States—now accept their obligation, as an international commitment, to help reduce and eventually close this gap.

How to make real progress in this great undertaking in the Western Hemisphere is surely more important than disputes over responsibility for its necessity and suspicions based in part on differing assessments of that responsibility. A basis of partnership has now been established in the great effort required. It would be more than a tragedy if the structure of such collaboration—I think particularly of the Alliance for Progress—were weakened, even destroyed, by lack of understanding or by mismanagement.

This unhappy result is, unfortunately, possible. A great initiative, noble and generous in concept, may be frustrated, not so much by a calculated assault on it by men of ill will for the furtherance of their own designs, but by carelessness, or a lack of understanding of the implications of genuine partnership, or even by failure to establish and communicate its purpose and its hopes—its mystique, if you like.

These dangers to cooperation for progress can be removed if, on the one side, exaggerated suspicions and oversensitiveness are avoided; if, to be specific, the generous policies of the United States are recognized, even if they are at times obscured by mistakes in method, or in mood. On the other side, it is vitally important to realize that attitude is even more important than aid; that grants do not necessarily mean, nor should they be expected to mean, gratitude; that an Alliance for Progress should not be confused with an alliance for military defense. It should also be accepted that good neighborhood in this hemisphere rests on the full acceptance of all the implications of partnership.

There is so much more than materialism in these tensions between rich and poor nations that they will not be eliminated, or even substantially reduced, merely by reducing the gap between standards of living. The spirit in which help is offered—and received—is as important as the help itself. So there should be a feeling of full participation on the part of all concerned. This may require taking certain risks, even sacrificing some aspects of efficiency, in the interest of full and acknowledged partnership. It will be worth it.

It is well to remember, also, that the positive effort to cooperate for progress, by joint operation of schemes for development, is bound to cause some tensions when so much in the way of material help is coming from outside, from the richest and most powerful country in the world, a country whose policies in the past have often created fears and resentments. There will be a feeling of dependence even when the theme song is interdependence. The word "intervention" has a bad sound even if it is for salvation. (The brave young man who jumps into the angry waters to rescue the beautiful maiden usually wants to marry her—or worse). Even in a tolerant, understanding, rich, and highly developed industrial nation like Canada, there is some uneasiness that we may be selling our pure Canadian soul for a mess of American pottage—or, in this case, United States dollars.

But it is not so. If we cannot protect our soul against this kind of financial pressure, it will not be so very pure and we will have only ourselves to blame. Meanwhile, I hope the dollars keep coming and I know that we will put them to good Canadian use for Canadian development.

So I beg of you, my Latin American friends, be careful; but don't misjudge the Americans. They are a wonderful and generous people—the least imperialistically minded people that ever had world power thrust on them. They have made lots of mistakes and will make lots more. So have we, the other countries of the hemisphere. If our mistakes are smaller ones, it is only because our countries are smaller. Remember, also, we can always blame the Americans for our own mistakes. This is another indispensable service the United States performs. We should not, however, presume on it too much.

More seriously, we should not expect quick and dramatic returns from a cooperative effort for hemisphere development. Perhaps an operation like the Alliance for Progress has already created too many illusions of spectacular results. I have heard the opinion expressed more than once that it has been oversold. But that is understandable. It is a political initiative, and political proposals, to be sold at all, must be oversold—especially to Congress or other legislative assemblies which provide the money.

It is also understandable that the leaders and the people of materially underdeveloped nations should be impatient for quick economic returns. There is, however, no way to ensure these, or any magic method by which they can be achieved through foreign aid alone. Even the most generous measure of such aid can only be marginal.

There is another problem that is full of potential tensions. Who is to be worthy of such aid? Must governments be reformist and democratic to qualify for membership in an Alliance for Progress club? Is the alliance to be one for democratic progress, or one merely for progress? Should the dictator not only be denied the embrace, but should the handshake be goodbye? I leave this problem to the OAS—in membership in which my country has become increasingly interested—and to the United States of America.

Here again I feel rather sorry for Canada's nearest neighbor. In this matter, they are bound to get into trouble, whatever course they follow. You cannot buy friends with aid, nor can you ensure democracy by withdrawing or refusing it. In any event, this would be a form of American intervention, and that is taboo. But if you help a dictator, are you not betraying democracy? I can only suggest that this problem be treated as a collective one, and that the solution to each manifestation of it should be taken collectively. There is nothing like a dispersal of responsibility in such cases.

One other very important matter was stressed in our discussions here: that Western Hemisphere problems and tensions— both political and economic—cannot be separated from those of the rest of the world.

Latin America, for instance, cannot escape the consequences of the Cold War, or of United States leadership of the free world coalition in that war. Yet this situation should not require— though it may result in—the linking of active collaboration in defense measures against the Communist menace with participation in any cooperative effort for development and progress. There is, however, a corollary to this. While you cannot buy friends and allies, or at least sincere friends and reliable allies, nevertheless no country has a right to share in the economic benefits of collaboration if it is actively working against that collaboration or working for others who are dedicated to its destruction.

Few of the economic problems and tensions of our hemisphere can be solved by hemispheric action alone. The development of the European Common Market is a good example of this. Europe is uniting. This *could* mean discrimination and diversion of trade, rather than the kind of expansion in which all countries of good will could share. We have been assured that the latter was the European objective, and that it could be, and would be, achieved. It is to be hoped so. Otherwise, an inward-looking, protectionist, discriminatory European Community would force Western Hemisphere countries to seek a hemisphere solution, which would likely be restrictionist and discriminatory.

This regional fragmentation of the free world would be a very unhappy development—politically and economically. No one could gain from it except those who wish to see our free democratic systems destroyed.

What is required is a recognition of the historic and positive significance of these European developments, and the necessity for their broadening on the economic side to include other countries in some appropriate way. This requires a positive and understanding attitude on both sides of the Atlantic. Instead of following the negative course of merely complaining about the problems raised by European success in building its own Community, the Western Hemisphere should establish close association with that Community and press hard for a better organization of markets in *all* parts of the free world; for world agreements, in particular, on agricultural products which would be fair to all producers and to consumers.

Latin America, as a community of its own, could even initiate such an approach. It should be taken now before the new patterns of the new European Community begin to set, or before other measures are advocated by those who have no constructive purpose in view and who would like to confuse the issue.

I think that North America would welcome such an initiative, looking to some broader economic association than the European Common Market. It would certainly reflect and strengthen the concept of interdependence which is as easy to laud in theory as it is difficult to work out in practice, but which is the only principle that makes any sense today. I believe also that such an initiative would be welcomed by the democracies of Asia, Africa, and Australasia, and, finally, by the Western European nations themselves who are providing the model from which we must build.

One other question is whether our system of free and representative democracy is equal to the tensions that come from development. Certainly the effort to meet the challenge of these tensions within the democratic concept is going to cause some disorder. In the process of achieving the quickened progress now demanded, there may even have to be restrictions and modifications of the democratic system as we know it in some of our comfortable countries. We must never, however, in order to achieve goals, think in terms of putting the clock back or of looking for alternative forms of rule, which history has shown to be, in the long run, both unstable and unworkable, and servile.

Developing countries today—under the furious urge to get ahead—often tend to be more disciplinarian in practice than those with longer established societies and more stable economies. It is foolish for us to expect such countries to show the economic flexibility and political give-and-take that are possible only after slow and prolonged development. The important thing, the essential thing that we want to preserve and *must* preserve within all our institutions is a respect for freedom and human rights; adherence to the rule of law, and to that spirit of tolerance and free enquiry which alone makes material progress worth-while. Without these, cooperation between states, for development, will be very difficult.

The Russian Communists faced this problem of the political control of forced development with relentless logic and ruthless methods. They decided to shut their people off from other and more prosperous people in the world and to lift themselves up by their own bootstraps, at any price. During this period, no citizen would be allowed to abandon his allocated task in the total, grueling endeavor. The verdict is not yet final, but the Russians seem to have shown that harsh methods can be effective in a limited and purely practical sense. People can be drilled and forced to accept austerity, to forego the immediate consumer pleasures in order to invest in the future, *provided* all easier alternatives are denied and force is used to make sure that the denial is observed.

Democracy is not the only form of government that gets immediate material results, but the price to be paid for the totalitarian alternative is too high to be acceptable to men who cherish freedom. However, and this is the point of importance, it is not necessary to pay that price in terms of political tyranny. The austerity which the British and some other West European peoples imposed upon themselves in the decade after the last war in order to invest in the future, and the remarkable resurgence of the West European economy after the destruction of war, have shown that parliamentary democracy is capable of the necessary self-discipline when it is required. It has been able to meet challenges and crises without the compulsions of total dictatorship.

There is little wonder, however, that new and underdeveloped countries are often impressed by the Soviet example of forced growth, even if not one of them has yet accepted it voluntarily as a model. The attraction of what seems to have been a dramatic material advance, combined with absence of those suspicions and tensions that can come from direct contacts and from historical association, can be a powerful combination. It has undoubtedly had a strong effect on many Latin Americans—especially young people. It creates a problem that cannot be solved merely by lashing out against Communist subversion but only by showing, not merely by words but by results, that there is a better way for progress.

I have a far better understanding of those problems than I had when I arrived for this Conference. I hope that we are now in a better position to utilize any opportunity we may have to do something about them. But I am also profoundly disturbed over what will happen to Latin America if something is not done, and done with all possible speed and effectiveness, to meet the challenge of the "revolution of rising expectations" which dominates the Latin American scene.

Time is against us in this effort because the growing consciousness that poverty and degradation are not to be tolerated has produced an angry impatience which is inflammable.

It is now a race between evolution and explosion.

River Plate in 1825, and in the British-French-Spanish expedition against Mexico in 1862. In its origin, the Monroe Doctrine was unilateral and nationalistic, expressing the traditional policy of continental isolationism contained in George Washington's famous Farewell Speech, but also reflecting the concern of the United States over the Russian infiltration along the Northwest coast and the interventionist policy of the Holy Alliance. None of the leading statesmen—Monroe, Adams, Clay, Polk—sought to convert it into a continental pact approved by the Latin American republics.*

Despite its nationalistic and unilateral formulation, the Monroe Doctrine was unhesitatingly accepted by the Latin American countries. Colombia and Mexico welcomed the new policy and Brazil, while never resorting to its protection, has sought repeatedly to transform this Doctrine from a unilateral policy declaration into a continental undertaking.

This "continentalization" of the Doctrine did not come to pass until after World War II, through the adoption of the Act of Chapultepec in 1945 and the Reciprocal Assistance Treaty of Rio de Janeiro in 1947.

Although the Monroe Doctrine was a source of tensions in the relations between the United States and Europe, it was generally welcomed by the Latin American states. The same cannot be said of some of its corollaries. The first of these is the so-called "Polk Corollary." In his message to Congress in 1845, after reiterating the principle of nonintervention, the then President Polk issued a warning to the effect that if a former colony, after declaring its independence, should wish to join the United States, this ought to be regarded as a "family question." The Polk Corollary was designed to prepare the ground for the acquisition of Oregon, Texas, and California. While directed mainly against Spanish intervention, it did in fact affect very deeply the interests of Mexico, the natural legatee of Spain's northern empire. The second corollary, named "the Roosevelt corollary" after its pro-

* G. Nerval, *Autopsy of the Monroe Doctrine.* New York, 1934, Macmillan.

ponent, Theodore Roosevelt, inspired several armed interventions in Central America and the Caribbean, by claiming for the United States the right to intervene in the internal affairs of the Latin American republics in cases where they failed to behave with reasonable efficiency and decency in political and social matters, to maintain international order, or to meet international financial commitments.

2. The second force idea was the Pan American movement, which unfolded in two phases: (a) the Hispano-American or Bolivarian phase, embodied in the Letter of Jamaica of 1815 and the Panama Congress of 1826, and (b) the Pan American Union movement, which found expression in the invitation in 1881 by the Secretary of State, James Blaine, for the conference of the Inter-American States, which was finally convened in 1890.

Even though in the implementation of the Bolivarian concept emphasis was given exclusively to the political and juridical problems of the Confederation of the Spanish Countries, Bolívar himself had thought in pragmatic economic terms, broaching both the idea of a single currency and that of a customs union. But the divorce between political structure and economic needs was to continue almost until our day. While the formation of a customs union was also among the main objectives of Blaine's convocation, the first Inter-American Conference in 1890 did not implement the idea, largely because of the protectionist sentiment then strong in the United States. Subsequent conferences in Mexico (1901), Rio de Janeiro (1906), Buenos Aires (1910), and Santiago (1923) were largely concerned with juridical matters and the creation of a juridical infrastructure for the system.

The political phase can be said to be ushered in by the Inter-American Conference on the Consolidation of Peace, which convened in Buenos Aires in 1936 and which benefited from the tension-reducing environment created by the Rooseveltian formulation of the Good Neighbor Policy. The economic phase of Pan American cooperation did not really assert itself until much later, with the launching of Operation Pan America, in 1958, followed recently by the Alliance for Progress.

3. The third force idea, the Good Neighbor Policy, with its corollary principle of nonintervention laid the foundation for a durable system of peaceful political coexistence; this was refined in its juridical aspects, though void yet of economic substance. During the Republican administration between 1952 and 1960, the Good Neighbor Policy found a revised expression in the policy of "good partnership," which was merely a conservative adaptation of the earlier theme.

4. The remaining key ideas of the Inter-American system were President Kubitschek's proposal for a Pan American Operation designed: (a) to bring to the foreground the problems of economic underdevelopment, and (b) to emphasize the collective responsibility of the Americas for their elimination. Subsequently, President Kennedy's Alliance for Progress, an outcome of and a complement to Operation Pan America, entered the beclouded inter-American scene. But more on this later.

Even though the pattern of North American political behavior, in the one and a quarter century elapsed between the Monroe Doctrine and World War II, may have assumed various shapes, its geopolitical underpinning remained unchanged. But political realities forced the United States to abandon its isolationism in respect to Europe, and in the interval between the eruption of the Cold War and the formulation of the Alliance for Progress, the geopolitical axis of the United States defense shifted to the European peninsular area.

THE PENINSULAR SCHOOL APPROACH

In the agitated postwar era, under General Marshall and Secretary Acheson, a new approach emerged which, for lack of a better phrase, I shall call the "peninsular school of thought." The crucial theme of United States foreign policy was then to deny to the Soviets the domination of Western industry and resources, and to preserve Western Europe from contamination by the Soviet ideology.

The working concepts of the peninsular school seem to have been twofold. The first was that the attention of the United States should concentrate primarily on the areas more exposed to Soviet pressure, either because of their vulnerability to armed conquest or because of their proximity to the center of Soviet ideological contamination. Thus, during the immediate postwar period, the European peninsula and the maritime fringe of the Eastern Mediterranean won top priority in the American design. The second concept was that, in view of the limitation of economic resources, public investments, loans, and grants should be channeled for the reconstruction and development of those danger areas; the needs of the underdeveloped countries of Latin America, Africa, and Asia should, insofar as practicable, be met by the operation of private capital. Furthermore, foreign aid should be handled as some sort of "ideological bactericide" and injected in such fashion as to prevent an abrupt fall in the European standard of living, with the subsequent proletarization and dissolution of the middle class by subversive pressures.

THE POLICY OF RESIDUAL TREATMENT AND THE PERILOUS LULL

Throughout this period, United States policy in relation to its southern neighbors was relegated to a residual position. This was the period of the "perilous lull." Viewed from Latin America, this policy seemed to rest on the following premises: (1) that Latin America had lost priority in relative terms because its war-time strategic importance had declined as a result of changing warfare concepts and of the displacement of the area of potential contamination; (2) that Latin American development was a task to be left to the responsibility of private funds, supplemented by such public loans as the Eximbank or IBRD (International Bank for Reconstruction and Development) might extend after meeting urgent reconstruction claims. This interpretation, though not completely unbiased, appears justified by the course of events.

It is clear that this "residual treatment" and the reversal of the traditional priority concepts was never accepted goodnaturedly by

Latin American countries, even when they recognized the realities of the situation and the danger of Soviet aggression. This also explains the cool and at times hostile reaction of Latin America to the Marshall Plan, a reaction which seemed at the time shocking and disconcerting to many Americans who expected a warmer recognition of their generous and self-sacrificing approach to the problem of European reconstruction.

The issue was further beclouded by the fact that the United States postwar policy suffered from a certain degree of indeterminacy, oscillating between the principle of uniform treatment and the "key country" approach. Initially it adhered to a pattern of standardized behavior, maintenance of the *status quo,* and balanced treatment for all members of the community. Two exceptions were made to this rule. The first was the Braden episode, which involved the application of economic sanctions against dictatorial regimes. The second, towards the end of the Acheson administration, was a brief essay in the application of the key country approach. The establishment of the Joint United States-Brazil Economic Development Commission in 1950 was a prematurely abandoned attempt to choose a special area for a concentrated economic development effort, with the double objective of strengthening the traditional political solidarity between the two nations and of testing the workability of a program for economic development within the capitalistic framework in contrast with socialist planning.

With the transition from the Truman to the Eisenhower administration, several postulates of the peninsular school of thought became outdated. The very success of the Marshall Plan lessened the Communist danger in Europe while widening the economic gap between the industrialized West, on the one hand, and the stagnant or slow-growing economies of Latin America, Asia, and Africa, on the other.

Feeling the need for a dramatic demonstration of interest in the fate of underdeveloped countries, the United States launched the Point Four Technical Assistance Program in January 1949.

This brilliant idea gave considerable satisfaction to the underdeveloped areas, including Latin America, which welcomed the
program as preparatory to an investment effort. The attendant
political risk was that technical assistance sharpens the hunger
for and increases the ability to use investment capital. Thus, if
investment programs are not forthcoming, the result may be increased disappointment.

THE NEO-GEOPOLITICAL APPROACH

The most important developments of recent years were the
abatement of ideological pressure from the Communists in
Europe, its recrudescence in Asia, and the problems created by
the emergence of new nations in Africa—nations deeply influenced
by Western culture but resentful of colonial domination.

In this changed scene, new patterns of foreign policy emerged.
During the Eisenhower administration, the trends of foreign
policy could be described as the "neo-geopolitical approach." This
new school of thought is not limited to this continent. Whether
Latin Americans like it or not, geopolitical postulates themselves
have changed *pari passu* with the assumption of world leadership
by the United States. The problem was no longer to deny to
Western European countries access to the continental preserve.
It was rather to maintain the influence of Western ideas in Asia,
the Middle East, and the newly emerging countries in Africa. It
is to prevent the ideology that now rules over the Eurasian heart-
land from taking hold of the maritime fringes of the Middle East
and Asia, the Far Eastern lands and the Indian subcontinent, as
well as of emerging countries of Asia. Thus the NATO organization came to be supplemented by SEATO, and the Marshall Plan
effort has been replaced by substantial aid programs for the
Middle East and Asia.

From the Latin American viewpoint, the approach of the neo-
geopolitical school presented no special merits over its predeces-
sor, except, perhaps, that it placed the United States in more
direct contact with the stark realities and the anguishing problems

of economic backwardness. The experience thus acquired could be useful in handling the Latin American underdevelopment problem, which is basically simpler and more readily tractable than that of some of the underdeveloped lands of Asia, the Middle East, and Africa.

THE PLURALISTIC APPROACH OF THE NEW FRONTIER

Until 1958 there had been in the United States postwar economic policy no change in the residual treatment ascribed to the Latin American countries. The era of the perilous lull was rudely broken by two shocks, the Nixon incident in May 1958 and the Cuban revolution in 1959. The first shock arose from incidents during the Nixon visit to Venezuela and Peru, which brought dramatically into the open the grave disintegration of inter-American relations. This created the opportunity for President Kubitschek of Brazil to launch the idea of "Operation Pan America," involving a much needed reappraisal of the state of relations between the United States and Latin America.

Although Operation Pan America was received in the United States with only surface cordiality, it led to a revision of long-standing behavior patterns in United States foreign policy, and ultimately to the formulation of the Alliance for Progress. The latter was born under the impact of urgency and the stress on social reforms arising from the Cuban revolution. Tracing back to 1958 the main steps of the revision, the following chain of events should be noted: (1) the declaration by Douglas Dillon, Under Secretary of State, in August 1958, of the United States intention to acquiesce in the creation of the Inter-American Development Bank, an aspiration present in half a century of inter-American economic conferences; (2) President Eisenhower's "Newport Declaration" of July 1960, in which he announced United States readiness to give financial assistance for social development programs if the Latin American countries would undertake some necessary institutional reforms; (3) the Act of Bogotá, precursor of the Alliance for Progress, in which the Latin

Americans committed themselves to undertake reforms in land structure, taxation, housing, and education, while the United States promised financial assistance for social progress; * and (4) the launching, on March 13, 1961, under a new Democratic administration, of the plan for the Alliance for Progress, multilaterally approved in August 1961 at the Conference of Punta del Este.

The inception of the Kennedy administration was marked by a broader approach which might be termed the "pluralistic" view of foreign policy. In many cases the new approach was merely the culmination of changes already in the offing during the latter part of the Eisenhower administration; in others, it represented a major departure from traditional behavior. In addition to a substantial revision of attitudes in relation to Latin America which is manifest in the Alliance for Progress, the pluralistic foreign policy has the following main characteristics: (1) A more pragmatic attitude regarding neutralism, contrasting with the moralistic view of the problem in the Dulles period in the State Department. Thus, neutralism in certain areas of border tension came to be recognized as acceptable, if not ideal. Greater emphasis is laid on the pursuit of independence by the under-developed countries than on alignment with the Western world. (2) A much deeper engagement in the promotion of economic and social development of the less developed countries, and simultaneously a much less inhibited support for the liquidation of colonialism, an objective hitherto pursued cautiously because of United States involvement in European alliances. (3) Bolder

---

* This promise was implemented through the appropriation by the United States Congress at the beginning of the Kennedy administration of $400 million for social development projects, of which $394 million were turned over to the Inter-American Development Bank for multilateral administration. This succession of steps is well described in a speech given in Philadelphia on May 24, 1962, "The Alliance for Progress at the City of Philadelphia," by T. Graydon Upton, Executive Vice-President of the Inter-American Development Bank.

utilization of foreign assistance as leverage for institutional and fiscal reforms, even at the cost of antagonizing governmental and social structures regarded as obsolete. (4) Greater acceptance of institutional pluralism in underdeveloped countries, in recognition of the fact that during the transition from colonialism to independence, and in the drive for modernization, authoritarian democracies, mixed socialist systems, and a substantial degree of government planning and orientation of the economy may be useful to accelerate structural transformation; correlatively, less emphasis is placed on the role of private enterprise and the pre-emptive role of foreign investment.

SOURCES OF TENSION IN INTER-AMERICAN RELATIONS

The following types and sources of tension, some of historical, some of current relevance, may be listed:

   I. Reactive tensions
  II. Ideological tensions
 III. Racial and cultural tensions
 IV. Institutional reform tensions
  V. Economic disputes.

I. THE REACTIVE TENSIONS

Reactive tensions have their roots in deep-seated resentments against (a) *geographic mutilation,* such as that imposed on Mexico by the annexation of California and Texas, or on Colombia through the fostered secession of Panama to facilitate the building of the Canal; (b) *armed intervention and occupation* in Nicaragua (1912/1933), Mexico (Vera Cruz, 1914), Haiti (1915/1934), Dominican Republic (1916/1924), and Costa Rica (1919); (c) *political intervention,* such as the special rights reserved to the United States under the "Platt amendment" to the Cuban constitution, enacted in 1901 and abrogated only in 1934; and (d) *economic domination* through the overwhelming influence exercised in the past by American private interests, such as the oil companies in Venezuela, the United Fruit Company in Central America, and the sugar interests in Cuba.

While United States policy in Latin America, particularly since the Good Neighbor Policy and the Rio de Janeiro Reciprocal Assistance Treaty, has moved in the direction of collective action, and the strength and influence of private companies have yielded in the face of stronger local governments and increased nationalist reaction, tensions still lurk below the surface. This explains the morbid sensitiveness of Latin America to United States intervention even when, in individual cases, there may be basic sympathy with its objectives, such as the toppling of an archaic dictatorial regime in the Dominican Republic or the containment of the Communist threat in Cuba.

II. IDEOLOGICAL TENSIONS

The second major source of tension linked mainly, but not exclusively, to the outbreak of the Cold War is ideological in nature. Such are the issues posed by Communist infiltration, nationalism, neutralism, and the "policy of independence."

Communist influence in Latin America is a major source of tension in the relations between the United States and Latin America, particularly because of its rather successful effort to instill in the indigenous nationalist movements an obsessive anti-Yankee fixation. The Marxian doctrine, preaching the international solidarity of the workers' movement and an internal class struggle within each country, is essentially anti-nationalist; but the pragmatic adaptations made by Lenin for the creation of Russian socialism, and particularly the Maoist revisionism, which replaces the emphasis on internal class struggles by the emphasis on national anti-colonial movements (enlisting the support of the petit bourgeois and national capitalist groups), greatly facilitated infiltration by Communists of nationalist movements in Latin America. The latter were then distorted into an anti-United States nationalism—a relatively easy task in view of historical resentments and other tensions arising from the economic and political imbalance between the colossus of the North and its weaker neighbors of the South.

Quite apart from the spurious marriage between nationalism and Communism, several strands of the nationalistic movement in most Latin American countries also increase tensions. These are, to use Simonsen's expression, the *phantasmagoric* and the *monopolistic* variants of nationalism.*

The first one rebels against colonialism, although colonialism is on the decline the world over and was never relevant, in its traditional form, in the relations of the United States with Latin America. Economic imperialism from the North is blamed for the evils inherent in conventional colonialism and is singled out as a target for nationalist tensions. Another variant of phantasmagoric nationalism is the opportunistic nationalism through which unscrupulous politicians manoeuver to shift the people's attention from the real causes of underdevelopment by transferring the guilt to foreign scapegoats.

Monopolistic nationalism is generally fostered by the so-called "industrial progressives" (or the "national capitalists," to use terms of the Maoist revisionism), who seek to use nationalism as a device to preserve national monopolies and stave off foreign competition, not only by tariff protection, but also by creating an investment climate inimical to the entry or survival of foreign investment in local industries. In view of the dominant trade and investment position of United States interests in Latin America, monopolistic nationalism seeks to mobilize public opinion against "foreign" (i.e., American) monopoly.

Independently of those aberrations, the very emergence of nationalism throughout Latin America is bound to create a certain amount of tension. This is because several of the components of the nationalist ideology run counter to prevalent beliefs and accepted tenets in the already industrialized nations, and particu-

* Mario Henrique Simonsen, "Tension in Underdeveloped Countries." pp. 137–38 this volume.

larly in the United States. This is indicated by Moreira's list of disconnected strands of nationalistic thought in Latin America: *

1. Absolute priority for industrialization. "To develop" is practically identified with "to industrialize."
2. Heavy reliance on the state as a direct entrepreneur.
3. The export of raw materials is generally considered as humiliating, and in certain cases the export of minerals as especially degrading because it robs the nation of irreplaceable wealth.
4. Distrust of foreign private capital, particularly in the form of direct investment or for the exploration of natural resources or public utilities. This suspicion does not apply, however, to capital in the form of loans, either private or public—a type of financial cooperation that is usually welcomed or even eagerly sought.
5. Over-all planning by the state is considered necessary. This belief is only of a general nature and often is not translated into a policy, even less a technical decision.
6. Agrarian reform is necessary, but merely as an instrument of social justice or as a pure ideological "must," the factors of increased agricultural productivity being usually undervalued.
7. The nationalist movements are often imbued with a high distrust of the "balance your budget" ideology and favor the "structuralist" interpretation of inflation and development.

The recrudescence of nationalism seems disconcerting at a time when Western Europe and the United States are seeking to escape its confines in a search for broader forms of supranational integration and interdependence. But this must be viewed in historical perspective and, if so interpreted, undue tensions need not arise.

The Western industrialized countries have, by and large, completed their process of national and social integration. The only major remaining pressure is the external threat of Communist aggression, against which the best defense lies in supranational integration. The Latin American countries, on the other hand, are still in the process of creating their national personality. There

* Marcilio Moreira, "Some Socio-Political Preconditions of Economic Growth." Unpublished M.A. Dissertation for Georgetown University, Washington, D.C., April 1962, p. 96.

is need of a cohesive force such as nationalism to maintain unity against the centrifugal pressure of heterogeneous regions and groups, and to abate inter-class tensions. In this context, nationalism may still be an important mobilizer of the national effort and a vital element in the drive for modernization, though fraught with the danger of ideological perversion.

It is a major task of social dynamics in Latin America to utilize the mobilization potential of nationalism without falling prey to its intoxicating perils. Very often the politicians' need for political excitement and for transferring guilt may channel nationalism into irrational detours, and may hamper development itself by adversely affecting the flow of investment funds. But if a sober view is taken of this phenomenon, if the legitimate historical grievances are recognized, if account is taken of emotional urges inherent in periods of the quick transformation of dependent economies into proud self-reliant nations, we shall find that nationalism in Latin America, as in Europe, where it was first born, may give ground to more balanced attitudes once the process of modernization is advanced and a greater degree of social integration is reached.

Another possible source of tension lies in foreign policy. The United States, as well as Western Europe, is likely to find a growing desire in the Latin American countries for an independent foreign policy, reflecting the need of those countries to assert their national personality and their differing interpretations of Cold War issues. It is altogether too simple, however, to dismiss the policy of independence, now spearheaded by Brazil and Mexico, as a mere manifestation of *neutralism,* or an exhibition of pro-Castro feelings. The independence policy of the Latin American countries differs substantially from Afro-Asian neutralism. First, they are not systematically nonaligned, since they remain faithful to the inter-American system. Second, they do not show interest in the formation of a third power bloc. Third, they have chosen Western institutions of representative democracy and capitalism, even though practicing them imperfectly, while the typical neutral country has not yet crystallized its choice between democracy and private enterprise on the one hand, and authoritarian socialism on the other.

The Cold War is also viewed differently. For the Western industrialized nations, the overwhelming problem is to protect their tested and workable institutions from the external Communist threat. For Latin America there is another chasm as relevant as the East-West conflict. It is the abyss that separates the prosperous industrialized countries of the Northern Hemisphere from the rest of us. The Western industrialized countries, for which external aggression is the only relevant threat, tend to view the Cold War as a problem of security; the Latin American countries, faced with internal threats of poverty and dissatisfaction, are less concerned with external security than with internal development.

It is thus no wonder that these countries, while conscious of their basic solidarity with Western ideals, view the Cold War from a different perspective and are readier to accept the competitive coexistence of the two systems. This is not only because coexistence seems the only viable alternative to global holocaust or to a rigid partition of the world into ideological compartments, but also because they believe that the competition with socialism will render democratic capitalism more humane and socially conscious and may prod the West into greater efforts in helping underdeveloped areas.

The Problem of "Fidelismo"

All of the foregoing sources of tensions have found a powerful condenser in the "Fidelista" revolution. It plays on the nationalist theme by mobilizing traditional resentments, particularly strong in Central America and the Caribbean area, against United States intervention and economic domination. It harps on the ideological appeal of Communism, with its emphasis on correction of social inequities and accelerated development through planning. It caters to the Latin American pride by asserting the national personality of a small country against a powerful neighbor.

It is thus no wonder that "Fidelismo" has become a major breeder of tensions in the hemisphere. Its appeal cuts across geographical frontiers and permeates several strata of the population. For the intellectual and professional groups the main allure is the mystique of "growth" and the magic appeal of collectivist planning as a shortcut to development. To the broad masses, the appeal lies in promises of redistributive justice and in the courageous break with the existing social order.

The tensions generated by the Fidelista movement affect not only the relations of Latin America with the United States but also the relations between the Latin American states themselves. Under the compulsion of the expansionist Marxian ideology, Castro has spared no effort to infiltrate neighboring countries and to spread subversion, not only against traditional oligarchic governments but against progressive governments of the moderate left. He managed effectively to cloud the inter-American scene with tensions unknown heretofore, such as the split vote at the Conference of Punta del Este on the handling of the Cuban problem. The countries more directly exposed to infiltration and subversive propaganda advocated strong action, while Mexico and five of the southern countries, for traditional reasons (the principle of nonintervention), juridical reasons (imprecision of the juridical instruments of the OAS to deal with new forms of Cold War aggression), or pragmatic reasons (fear of aggravating domestic tensions, or skepticism regarding the effectiveness of sanctions), followed a more moderate course, while joining in the condemnation of Castro's allegiance to the Soviet bloc as incompatible with the inter-American system.

Though still important as a source of tension, Fidelismo has lost some of its original luster. The appeal to nationalistic sentiment in Latin America and the pride of asserting independence vis-à-vis the United States was sapped by growing evidence of submission to the social and political patterns and the foreign policy of the Soviet.

The unabsorbed complexities of socialist planning failed to provoke a miracle of rapid growth; the agrarian reform based on collectivization of land, rather than on its redistribution, failed, as it did elsewhere, to solve the food problem, for it did not yield the production stimulus which has been so successful in the redistributive experiments of land reform in non-socialist countries. In this whole context, ideological repression by a police state, which might be accepted as a price for rapid social reform and regimented economic growth, has become a grave social irritant.

Finally, by promising an alternative and more humane road to social reform and economic development, the Alliance for Progress, though yet untested by performance, is beginning slowly to erode the Castro myth.* But the Castro revolution has not so exhausted its vigor and resourcefulness as to be judged ineffectual, nor has the Alliance for Progress yet proved its mettle. This, then, is the great confrontation of the next few years, with its tensions, perils, and promises.

III. RACIAL AND CULTURAL TENSIONS

It is easy to exaggerate the importance of racial differences and of the divorce between Anglo-Saxon and Latin cultural forms as sources of tension. Those factors cannot be neglected, but there is little doubt that they are declining in importance. With the advance of racial integration in the United States there has been an abatement there of the racial discrimination against nationals of some Latin American countries, particularly Mexico, thus narrowing this source of tension.

The cultural divorce is also narrowing because the very process of economic development is bringing to Latin America an absorption of modern technology imported largely from Anglo-Saxon sources, and also because in the United States knowledge of the language and cultural patterns of Latin America is increasing.

* Editor's Note: This was, of course, written before the missile crisis of October 1962.

IV. INSTITUTIONAL REFORM TENSIONS

Tensions may arise from attempts by the United States to influence the political systems and/or to promote or stimulate reforms in the institutions of its neighbors in the South. Those tensions may be classified according either to *means* or *objectives* into three groups:

1. *Use of armed pressure to affect political systems.* Most of the armed interventions to "restore civil order" in the Central American republics and the Caribbean area from 1912 to 1934 had an implied objective of discouraging the implantation of dictatorial regimes, although in a good many cases the more pragmatic reasons of protecting United States property and assuring financial solvency were dominant. More recently, the military and logistic support for the overthrow of the Arbenz Guatemalan regime, the abortive Cuban invasion, and the display of naval force in Santo Domingo to prevent the restoration of the Trujillo family rule exemplify attempts to induce the modification of authoritarian systems—of the left and of the right—by resorting to military pressure.

2. *Use of economic pressure to enforce canons of monetary stability and fiscal discipline.* Throughout the postwar period, the United States Government has repeatedly sought, either bilaterally or through the International Monetary Fund (in the latter case with the support of Western European countries, which have in fact become more rigid and uncompromising than the United States), to use the leverage of economic and financial assistance for the adoption of "sound" fiscal, exchange, and monetary policies.

This apparently reasonable linkage of financial assistance to requirements of sound monetary and fiscal behavior has been a major source of tension. It reached an explosive point in July 1959, when Brazil interrupted discussions with the Monetary Fund. Here again the Latin American behavior is ambivalent, since inside the countries themselves there is a sharp policy clash between the "monetarists," who might accept the validity of monetary discipline as a means to attain effective utilization of resources, and the "structuralists," who believe that the inflation problem in Latin America is institutional and structural in nature. They think it cannot be curbed except through gradual action, based on investment programs supported by foreign assistance and institutional adaptations designed to increase flexibility of supply.

While there is merit as well as heat on both sides of the argument, the rigid subordination of monetary assistance, particularly in the form of balance of payments loans, to the approval of programs of monetary stabilization and demonstration of performance, frequently creates a vicious circle. This is because monetary authorities do not operate in a political vacuum. Sound plans for combating inflation often find political obstacles that can be surmounted only slowly. This is likely when, during the early phases of stabilization, distortions must be corrected by letting subsidized prices rise, the exchange rate depreciate, marginal industries wither through credit restrictions—all of which may injure large groups able to mobilize political power. Or the instability of export prices of primary products may play havoc with stabilization programs by rapidly canceling the borrowed exchange resources or decreasing tax receipts. In these circumstances, a rigid insistence on undeviating performances in an adverse political context may further weaken those who fight for monetary stability. This may bring about a retrogression in financial and fiscal policies and compound the evil by slowing growth without achieving price stability, until a much greater financial involvement must be accepted under semi-catastrophic conditions.* In recent years this has been only too frequent an experience in Latin America. A

* Professor David Felix notes that to maintain a consistently orthodox set of economic policies against strong redistributive pressures, dictatorial governments are usually required. "It was the error of the Eisenhower administration," he says, "in its zeal to promote economic orthodoxy and a favorable investment climate, to become too closely identified with unpopular dictatorships." Cf. "The Alliance for Progress, the Long and the Short View," in *Centennial Review*, Vol. I, No. 3, p. 325.

much more sophisticated handling of this problem is called for on the part of the United States financial authorities, the International Monetary Fund, the World Bank, and last but not least, the Western European governments. The latter, absorbed in the problems of the Common Market or of their African and Asiatic associations, have been indifferent or rigidly orthodox in dealing with Latin American finances.

3. *Use of foreign aid programs to promote basic institutional and structural reforms.* As a means of reducing the level of tensions, while promoting political change and institutional reforms in Latin America, the United States has sought throughout the years to utilize multilateral mechanisms or to get agreement from the Latin American countries on the reforms desired. In the political field, the principle of representative democracy has been written both into the Charter of the OAS and into the financial cooperation programs, such as the Act of Bogotá and the Charter of Punta del Este. Similarly, the requirement of basic structural reforms was made an integral part of the compact of the Alliance for Progress.

Analysis of the tensions of institutional reform presents tantalizing problems, due at times to inconsistencies in United States behavior but more frequently to the ambivalent position of the Latin American states themselves. In the political field, for instance, despite widespread disapproval of totalitarian regimes operating in violation of the principles of the inter-American system, there is hesitation and fear when pressure is applied by the United States to concrete cases, such as the toppling of the Trujillo dictatorship or the recent military coup in Peru. Thus the traditional fear of intervention leads Latin American countries to the contradictory attitudes of denouncing totalitarian regimes but refusing to support concrete steps to discourage their implantation; or, after blaming the State Department for supporting dictatorial oligarchies, they recoil when the United States takes the opposite position of mobilizing economic and political pressure for the effective defense of the principle of representative democracy.

The institutional reform tensions arising from the bold program of social transformation envisaged in the Charter of Punta del Este—land, fiscal, educational, and housing reforms—are of a still different nature. They are, in a way, "consented," since by subscribing to the Act of Bogotá and the Charter of Punta del Este the Latin American countries accepted those tensions as unavoidable in the process of promoting structural transformation. But although many of the governments gave formal consent to those valid reform objectives, they may find it difficult in concrete cases to mobilize enough popular support to overcome entrenched interests of politically powerful groups. In a few instances the acceptance of the Punta del Este objectives may have been less than sincere, and eroded by the realization of a difference between the interests of the traditional ruling groups and the egalitarian and distributivist aspirations embodied in the Charter.

V. ECONOMIC DISPUTES

Throughout the post-World War II period, during which the treatment given to Latin America was in a sense "residual," several issues arose in the economic dialogue between the United States and its neighbors to the South. Many of those sources of tension have recently abated, but it may be useful to review them briefly:

1. *The controversy on lending policies.* The United States adhered, almost until the signing of the Act of Bogotá, to the concept of restricting foreign lending to the imported components of economic development projects, while Latin Americans pleaded for more flexibility in order to permit the financing of social projects in housing, education, and health, and also the coverage through foreign lending of the local costs of investment projects.

Also, the Latin American countries emphasized the need for flexible loans of the "soft" variety, a principle which before Bogotá and Punta del Este had been only reluctantly accepted through the establishment of the IDA (International Development Agency, a subsidiary of the World Bank) and of the Development Loan Fund.

2. *The controversy on financial mechanisms.* Over the last half century the Latin Americans proposed on several occasions the creation of a specialized inter-American financial institution, over whose policies they would enjoy substantial influence and which would concentrate on the problems of the area. Only in 1958 did the United States agree to the idea, which materialized in the foundation of the Inter-American Development Bank in April 1959.

3. *The controversy on commodity prices.* The Latin Americans laid great emphasis on the need to stabilize commodity prices, on parity schemes linking prices of primary products to those of manufacturers in order to prevent terms of trade from deteriorating, and on international cooperation, through commodity agreements or compensatory financing, designed to regulate the market and/or assure stability of foreign exchange earnings.

Until recently the attitude of the United States was sympathetic to studying the problem, but noncommittal as to action.* The policy has been substantially modified since Bogotá and Punta del Este, leading to more active United States participation in the effort to stabilize coffee prices, to formulate programs for the creation of funds for compensatory financing, and finally to press the Europeans for adoption of more liberal and nondiscriminatory trade practices in relation to Latin American products.

4. *The controversy on the role of private investments.* It may be recalled that throughout the period of "residual treatment" the main responsibility for cooperating in the economic development of Latin America was ascribed to private capital, while official financing agencies would play only a complementary role.

* In the Inter-American Economic Conference of Finance Ministers at Petropolis, Brazil, in October 1954, a Latin American proposal to stabilize raw material prices was rejected by the United States as a "threat to free enterprise."

This on the grounds that private investment (a) is guided by productivity criteria and not by political or social considerations; (b) carries a built-in contribution of know-how and organizational experience when it takes the form of direct private investment; and (c) is a much larger reservoir than that of public funds and not subject to budgetary vicissitudes.

Latin Americans, on the whole, tended to assign a much larger function to public capital, at least in the initial stages of development. The argument proceeds thus: (a) the most urgent need at this phase of their growth is for investment in the creation of the economic and social overhead, a task usually unattractive to private capital; (b) private portfolio investment has practically disappeared, while direct investment, though involving no rigid debt obligations, tends to be burdensome in balance of payments terms because it requires enough remuneration to attract funds in competition with profitable domestic investments within the United States or in the Common Market area; (c) paradoxical as it may seem, public loans are held to involve much less danger of political attrition than the presence, within the country, of big private investors. Finally, private investment is subject to imponderables—psychological, political, and economic—that cause its flow to be uneven and erratic, thus rendering difficult the formulation of development plans and programs.

Developing a trend of thinking already discernible in Eisenhower's "Newport Declaration" and in the Act of Bogotá, the Kennedy administration took a more flexible view. While stressing the importance of private capital, it also recognized the validity of the insistence of Latin Americans on the assignment of a larger role to public funds (a) because of the nature of the investments urgently needed—economic and social overhead projects; (b) because of the erratic behavior of private capital and its susceptibility to short-term political shocks; and (c) because of the "vicious circle" problem: the expansion of private investment requires an improvement of the investment climate in terms of political and monetary stability which, in turn, would presuppose a rise in the level of investment. If unable to count on adequate foreign assistance, the governments would endeavor to raise the level of investments by inflation, thus further impairing the investment climate.

This shift of the main responsibility for financing Latin American development from private capital to public funds has been expressly set forth in the Punta del Este Charter, which says in Title II, Section 4: "The greater part of the sum (a supply of capital from all external sources of at least $20 billion in the next ten years) should be in public funds."

While there has been a great conceptual improvement through the realization of the limitations of private financing, some points of friction remain: (a) the policy of the Washington financing agencies in refusing to lend for state oil monopolies in Latin America, and (b) the controversy over expropriation of United States properties.

Regarding the first of these problems, United States policy appears to have evolved from a complete denial of public loans for state oil enterprises to restricted financing of certain phases of the operation (transport, refining, and distribution) for state companies where countries also allow the functioning of private enterprises in prospecting and refining (Argentina, Bolivia), and preferably in joint investment schemes with private capital. There appears to be no restriction, however, on the financing of research and development of nonconventional petroleum sources such as bituminous shale. The alleged rationale for the policy of restrictive public lending in the petroleum field is the availability of private capital, which would justify husbanding scarce public funds for investments unattractive to private capital. This contention is disputed by some of the Latin American countries, which point to the unreliability of investment decisions by the private oil companies, their lack of interest in opening up new fields of production that might compete with excess capacity owned elsewhere, the subordination of their exploration and pricing policies in Latin America to their world-wide market interests, and, finally, the political inadvisability of foreign operations in a field of strategic importance.

5. *The controversy on expropriating United States properties in Latin America.* The trend toward expropriation has been exacerbated by Cuba's wholesale nationalization of foreign companies, but in varying degrees it was present in most Latin American countries even before the Cuban experiment. The fields most vulnerable to the expropriation drive are public utilities, public transport systems, and oil production and processing facilities. Unlike the petroleum field, where the drive for nationalization is basically political and strategic, in transportation and public utilities there are technical problems related to the near impossibility of private operation under rate regulation in periods of prolonged and sharp inflation. The lag of rates behind cost (prompted by demagoguery or by the administrative complexities of frequent rate revisions) deters private investment, leading to deterioration of the services and the creation of bottlenecks which, in turn, aggravate political opposition to rate increases and generate public clamor for state intervention, particularly in foreign enterprises which are targets of nationalistic pressure.

State intervention does not, of course, solve any of the technical problems arising from inflation (often it increases real costs and decreases efficiency), but it permits the continuation of investment by dividing the burden between the direct user and the general taxpayer.

The expropriation controversy does not concern the right of expropriation itself. It refers to (a) the economic wisdom of allocating resources for absorption of existing operations rather than for new investments; (b) the determination of what is "fair and adequate compensation" in terms of valuing properties and of payment currency; and (c) the degree of acceptable diplomatic action by the government of investor countries to protect the interests of expropriated companies abroad.

On the question of defining expropriation, the usual inclination of the private investor is to resort to "reproduction costs" as the method of valuation and to require prompt payment in convertible currency; if strictly interpreted this would in fact impede expropriation, in view of the financial stringencies of most Latin American countries. The Latin American tendency is to advocate the payment of compensation in installments, with a major proportion to be paid in local currency independent of convertibility provisions, and often with tied-in reinvestment clauses. As for the degree of diplomatic protection, the position of the Latin American countries is generally that only in the case of denial of justice by local courts does the problem become a legitimate case of "protection of nationals" under international law. As long as internal legal remedies have not been exhausted, diplomatic protection is regarded as improper.

In practice, the United States Government has taken a pragmatic and moderate course on this matter, at least since the Rooseveltian handling of the Mexican expropriation of oil companies in 1934—a case in which the claims of the companies obtained only a modicum of support from the administration, since political reasons for a settlement were judged to overwhelm private interests. This tradition has been maintained with minor changes. During the 1962 discussion of the Foreign Assistance Bill, provisions were inserted directing the United States administration to suspend aid in cases of expropriation not followed by "appropriate steps" to provide "equitable and speedy compensation in convertible foreign exchange, as required by international law."

Such a provision, unless wisely administered, may become a source of interminable friction in United States relations with the Latin American countries, which are likely to question (a) the implied assumption that compensation in convertible foreign exchange is required under international law when legal tradition supports only the requirement that compensation be made in a "useful" form of payment; (b) the premature internationalization of disputes, in view of the fact that, unless and until denial of justice by local courts is demonstrated, litigation between individual companies and sovereign states remains a matter of internal and not international law; and (c) the possibility that foreign assistance programs may be transformed into a dangerous leverage by private interests in support of exaggerated claims on foreign governments.

THE CONTROVERSY ON PLANNING

A useless and frustrating dispute on planning versus free enterprise lurked below the surface during several of the inter-American economic conferences of the postwar period.

Various Latin American countries, desirous of (a) assuring continuity of financing arrangements; (b) obtaining global financial commitments on a program basis rather than on a project-by-project basis; (c) expanding governmental investments in the infrastructure; and (d) utilizing planning as an instrument for mobilizing popular support for economic development, pressed for recognition of the principle of planning and programing and for the acceptance, by the United States, both in its own financial agencies and through its representatives in international organizations, of long-term financial commitments.

At first the idea of long-range planning and programing found reluctant ears among United States policy makers, who were preoccupied with avoiding a massive involvement in financial commitments for aid to Latin America and were fearful that the endorsement of the planning philosophy might encourage or hasten state-minded or socialist tendencies in Latin American governments, thus stifling private enterprises. This attitude began to change after the launching of Operation Pan America, and particularly during the discussion of the Committee of Nine and the Bogotá Conference in June and September of 1960. But only in the Punta del Este Charter was there a frank and strong endorsement of the principle of global planning and United States commitment for Latin American development on long terms.

This shift in policy has not been devoid of paradoxes. After having insisted on United States acceptance of the planning philosophy, many Latin American countries found themselves administratively and technically unequipped for undertaking the planning job when the principle was finally recognized at Punta del Este. Substantial progress is now being made in this direction, and one of the major tasks of technical assistance in the near future will be the improvement of the planning machinery on this continent.

THE ALLIANCE FOR PROGRESS

By far the most important recent event in inter-American relations is the launching of the Alliance for Progress. This was built on the foundation laid by President Kubitschek's Operation Pan America. The two have points of contact and points of dissimilitude. Both aim at setting quantitative growth objectives for Latin American countries, at determining needed rates of investment and the magnitude and sources of the required external assistance. Both recognize the collective responsibility of the Americas in the fight against economic underdevelopment. They differ in that the Alliance stresses immediate promotion of social investment and long-run institutional and structural reforms, which had not been emphasized in Operation Pan America. The latter envisaged social development as a by-product of economic development and held that reforms should be a result rather than a precondition of the global investment effort.

The simple statement of the Alliance for Progress has contributed to a significant short-run reduction of tensions in the hemisphere. Many of its postulates recognize long-standing claims of enlightened Latin American statesmen and economists. Whether its final result will be a permanent abatement of tensions depends on methods, pace, and success of implementation.

As is inevitable in programs of social transformation, internal tensions are generated during and within the very process of change. In a classification of tensions, one might distinguish between the *transformational* tensions and the *operational* tensions. The first are unavoidable and necessary, for they are at the very core of the problem of changing social aims, attitudes, and values. The process of modernization of societies is never spontaneous but is a promoted change, in which the elements of the old social order are subject to transformation or destruction. The operational tensions are those generated by the imperfections and strain of the machinery for implementation of a complex program of social change and economic development, operated on an international scale. In a sense, the transformational tensions refer to *terminal* values and the operational ones to *instrumental* values. Here we might discuss several antinomies that beset the Alliance for Progress.

1. *The contrast between the instrument and the objective.* The Alliance for Progress is a bold program for economic development and social change, with a strong egalitarian bent. But a few of the governments that signed the Punta del Este Charter still represent traditional rural oligarchies whose allegiance to drastic social change is superficial or timid. Here the implementation of social reforms will be impelled much less by the carrot of social justice and economic development than by the stick of fear of social convulsion.

2. *Contradiction between the need for an impact effect and the conditions of maximum effectiveness.* In order that investments may attain an optimum yield and to assure a proper coefficient of self-help, there must be an adequate institutional framework, structural reforms of tax and land tenure systems, and a coherent set of monetary and fiscal policies. On the other hand, it is often necessary, for social and political reasons, to direct some initial investment to several sectors of the underdeveloped economy even before social reforms are enacted and effective economic policies are adopted. A certain risk of initial waste must therefore be accepted—almost, we might say, as the political cost of breaking inertia and arousing public support and participation. There is no way of avoiding a partial misallocation of resources, except at the much higher cost of generating skepticism and mistrust regarding the purposes and effectiveness of the Alliance.

3. *The controversy between social and economic development.* The Alliance has been criticized, particularly in Brazil, as a method of dealing with social problems by means of social remedies, while those problems require basic economic solutions. Yet, when the prevailing social environment is such that the available labor force cannot be fully engaged in production because of social unrest, squalor and disease, it is sensible to supplement massive economic investments with allocations of capital for social development projects. Economic and social investments, instead of being mutually exclusive alternatives, are complementary.

4. *Consented reforms versus revolutionary change.* One could easily picture the cleavage of contemporary social action and thought in Latin America as coinciding with the gap between the will to bring about basic economic, social, and political reforms by means of democratic change, and the desire to subvert existing institutions in order to impose upon social reality new patterns and new values. We find the extremes of left and right, the revolutionaries and the defenders of the *status quo*, fighting in the same trench, although for opposite reasons, against the Alliance for Progress—the former because they are too impatient to work toward gradual progress; the latter because they do not want to lose the comfortable status they have enjoyed for so many years in our unjustly organized societies.

5. *Government planning versus free enterprise.* Social pressures for development in the modern context require a large degree of government intervention, which, if not skillfully handled, may have restraining effects on the vigor of private initiative. Political factors may impose the reservation of special areas for national operation. It is far from easy to maintain a correct balance between private motivation and planned growth, and it may be expected that tensions will arise between governments and private enterprise, particularly foreign enterprises. The use of the leverage of external assistance to interfere with a government's freedom of choice in allocating tasks between the public and the private sector may generate dangerous frictions which must be avoided if

the Alliance for Progress is to succeed.

6. *The conflict between political inspiration and bureaucratic inertia.* The new mood, the new tempo, the new magnitude of effort finds enemies in the conventional attitudes of Washington lending agencies that adhere to conventional banking criteria, that are always prone to reduce their own effort when new sources of funds enter the field, as well as in the incoherence of receiving countries unable to modernize their administrative and planning machinery. In fact, bureaucratic attitudes threaten to sap the vigor of the political inspiration of the Alliance.

7. *The antinomy of trade versus aid.* The decline in the dollar receipts of Latin American countries, as a result of declining prices of their exports to the United States, is comparable to, and in some instances greater than, the amount of dollars received in loans and grants from the United States. Since 1953, the weighted U.S. average price of Latin American imports (excluding Venezuela and Cuba) declined by 20 per cent, while U.S. export prices rose by 10 per cent. The value of exports of Latin America to the United States in 1961 (assuming a relatively low price elasticity of U.S. demand for those exports) could have been higher by some $1.4 billion if prices had remained at the 1953 level, a year which may be taken as a reasonable basis for comparison because it was not distorted either by the abnormal demand of the preceding Korean boom or by the coffee valorization prices of 1954. This sum is more than the combined flow of funds from all sources into Latin America last year. Thus, despite an apparent substantial flow of funds to Latin America in the last decade, the perilous drift toward stagnation or abatement of the growth rate of the countries south of the Rio Grande has not been stopped.

It is true that the price decline is a market phenomenon and not the result of an international conspiracy, and that to a certain extent the Latin American countries themselves, through unrealistic production and trade policies, contributed to the weakening of their terms of trade. The problem, however, is not to allocate guilt but merely to verify objectively that in a net sense there has not been a transfer of real resources to Latin America, and that neither the United States nor the industrialized countries of Western Europe (which unlike the United States have benefited from improved terms of trade without an offsetting lending effort) have lost treasure or substance in helping Latin America. It should be noted that while both the American taxpayers and Congress acted generously in accepting the burden of taxes for foreign aid, there is a tendency to forget the savings which the American consumer realized through lower prices paid for imports from Latin America. The financial effort imposed by the Alliance for Progress represents, at currently estimated amounts, less than one-fourth of the yearly outlays for the Marshall Plan, and it comes at a time when the American economy does not suffer inflationary pressure but has substantial idle industrial capacity, food surpluses, and unemployed human resources.

The solution of these antinomies will be of fateful import for the Alliance for Progress. They affect and involve both North Americans and Latin Americans. Anguishing contradictions and conflicting motivations are not a privilege of either side, but part of the human burden that can only be relieved by joint effort.

But more is required. There are political and psychological preconditions. Among them, the most important is the creation of a *mystique*. I prefer to talk of mystique rather than of ideology because the latter word has been often tainted by the evil scent of regimentation and intolerance.

The Alliance is not an exercise in a political vacuum. It is a work of social engineering, requiring from the people a passionate involvement. In this sense it has to act as counter-myth to the Communist ideology which, despite its wanton brutality, has been rather successful in conveying to neglected masses a feeling of participating in the construction of new societies. That the program of the Alliance may succeed, men's minds and hearts must be mobilized, old traditions crushed, privileges waived, social injustices corrected.

The problem is to instill in the masses in Latin America a sense of *personal* as well as of *national commitment*. This personal in-- volvement would require the breaking of inertia and skepticism. In other words, we must improve the *credibility* of the Alliance. That is why actual deeds in the form of well-chosen impact proj- ects to reach the masses are needed immediately, independent of social and structural reform, and independent of prior satis- faction (by governments often paralyzed by strife or insufficiently committed to the reformist purpose of the Alliance) of require- ments of planning and financial stability.

But a sense of *national involvement* must also be created. As Governor Muñoz Marín of Puerto Rico has put it, the "ideals of the Alliance must be fused with the national ideals of each coun- try." Those national ideals may take the form of plans, programs, or simply a development strategy. What is essential is that they represent national aspirations and not the importation of a for- eign mold; otherwise they would not provoke a national involve- ment in the concept of democratic reform and change.

Finally, since the Alliance is a cooperative continental under- taking, the organs for political expression and multilateral action must be strengthened. In the European case, a "mystique of unity" was created by a succession of associative organs, both in the eco- nomic and in the political fields—the OEEC under the auspices of the Marshall Plan, the Council of Europe, the Coal and Steel Community, the Western European Union, and above all the Common Market. Hence the frequent suggestion for the creation in the inter-American scene of executive organs to promote eco- nomic integration (fashioning perhaps a "hemispheric national- ism," to use Felipe Herrera's expression),* as well as of a political body, possibly in the form of a Western Hemisphere Parliament, that may prove instrumental in fostering the mystique of the Al- liance. For the political strength of the Alliance is just as impor- tant as its economics.

* Felipe Herrera, President of the Inter-American Development Bank, "The Economic Aspects of the Alliance for Progress." Address at Georgetown University, June 27, 1962.

The Alliance for Progress offers what may be the last chance to reduce economic, social, and political tensions of the impatient and impoverished masses of Latin America to levels compatible with democratic reforms, without the painful and often uncontrollable surgery of authoritarian revolution.

Bold faith is needed no less than patient toil. There must be a search for constant understanding, and there must be courage to make mistakes because of excessive faith, rather than stagnate through caution or conventional wisdom.

To make the Alliance succeed is the great and perilous but rewarding travail of the Americas in this fateful decade.

INTER-AMERICAN TENSIONS AND THE ALLIANCE FOR PROGRESS

LINCOLN GORDON

Ambassador to Brazil,
United States

In considering the tensions apparent in the development of the Western Hemisphere, we are all aware that tensions can be either constructive or destructive. Modern psychologists tell us that all life is an alternation between tension and relaxation. War involves disagreeable tensions. Love involves highly agreeable tensions. And work involves necessary tensions. In his classic book on *The Strategy of Economic Development,* Professor Albert O. Hirschman has shown how unbalanced economic development, which many economists consider wasteful and which certainly does create tensions, can be a powerful spur to growth, provided that the sectors in the lead are of the type which drag along the others more rapidly than they would move in the course of non-tensional, vegetative, relaxed development.

Title I of the Charter of Punta del Este states: "It is the purpose of the Alliance for Progress to enlist the full energies of the peoples and governments of the American Republics in a great cooperative effort to accelerate the economic and social development of the participating countries of Latin America, so that they may achieve maximum levels of well being, with equal opportunities for all, in democratic societies adapted to their own needs and desires." The Charter then specifies goals of economic and social progress and ways and means for achieving those goals. These include national programs of coordinated public investment and stimulated private investment, special attention to social progress, institutional reforms and improvements, action to improve Latin American trading conditions, and systematic support through external technical and financial assistance. The last paragraph of the *Declaration to the Peoples of America*, which was adopted simultaneously with the Charter, refers to a new era for the inter-American community, supplementing its institutional, legal, cultural, and social accomplishments "with immediate and concrete actions to secure a better life, under freedom and democracy, for the present and future generations."

How does all this look a year later? Candor compels us to recognize that it is a very mixed picture. On the technical side of developing programs and projects, a good deal has been done. The Inter-American Bank, under Dr. Herrera's direction, has played an indispensable part in speeding up this process. Some Latin American governments have greatly strengthened their administrative machinery for program making and selection of priorities. On the side of the United States Government much headway has been made in building a new organization and in gradually converting the working methods of bureaucracy to the new spirit called for by the Alliance for Progress.

The lists of specific institutional reforms and improvements in Latin America make an impressive showing. Yet it is clear that the "full energies of the peoples and governments" have not yet been enlisted in this effort. There is not yet a sense of a great cooperative effort as the highest priority of the inter-American community, securing the devoted efforts of the most talented leaders in public and private life throughout the hemisphere. Democratic institutions remain under very great pressure, and in some cases they are temporarily in eclipse, although not irrecoverably.

Why these shortcomings? In my opinion, the basic shortcoming has been squarely identified by Ambassador Campos when he speaks of the need for a political mystique. Unless the pursuit of economic and social progress, in the terms of the Charter of Punta del Este, becomes a major part of the national political life of each participating country, and unless the great majority of people and organized groups and leaders of influence feel themselves involved and committed to these goals, the Alliance for Progress will not succeed, regardless of the technical soundness of individual projects and the amounts of foreign financial support made available to Latin America. The Alliance then will become simply another American aid program, no doubt larger and better than its predecessors, but not a cooperative process for bringing about a real sea change in the actual standards of living, in the sense of participation in progress by all classes and regions of the national communities, and in the security of civil liberties and the institutions of representative democracy.

The underlying will for accelerated economic and social progress under free institutions clearly exists in Latin America. To be sure, there are minorities in opposition. There are vocal minorities on the far left, whose main interest is in overthrowing free institutions. They fight the idea of democratic progress, just as the Communist parties in Western Europe fought the Marshall Plan fifteen years ago. There are less vocal, but powerful, minorities in the traditional oligarchies, and sometimes among the newly rich industrialists, who are too satisfied with things as they are to be receptive to any kind of change, even though experience elsewhere might suggest to them that they could find a useful, satisfying, and rewarding place in a progressive democratic society. But I would guess that taken together these minorities account for no more than 15 or 20 per cent of the peoples of Latin America. The problem is to find and encourage articulate and effective leadership for the aspirations of the vast majority, and to relate a political mystique to the technical problems that must be objectively diagnosed and solved.

That sort of leadership clearly must be Latin American; it cannot come from outside. This was the supreme merit of ex-President Kubitschek's idea of Operation Pan America. He thought of a cooperative movement led by Latin American nations, and supported by the United States and other friendly countries, to make expanded economic development the central objective of organized public and private effort in this continent for this decade. I have always regretted that my own Government did not fully recognize the potency of this idea when it was launched four years ago. It did win partial recognition in the decision to establish the Inter-American Development Bank and in the Act of Bogotá, and full recognition in the Charter of Punta del Este. Nevertheless, it has not yet developed the political drive which its success required.

The Alliance for Progress is often compared to the Marshall Plan. The differences are greater than the similarities. Development is a far more difficult undertaking than economic recovery, and the administrative institutions of Latin America, as well as the economic and social infrastructure, are much less developed than were those of Europe in the late 1940's. But the European experience does contain some useful pointers. At a certain point in the development of the Marshall Plan, there became evident a compelling need for European political leadership at a high level as part of the formal cooperative machinery. And when the idea of European integration was conceived as the basis for a great new move forward on the foundation of postwar recovery, it was given vital political leadership by Jean Monnet and his Action Committee for the United States of Europe, a necessary informal prerequisite to the later establishment of formal institutions for economic and political unification. Nor were these movements limited to cabinet ministers and public officials. They sank their roots into the national communities, enlisting members of parliaments, political parties, organizations of businessmen, labor unions, and the liberal professions, universities, the press, and other organs of mass communication. Is there not in this experience something to be drawn on for guidance in the contemporary Latin American scene?

In his discussion of the relationship between Operation Pan America and the Alliance for Progress, Ambassador Campos' paper notes two other points of difference: (1) the inclusion in the Alliance of immediate social investment, along with large-scale economic investments, and (2) the emphasis on institutional and structural reform. Like Ambassador Campos, I believe that social investments, properly conceived, are complementary to economic investments and are major elements in an effective development program. I would argue, moreover, that both social investment and structural reforms are essential to a full sense of participation in the development process by all elements of the population, and therefore essential to the national cohesion and sense of popular identification.

But there is much misunderstanding on this point, certainly in Brazil. I often hear criticisms of the so-called "assistencial" character of the Alliance, as if it were only a program for charitable palliatives of the misery which is so widespread in this continent. This is a gross misunderstanding. The term "assistencial" may perhaps be applied to a campaign to eradicate malaria or to eliminate the many debilitating diseases which come from impure water, but public health measures of this type are essential to an economically productive population as well as to a happier one. And education, which is conventionally considered to be social investment, has been proven to be one of the most economically rewarding forms of investment that any nation can make, provided that it is properly designed to meet the needs of a rapidly modernizing society.

The most acute problems of internal tension in carrying out the Alliance for Progress arise in connection with structural reforms. Agrarian and tax reform are cited most frequently, but I would consider equally important reforms in the organization, working methods, and attitudes of public administration; reforms to modernize the administration of private business; educational reforms; and reforms in the financial institutions which stimulate savings and channel them into constructive investment. All these types of reform are indispensable to economic and social progress. Perhaps the Act of Bogotá and the Charter of Punta del Este can be given some credit for the fact that discussion of basic reforms has become a commonplace of Latin American politics.

Many discussions of the politics of reform seem to me to be oversimplified. It is often assumed that there is a one-dimensional political spectrum, running from revolutionary reformers on the far left, through a center of varying breadth composed of democratic reformers, and ending with reactionary anti-reformers on the far right. No doubt this spectrum exists, but it is certainly not the only political dimension. Cutting across it are conflicting ideas on the nature of governmental institutions. There is one well-entrenched tradition of government as a patron of special interests, serving not only wealthy oligarchies, but also specially privileged labor unions, and furnishing innumerable useless jobs for protégés of various political parties. This contrasts with the concept of government as a body of efficient public administrators serving the broad public interest. There is another dimension which separates demagogues who prefer attractive but meaningless slogans (which may be of the left, right, or center) from political leaders who seek real remedies for the social and economic problems crying for solution. And there is a further dimension which separates distributive reformers from expansionist reformers.

In any society where great wealth exists in the hands of a few, the idea of dividing their wealth among the many has an obvious popular appeal. In societies with low average incomes, the contrast between poverty and wealth is especially marked because the middle class is small and the wealthy few may be, like the princes of India, wealthy to a degree wholly unknown in modern industrialized societies. No one could claim that such societies are socially just, and distributive measures obviously must play some part in their modernization. But where average standards are low, mere distributive measures add no significant real income to the masses. They add only the psychic income of seeing the once mighty laid low. If the desire is for genuine economic and social progress for the entire community, the main thrust of reforms must be directed toward development, growth, investment, and higher efficiency in production and distribution.

The reformist philosophy of the Charter of Punta del Este embraces both developmental and distributive objectives. In translating these principles into practice, obviously each nation will have to find its own patterns, suited to its geographical and social conditions and its popular aspirations. But unless the primary emphasis is placed on expansion, the wherewithal to meet those popular aspirations simply will not exist.

In this connection, the North American New Deal of a generation ago seems to me a highly instructive experience. The New Deal brought about major transformations in the structure and attitudes of United States society, most of which have long since been accepted by both political parties and all sectors of opinion. Reviewing the principal features of the New Deal, with the advantage of a generation's hindsight, it is clear that its great successes were those measures which looked toward economic expansion and growth, and the reshaping of institutions within a context of such growth. Its failures were the measures which reflected the gloomy view—quite widespread at the time and later wholly disproved by history—that the American economy was already overbuilt and that reforms must simply distribute what could be produced under a regime of perpetual stagnation.

The measures looking toward growth were able to create new harmonies among interest groups and classes which would have been condemned to civil warfare against one another within a context of stagnation. Let me mention a few examples. Regulation of the stock market was not designed to destroy Wall Street and the investment bankers; it was designed to reform the capital market, to replace speculation by true investment, and to open the way for democratization of stockholding in the large business corporations. The systems of housing and farm credit insurance were not designed to socialize the housing industry or agriculture; they were great social inventions in collaboration between government and private enterprise, which made possible the enormous postwar programs of rehousing and of higher agricultural productivity. The Tennessee Valley Authority was born of a refusal to accept the inevitability of backwardness in that very underdeveloped region; it sought instead to promote balanced growth through efficient use of water and land resources and systematic community development. The social security system met the most pressing needs of old age and unemployment insurance, and added important stabilizing influences to the economy as a whole, but it could never have been afforded under conditions of economic stagnation. The public utility holding company law rebuilt the financial structure of the electrical supply industry, not by punishing or expropriating the operating companies, but by placing them on a firm foundation for future expansion and improved service.

The New Deal contained many faults, including a spirit of undiscriminating antagonism toward the business community at large. But it also had the great virtue of a political mystique. It asserted the self-confidence of the nation in its capacity to cope constructively with its economic and social problems. It expressed a passion to include fully in the national society certain formerly forgotten groups—the Negroes, the migratory farm workers, the marginal farmers of the South, and the urban workers not yet organized into trade unions. And it applied a highly pragmatic and realistic approach to specific problems of social engineering. All these elements seem to me very relevant indeed to the contemporary Latin American scene.

The need for realism in social engineering poses a special challenge to Latin American universities, which are another focus of internal tensions in the development of the hemisphere. It is from their student ranks that leaders must come for the continuing struggle for economic and social progress.

During the past few decades, Latin American faculties of medicine and engineering have felt compelled to adopt truly professional standards, with rigorous training and strenuous devotion to studies by the student body. The reasons are evident. Without such training, the medical patients die and the bridges and buildings collapse. In many parts of the continent, however, the illusion remains that social engineering is still a matter for dilettantes—for part-time students of law and of economics taught by part-time professors. Young men can graduate with honors, persuaded that glibness in verbal expression is an adequate substitute for respect for hard facts and for rigorously objective thinking. They are encouraged to confuse the *ought* with the *is*, to believe that a social structure has been built when an esthetically pleasing design, or even an impressionistic sketch, has been drawn. But if effective development is to take place, the faculties of law and economics must develop the same toughness as the faculties of medicine and engineering. Without this, one can expect continued diseases in the body politic and continued collapses in the social structures.

Let me mention a few examples of this problem of realism in social engineering. In facing the problem of chronic inflation, the realists will look for the basic causes in budgetary imbalances, excessive credit expansion, wage increases without regard to productivity, and structural bottlenecks in critical areas of production. They will not be satisfied with emotional outbursts against such convenient scapegoats as foreign investors or greedy speculators.

In dealing with public utility services, the realists may choose either management by government or management by private enterprise, but they will insist on efficient management and on the service's paying its own way. They will recognize that when a telephone or power service is subsidized, that subsidy is not truly free. It is a gift to the fortunate users at the expense of much poorer non-users, who pay the cost either through general taxes or through inflation. Such a policy not only contradicts economic sense; it violates the most elementary canons of social justice.

The realists, similarly, will be most interested in agrarian reform, but they will not be satisfied with mere promises to give land to the landless. They will insist first on securing the facts as to how land is owned and used, on devising patterns of productive use which will raise agricultural productivity and permit the earning of a decent living by farm families, and they will combine reforms in land tenure with the organization of agricultural credit, supplies of seeds and machinery, and effective mechanisms for storage, marketing, and distribution.

Such an approach to social engineering will not dissolve all the tensions implicit in economic and social change. But it would give the constructive tensions the pre-eminence they deserve. Surely this is a challenge to enlist the passions and the intellectual energies of the university youth who are rightly dissatisfied with things as they are. If they were to analyze coolly the human and material resources of this continent, they would see that the objective problems of social and economic development are far more readily soluble here than in the other great underdeveloped continents of Asia and Africa. They would also see that development cannot be achieved by waving magic wands, by exorcising foreign scapegoats, by drafting five-year plans without the necessary machinery to put them into effect, or by distributing poverty without creating new wealth. And they would see that steadfast cooperation among the Latin American nations can bring much greater results than isolated national efforts, and that the effective collaboration of friendly foreign nations can make a critical difference between success and failure in a limited period of time.

I said at the start that a political mystique is indispensable to the success of the Alliance for Progress, and that leadership in the creation of this political mystique must come from Latin America. I do not mean by this to suggest that we North Americans have no useful role to play. On the contrary, we have an indispensable role. We are the major source of outside technical and financial support, and it is no easy job to organize ourselves to supply that support promptly and effectively. We need to convey a much better understanding than now exists in Latin America of the nature of our own society and the reasons that impel us, perhaps somewhat belatedly, to join in this great cooperative partnership with Latin America. We must also dispel certain suspicions and doubts, some deliberately fostered by the Communists and their allies, but others which result from the historic tensions within the hemisphere so well described by Ambassador Campos. There exists, for example, a concern that the Alliance for Progress might undermine the sovereignty and independence of Latin American nations. I know that I speak for our Government as well as for myself in saying that we do indeed believe in ultimate interdependence, but it is the interdependence of freely cooperating peoples and nations, each independently making its own decisions to work with the others in its own deepest interest.

It is also true that we in the United States have our own real national interest in the success of the Alliance for Progress. This is not a selfish interest, however. It is our interest that there be a Western Hemisphere of prosperous, self-reliant, and securely democratic nations. And if we look ahead, our imaginations cannot help but be inspired by the idea of a great triangular Western community in which Latin America, Western Europe, and North America are the firm foundation units for an ever-widening area of peace, of freedom, and of liberation of the human spirit in the world as a whole.

ECONOMIC DEVELOPMENT: THE LESSONS AND THE CHALLENGE

DAVID ROCKEFELLER

President,
The Chase Manhattan Bank, United States

In a sense, I suppose, any North American venturing into South America to talk about economic development is in a position memorably described by the seventeenth century nobleman, Lord Rochester, who said: "Before I got married, I had six theories about bringing up children. Now I have six children and no theories."

I, too, have six children, but being a somewhat less prudent man than Lord Rochester, I still have a few theories left. Some of them relate to the central theme of this Conference.

In the widening spectrum of current economic problems, none is more compelling than that of supporting the modernization of the developing areas—compelling in the opportunity presented, in the novelty and complexity of the challenge to Free World governments and businessmen, and in the formidable demands made on our stamina, our vision, our leadership. To help fulfill the thrusting aspirations of the less developed nations is an opportunity that fires the imagination and kindles the humanitarian impulses of people everywhere.

69

The industrial nations have now had experience in attempting to support and encourage economic progress in the developing areas since the end of World War II. In human terms, the advances in these areas in recent years have some impressive aspects. In financial terms, the flow of assistance from the industrial nations to those in the difficult midpassage of economic development has increased substantially—from a 1950–1955 average of 3½ billion dollars a year to better than 8 billion now. Progress is being made, too, in fashioning mechanisms in various parts of the Free World to coordinate the aid efforts—through the World Bank, the International Monetary Fund, the Special Fund, the Organization for Economic Cooperation and Development, and, of course, the Alliance for Progress.

All this adds up to a promising start—but no more than that. The harsh fact is that too little progress has been made in generating the vital spark of hope for the 1½ billion individuals now living in the developing areas. The appalling contrasts between rich nations and poor have primed many areas for revolutionary ferment.

The obstacles to development most clearly attested by our experience fall into three broad categories. One is the instability of commodity prices and export earnings. Another is the upsurge of population. A third is the attitude and responsibility of the developing areas themselves.

The first category of problems—those relating to commodity price trends and fluctuations—has been brought into sharp focus in recent years, especially in Latin America where most nations depend on a few primary products for a major portion of their export earnings. Indeed, in sixteen of the twenty Latin American republics, one or two commodities account for more than half of total exports. Thus, wide price swings in commodity markets can imperil the very structure of a national economy.

Still more serious is the general decline in commodity prices during most of the 1950's. The result has been an adverse trend in the terms of trade of the Latin American nations. A given volume of exports now buys only 89 per cent as much from the industrial regions of North America and Europe as it did in 1957. In a number of cases, this decline in the terms of trade has meant a loss in export earnings considerably larger than the inflow of outside assistance.

Recognizing the importance of this commodity price problem is, of course, far easier than devising effective counter measures. Past commodity stabilization agreements have not proven notably successful. There is a great deal of experience, including that acquired under the United States agricultural support price program, which shows that attempts to hold prices above the level dictated by supply and demand can prove exceedingly costly.

However, it is contrary to common sense for coffee growers, for instance, to be encouraged to continue producing enormous surpluses when the warehouses in Brazil already bulge with enough coffee to supply the world for a full year. A step in the right direction is the Brazilian Government's present program to persuade coffee growers to reduce the number of trees under cultivation.

Despite the complexities of the commodity problem, I believe that men of good will can find a workable solution through cooperative effort. It may be possible to work out international control arrangements which will help reduce sharp or speculative fluctuation in commodity prices and hence cushion the abrasive impact of price spirals on the developing areas. So vital is this issue that the industrial nations have no alternative but to demonstrate their sense of responsibility by joining the developing areas in a tireless quest for effective action.

The second broad range of problems concerns population trends. Somewhere in the world three babies are born every second, nearly 2 million every week. The increase in world population so far this year is almost equivalent to the total population of Brazil. This population explosion exerts its strongest impact on the developing countries. Latin America's population is growing at a faster rate than that of any other major area of the world—2.4

per cent annually, compared with Asia's 1.8 per cent and Africa's 1.9 per cent.

In the early stages of modernization, the rate of population growth quickens rapidly. As disease control, sanitation, and medical care are improved, the mortality rate drops sharply while the birth rate is usually little affected. Thus a major effort is required merely to keep over-all production rising in pace with population. During the decade of the Fifties, the income of the developing lands increased by 3 per cent a year. But two-thirds of this gain was canceled out by the 200 million new mouths to feed. President Eugene R. Black of the World Bank has remarked grimly that "we are coming to a situation in which the optimist will be the man who thinks that present living standards can be maintained."

Underlying the population problem is a tragic dilemma: the developing nations cannot achieve a higher standard of living without some form of population control, but they cannot achieve population control without a higher standard of living. In areas where human labor is still the main force of a society, many parents consider large families indispensable as helpers in the fields and as security for old age. It is only when people see more opportunities for a higher standard of living that they begin to consider whether a smaller family would not be desirable.

In the nineteenth century, the French decided in favor of smaller families when they were confronted with new laws on the inheritance of property. More recently, the Japanese, after a period of swift expansion, appear as a result of both personal choice and government legislation to be stabilizing their population. Thus does history suggest that a certain degree of economic development must occur before smaller families seem desirable.

Population growth has been more of a problem in terms of human welfare than had been anticipated. More study must be devoted to the relationships between population factors and general development problems. The most valuable resources of any country are the skills and character of the people. If bodies multiply faster than skills, then all that we have worked to gain is gravely endangered, and the possibility of further progress is tightly circumscribed. The Free World must keep constantly in mind the question of whether the rise in sheer numbers is obstructing the rise in trained quality of human beings.

The third set of obstacles to development—those relating to the attitudes and policies of the emergent nations themselves— has proven the most difficult. In some cases, political and economic instability has created a climate stifling to economic growth. In others, an emotional nationalism has led to domestic actions discouraging the flow of outside assistance from private sources.

We have seen examples of this during the first year of the Alliance for Progress. In concept, the Alliance emphasizes the primacy of private investment. The architects of the Alliance advocated that fully one-third of the capital from outside the region and two-thirds of that generated domestically should come from private sources, and they believed this to be a realizable goal. Yet, in practice, the programs encouraged thus far have been concerned mainly with government action. This has been due in part to governmental attitudes both in the United States and in Latin America, and in part to a deteriorating economic and political climate which has not been conducive to private investment. In concentrating on the government sector, the Alliance has tended to stress reform movements which cannot be carried out swiftly without great social unrest and political uncertainty. This completes the vicious circle, for these are precisely the conditions least likely to provide a hospitable climate for savings and investment.

The tax reform effort under the Alliance is another case in point. Tax reform is a bewilderingly complex matter in any country—as we are finding out in the United States. In Latin America, it would be helpful if the pressure of the Alliance could streamline tax collections and combat tax evasion. However, it would be a grave mistake to alter tax rates so as to reduce the very business incentives needed to draw out private savings and investment. If Latin America is not to embrace doctrines which give central governments authority over national resources and diminish individual freedom, incentives must play a more important role.

One of the most formidable barriers to private investment abroad is the barrier in the minds and emotions of those who need foreign investment most. Because they wrongly tend to equate it with colonialism, they are reluctant to accept it. They veer toward a coldly anti-capitalist attitude and they scorn the profit motive which in the industrialized nations of the Western World has been the prime generating force producing economic growth since the industrial revolution in the late eighteenth century.

This hostility to profit on the part of many people in Latin America is based, in part at least, on misconceptions of the magnitude of profits made by foreign investors. It is generally believed that profits have been exorbitant and have resulted in the exploitation and impoverishment of the host country. This attitude was pointed up in a special Gallup Poll taken in fourteen nations of the non-Communist world. Participants were asked what per cent of profit they thought a typical United States industrial firm earned. Answers ranged from 25 per cent in Rome to 60 per cent in Montevideo. Actually, over the past thirty years, industry in the United States has earned less than 5 per cent profit annually on the sales dollar, and less than 10 per cent on the investment dollar. Earnings on foreign investments have not been significantly higher.

A country can achieve rapid growth and modernization only if it is willing to encourage savings and investment, adapt itself to the changes demanded by modern technology, and support the general education and social betterment of the entire population. These requirements can be met only by stable governments with both the wisdom and the courage to carry out responsible economic policies, including those which will maintain domestic price stability.

The record shows that nations refusing to adopt such policies have achieved little progress, even with massive public assistance from abroad. Political instability, inflationary policies, threats of expropriation, and discriminatory taxes have largely checked real economic growth. Hence, one cannot overemphasize the fact that economic development is a product of a nation's own policies and attitudes. This is often insufficiently appreciated in some governmental circles in the United States, and it certainly is not understood by those who press for ultranationalistic and leftist policies in Latin America. The alternatives to policies that encourage private savings and investment are either a stultification of economic growth or a fully controlled economy where the state, rather than the consumer and the investor, determines the level and character of consumption and investment. Such a system can work efficiently only in a police state.

I have reviewed the major lessons which seem to me to emerge from our experience in order to point towards a more constructive approach to the realities of the future. Today the resources and knowledge are at hand to eliminate hunger in nations of the Free World willing to cooperate; to eradicate most epidemic diseases and provide minimum standards of medical care; to extend elementary education to virtually all individuals, and secondary and higher education to a rising proportion of talented people; to provide decent housing for the vast majority; and to double average per capita incomes roughly every generation.

How can we go about the pursuit of these exhilarating goals? Three steps seem to me pre-eminently important.

First, we must develop a more imaginative and effective strategy of economic aid. The basic problem is to use foreign assistance in a manner that will excite and enlist increasing local efforts. This assistance should be regarded as seed capital. As such, it should be directed into channels where it will support and encourage local investment and technical advance. Proper direction and use of economic aid are far more important than its sheer quantity—a fact which we in the United States have been slow to learn.

Second, we must devote increased attention to forward planning.

A developing nation needs broad objectives and an omnibus plan for achieving them. It needs national policies which, within the framework of the free pricing system, will direct its scarce resources toward the attainment of those objectives. Out of a give-and-take process between business and government can come a development program that will produce sustained progress without sacrificing the freedom of individual choice.

Third, we must place greater emphasis on private investment. There is much to be said for asking the developing countries to recognize the desirability of foreign private investment through their endorsement of some form of multilateral convention. Such a convention would state specifically that foreign investors were to be given the same rights as their domestic counterparts. A related suggestion, which has great merit, involves setting up a multilateral institution financed by both industrial and developing nations to provide guarantees for private foreign investment. These steps would represent a degree of maturity in the attitude of the developing countries which must be realized sooner or later if their own best interests are to be served.

In the Western Hemisphere, economic development has taken on a new and fateful meaning. Under the Alliance for Progress, we share a common goal of economic advance; a common belief that man can shape his own economic destiny; a common commitment to raise living standards throughout the hemisphere. As Walter Lippmann pointed out recently, the Alliance is a "unique experiment," rooted in the realization that "without a rise in the standard of life of the mass of the people, there can be no enduring stability." It represents a pioneering attempt to attack underdevelopment on a massive scale; on a broad economic, social, and political front; and on a basis of respect for man's eternal yearning for freedom.

Communism boastfully claims that its revolutionary measures offer a surer route to equality, material well-being, and the achievements of technology and capital. But it should be recognized that revolution and Communism are far from synonymous. The

United States went through a successful revolution in the eighteenth century with ideas and principles far more revolutionary than the tenets of Marxism. Its example of a prosperous and socially conscious nation, operating under a mixed system of free enterprise and government, can be an inspiration to pacific revolution by less favored peoples everywhere.

The challenge, as I see it, is twofold:

For the industrial nations, to work creatively to assist the emergent lands in making their revolution peacefully and democratically.

For the developing countries, to mobilize their natural resources more effectively; develop the skills and talents of their people; and improve the climate for private investment, both domestic and foreign.

It is up to us to measure our responsibility and determine our response. If we have the stamina, the vision, and the leadership to apply ourselves zestfully to these tasks, we can broaden and brighten our horizons beyond all expectation. In so doing, we shall contribute enormously to the peace, security, prosperity, and freedom of all mankind.

COMMERCE BETWEEN RICH AND POOR COUNTRIES AS A SOURCE OF TENSIONS

JOSÉ FIGUERES

**Former President of
Costa Rica**

The common civilization that will cement humanity together will be a product of many cultures and many ages, each of which contributes certain values that attain general acceptance. In the twentieth century the eradication of poverty, disease, and ignorance, called economic and social development, has become such a universal value.

With advancing technology, all countries, all races, certainly both sides in the Cold War, consider economic and social development as an aim to be achieved in our time. Several nations have already achieved a high level of development, partly as a result of the spirit of solidarity established among their citizens—a spirit unknown in previous times. Most countries are still lagging, but a new phenomenon has appeared which may accelerate their development and integration: a new feeling of solidarity, this time between country and country.

During the period when solidarity was being established within those advancing lands, misjudgment of evolutionary tendencies created opposition and tensions. It took painful deliveries to give birth to integrated societies. Now, in a large number of less developed countries, with internal solidarity emerging and international solidarity simultaneously appearing, there exists a double source of misunderstandings and tensions.

I shall deal first with the characteristics which relate to the tensions impeding our progress toward internal and external solidarity.

1. Latin America is European in culture. Even the pre-Columbian groups have adopted European aspirations.

2. Latin America has fought for democracy as it is understood in North America and Western Europe. The present adult generation considers freedom precious and costly, and takes its advantages for granted. The only other avowed creed is Communism, held by a vigorous minority, especially among the younger generation, which is not satisfied with the economic fruits of democracy.

3. The Latin American republics have "exchange economies," based on heavy imports and exports, unlike the "closed economies" of the United States and India, where the foreign sector of commerce is relatively small.

4. The exchange economies of Latin America are drained by selling cheap and buying dear, reversing the fruitful relation by which countries like nineteenth-century Britain accumulated their wealth.

It is obvious that you cannot develop a country in political turmoil. Order is indispensable to productive work. It is less obvious, though equally true in our time, that you cannot maintain democratic government under conditions of extreme poverty. Economic development and political stability are today like the hen and the egg.

When an honest, progressive group reaches power in Latin America, exaggerated expectations, impossible to fulfill quickly, soon produce a degree of disappointment. Influential newspapers owned by the propertied class fan this disappointment. Leftist agitators, with international help, exploit the frustration. The rich and the poor get together in criticizing the government. The rich want subversion, hoping that a military dictatorship will re-establish their privileges. The extremists want subversion, expecting to take the leadership of the anti-military movement which is bound to ensue. The poor want subversion, dreaming that a destruction of the established order will open the way to a better world. Few seem to realize that economic development, with fruits for all, is not a fast growing tree.

Undoubtedly the people would be less inclined to despair if they were not prodded simultaneously by reactionaries who irresponsibly create trouble in the country, politicians who irresponsibly want power everywhere, and extremists who irresponsibly create turmoil in the world. World tensions are not spontaneously generated.

The freedom of the press, though indispensable to democratic society, is a mixed blessing when development plans call, on the one hand, for agrarian reform, taxes, and social justice, and on the other hand, for a slow growth in the standard of living, so as to make capital formation possible. What we call freedom of the press is mainly, in fact, the freedom of the publishers, and particularly the freedom of the advertisers. The very same business people who benefit from the increased purchasing power of the majorities, and from social peace, abuse their power over the press to discredit democratic government, because they oppose the short-range sacrifices that economic reforms demand. The very same underprivileged people for whom the reforms are made supply ammunition to a hostile press and votes to opportunist politicians, because they expect their condition to improve faster than even a rapid growth permits.

At the root of popular dissatisfaction in underdeveloped countries lies the desire to consume the niceties of the industrial nations which are not locally produced. I once asked President Paz Estenssoro why we had no problems of balance of payments in our America before Columbus came. He answered, "Because no Bolivian had ever thought of using a toothbrush."

The desire to use toothbrushes appeared long before the new countries had the technology and the capital needed to make them. They had to be imported from countries with a higher standard of living. They had to be paid for in tin, or coffee, or cocoa, produced by cheap labor. Automatically, one hour of work abroad had to be exchanged for many hours of work at home. The problem of terms of trade between developed and under-developed countries had been born, and it was bound to increase.

If all the citizens of nonindustrialized countries were to use toothbrushes and other refinements of industrial society, covering their costs by exporting local products, one hour of work should then be exchanged for one hour of work internationally. Since this condition does not prevail, the work of the poor nations can pay for the toothbrushes of only a few of their citizens. The majority has to do without them. The ancient problem of privileged minorities has appeared in a worsened form.

Social justice is the remedy recommended for the tensions caused by the privileged minorities. Some people own more than one toothbrush, while others have none. Let us distribute the toothbrushes equitably. Soon we shall find, as a result of distributive justice, that only 80 per cent of the people, instead of 85 per cent, have to do without toothbrushes. Or that we have available only a fraction of a toothbrush per person. Scarcity is more prevalent than maldistribution.

Another remedy suggested is diversification, industrialization. Let us make the toothbrushes at home. All we need is a factory and some technology. But a factory means capital, which comes from savings, which come from reduced consumption. And technology means an expenditure in education, which means a reduction of other expenditures. Therefore, some of the man-hours of work which are now exchanged for the toothbrushes of 15 per cent of the people should really be exchanged for the machines necessary to build the factory, and for the books and teachers necessary to prepare the workers. In order to industrialize we should reduce from 15 per cent to 10 per cent the proportion of our people who can afford toothbrushes. *Industrialization pre-supposes sacrifice.*

But, we are told, we can lessen these problems by receiving foreign aid. Part of the cost of the factory will be given to us by rich nations who underpay us for our work. Thanks to their gifts (or loans), instead of reducing from 15 per cent to 10 per cent the proportion of toothbrush users, we can build the factory by merely reducing this proportion to 12.5 per cent. *Aid can never compensate for the inequity of the terms of trade.*

In the meantime, importers and advertisers will stimulate *all* our people to use toothbrushes. Agitators will encourage *all* our people to grab the toothbrushes of the 15 per cent who have them, and make everybody happy by giving one-tenth of a toothbrush to each person. Simultaneously, in the aid-giving countries newspapers will criticize the handouts of foreign aid, and politicians will defend the taxpayer's money by calling friendly nations "beggars." Day by day, in the rich and the poor countries, *the seeds of world tensions are being planted by international trade.*

"The new city," said Plato in the fourth century B.C., "must be placed inland, lest foreign ideas undermine its faith, foreign trade its peace, and foreign luxuries its self-contained simplicity." In April 1962, a reform-minded military ruler who probably knows few philosophers, General Park of South Korea, creator of the "New Life," proclaimed: "The sight of foreign goods arouses wanton desires in the minds of the people. Burn them!"

According to *Time* Magazine, "condemned to the fire were French cosmetics, Hong Kong brocades, Swiss watches, German phonographs and records, American neckties and shirts, Japanese toys—more than 200 items in all, with a dollar value of $230,-000."

The industrial nations of today have reached a stage where consumption is considered an economic virtue; consumption of almost anything stimulates production. "Business is good" when people are buying heavily. It is taken for granted that the production facilities are there, awaiting the call of demand. Few people stop to think that this is a recent phenomenon in economic history. All through the millennia of man's struggle to earn a living in organized society, in spite of what individual merchants might want, consumption was a thing to be avoided or reduced to a minimum.

Only during the last half century, and in a few countries, have machines and techniques multiplied man's productive ability to a point where it is often desirable to encourage consumption in order to keep the economy functioning. Even in those happy countries demand sometimes overreaches the capacity to produce, because of high wages, excessive credit, or other factors. From that point on there is no increase in the flow of goods and services —just an increase in the circulation of cheaper money.

Furthermore, in wartime, when demand for all things is extremely high, the rich nations stop considering consumption as a virtue. Demand is curtailed by rationing, quotas, and appeals to patriotic austerity. Business is discouraged. The tourist agencies should conserve, as a reminder and consolation in periods of slack business, the signs posted on the walls of airline offices in the United States during World War II: "Is this trip really necessary?"

In the nonindustrialized nations, where so many of the modern conveniences have to be imported, and paid for in low-priced exports, the effects of consumption more often resemble wartime stringencies than peacetime affluence. True, the demand for certain local goods, for which the necessary resources are available, may have a beneficial effect. Even the waste of the rich, if it be restricted to indigenous luxuries, may be welcome in some cases. But generally the tendency to consume, to raise the standard of living prematurely, slows down rather than accelerates economic development, not only because savings and capital formation are curtailed, but also because the economy is obliged to produce more and more primary goods for export, thus weakening the foreign market.

Theoretically, it is conceivable that the retarded countries would develop in social peace if they could induce their people to maintain Plato's "self-contained simplicity." Leading a bucolic life for a time, they would import almost exclusively machines, trucks, and other capital goods. Practically nothing for consumption; none of the niceties that "arouse wanton desires." To pay for the bulldozers and the power plants, they would have to export a relatively small amount of coffee, or wool, or bananas. Limited shipments would keep prices up. The exchange then might even be man-hour for man-hour of work, instead of ten to one as it is today, in the trade between industrial and nonindustrial nations.

Assuming sound economic and social management in this Arcadia, the work that is now devoted to producing cheap exports to pay for expensive luxuries would be used to provide more local food, better houses from indigenous materials, handmade roads, schools, and health centers, in the simple, pre-industrial ways. Gradually the cement plants, diesel engines, and other imported capital goods would change the landscape, the customs, the productivity. The people could then consume more and more of the amenities of the industrial era, locally produced. Through privation and austerity, the country would have been developed.

However, the road to Utopia is not as clear as all that.

Perhaps the military dictatorship of South Korea will be able to enforce its "New Life" upon its people. The smaller the amount of gasoline, American breakfast cereals, plane tickets, and cablegram services used by the well-to-do minority, the smaller will be the amount of poorly paid export rice that the majority will have to harvest to pay for imports. The utilization of the labor force will be better, in physical production, education, and public health. At an initial stage of development, the slower the growth of the middle class with its consuming habits, the faster will be the increase in imports of capital goods. Diversification and industrialization, the recipes often recommended under a stern plan, will probably be effective in a short time. No foreign sales-

men or advertisers, no reformers, no "free press" should be allowed. Few social tensions will manifest themselves under an
autocratic regime.

The Soviet Union has enforced economic development with a
minimum of imports for nearly half a century. The country is so
large and so varied in latitudes and resources that the exclusion of
foreign luxuries is probably a less severe hardship than it would
be for a smaller nation, where fewer things are locally produced
from the start.

By Western standards, the Russian effort has not yet produced
an abundance of consumer goods. Under central planning, and
disregarding consumer demands, the country has devoted a high
proportion of its output to education, technology, heavy industry,
and war. To some extent the economy must have suffered from
the lack of diversified initiative and management. Presumably,
however, if peace prevails, these past decades of forced austerity
in consumption and largess in capitalization will eventually produce an affluent society of some kind.

The trouble with the Latin American republics and similar
nations is that they want to drink the milk and eat the cow at
the same time. They want development, but they also want
democracy, however imperfect the government, and freedom of
choice for consumers, however modest the national income. They
want economic growth, which requires capital formation, but
they also want to consume all their income, or a little more, which
impedes capital formation.

Even under democratic government, capital formation would
not be so difficult if these peoples had only *internal* problems, if
most of the articles they want to consume were locally produced,
if their countries were larger and therefore their economies more
varied—if, for example, there had been a Latin American common market for the past fifty years.

Indeed, in a "closed economy," with few imports and exports,
the difficulties of capitalization are not so serious. Landowners
and businessmen are always powerful, whatever their complaints,

and their tendency is to keep wages low and profits high. Part of their profit is wasted, but much of it goes into capital formation. Wage earners are also powerful nowadays, as union members or as voters. They tend to push salaries up and profits down. At some moment their pressure may increase the over-all purchasing power too much and provoke excessive demand. But normally it has stimulated efficiency, investment, and output. Growth has been the result of the equilibrium of forces in the struggle between business and labor in modern industrial democracies.

However, different things happen in underdeveloped countries with "exchange economies" when the "wanton desires" to consume the products and services of foreign industry are aroused.

Privileged minorities exist in every society. Justly or unjustly, they manage the wealth of the nation, whether in exercise of prerogatives, as in old aristocracies; or in exercise of ownership and its administrative instruments, as in the West today; or in exercise of political power, as in Russia now. Such minorities live high. They enjoy the conveniences and luxuries made possible by contemporary civilization.

Before the industrial revolution, the economy could support only a minority at a high level of living. Nowadays, with technology, social aspirations, and the science of development, those minorities are the spearhead of a way of life that tends to spread and to become generalized. A few countries have already transformed themselves into affluent societies, and a dozen welfare states have at least eliminated poverty. Those nations constitute the developed world.

In the poor sector of the world, the privileged minorities manage to keep up with the Joneses abroad, but at the expense of the local majorities. The chief of the most illiterate Arab state has a fleet of Cadillacs. The capital of any starved country has air-conditioned hotels to welcome the visiting European or North American. All the Latin American republics have fully developed urban areas. There exists around the globe a society of people who seldom sleep in a room without a private bath wherever they go, and who are seldom away from the telephone. The world economy supports that international society, composed of large numbers of people from the developed countries, plus the fortunate minorities of the poor nations.

How do the economies of the poor nations pay for the imported automobiles, nylon shirts, and all the modern goods and services that allow their local minorities to mingle with the affluent foreigners? There is the rub! They have to pay with coffee or tea, or jute or sisal, or any other of the few articles that cannot be produced in the temperate zones, where most of the industrial countries lie.

The demand for these primary articles is limited. As they are produced and exported in larger and larger quantities to pay for the products of an ever advancing technology, they flood the markets, depress the prices, and retard local development.

New conditions also upset trade relations. Take, for example, the coming of the jet plane. Suppose that the economy of Ecuador is buying 100 tickets a day, from Quito and Guayaquil to the United States and Europe, at an average of $500 a ticket, in propeller planes. Whether the airline is local or foreign makes little difference, because one major cost is the amortization of the plane, which is built in a developed country.

The economy of the poor nation, as a whole, is paying $50,000 a day to the economy of the industrial world for the service of plane travel. Ecuador has to export 250,000 pounds of cocoa daily at 20 cents per pound to cover the cost of this service.

Suddenly the propeller planes are changed for jets, which cost several times more to build. Plane fares jump 40 per cent. The bill presented by the developed nations to Ecuador goes up to $70,000 a day. Where is the corresponding increase in the dollar income of the Ecuadorean economy to pay for the $20,000 difference? Nowhere! The tendency will be to ship more cocoa; 350,-000 pounds at 20 cents would bring in the $70,000 needed to cover jet transportation. But 40 per cent increase in the supply of cocoa may depress the price 5 per cent, if only one supplying country increases exports, or 50 per cent if all supplying countries are forced to do the same. Suppose that few countries pay for jet transportation with cocoa, and that prices drop only 10 per cent, to 18 cents per pound. Ecuador will still have to export $70,000 worth of cocoa if 100 jet tickets are to be consumed. It will take nearly 390,000 pounds to cover the daily bill. Again, the 40,000 extra pounds may bring the price down to 17 cents per pound. Still more cocoa will have to be shipped. And so on and on. Unless fewer people travel by jet, unless the minority who can afford to travel is reduced to a smaller proportion of the total population, the majority whose work is needed to produce the cocoa will have to reduce its standard of living, adjusting it to a price of 17 cents per pound, as a result of the coming of the jet.

Looking to the future, some people hope that the trends will change, and the dependence of the poor countries on exports of primary articles will be reduced as a result of common markets, planned development, and international aid. Undoubtedly, all these useful means of development must be encouraged. But unless more basic measures are taken, their effects will be slow. The gap will not be closed, because the advanced nations are advancing fast.

The more the new nations develop, the higher their imports will be. In the foreseeable future the countries that have taken the lead in the industrial revolution will continue to supply the articles that require heavier equipment, more advanced technology, and higher investment.

What will the Latin American republics export, after they develop, to pay for their new imports? To some extent they may do as Japan does now; try to compete internationally in automobiles and electronics. But the bulk of their exports will still be coffee and cocoa and bananas from the torrid zone, minerals from the mining areas, and meat and wool and off-season grapes from the extreme South. There is such a thing on earth as a natural distribution of resources. As long as coffee and bananas are wanted by people in the temperate zones, they will be the logical exports of the tropical latitudes.

In 1962 it is permissible to ask: What would happen if Russia should win the Cold War in Latin America? If that meant the disengagement of our economies from the United States and Western Europe, to be coupled with the Communist countries, as Cuba has done, certainly our international trade would be a great deal worse than it is now. Russia and China are poor markets for the exports of Latin America, and for a long time they would be poor suppliers of her needs.

There is a still more fundamental question: What makes anybody believe that the Communist nations, even if they could replace the Atlantic countries in their trade with Latin America, would be more enlightened and more inclined to international solidarity? Has Russia established a healthy precedent in her business relations with the satellites of Eastern Europe or Asia?

The pro-Russians of Latin America may ask: Why should we switch our trade connections from one world to another? Why can we not deal with East and West simultaneously? This is a good question. Unfortunately, however, it is as good or as useless as asking: Why should there be a Cold War?

Perhaps there are more pertinent questions for us to ask at this moment: Why should the West allow a rudderless international commerce to play havoc with all the efforts that are being made to bring order and to reduce world tensions? Why waste most of the effort of foreign aid when world trade continues to drain the poor nations? In fifty years or more, after the majority of nations will have been developed, in spite of international trade, it is expected that the work and resources of all countries will be compensated equally. Why not accelerate the process and start equal compensation now?

The advanced Western nations have established justice among the various segments of their populations. Industrial workers are no longer proletarians; farmers have ceased to be peasants. This solidarity among groups, equalizing their incomes, has brought about a great internal market, making mass production profitable.

Nothing indicates that solidarity among countries would not bring the same benefits to all.

The minimum legal wage is one of the best examples of enlightened policy, and of ethics applied to economics. Countries like the United States refuse to import workers and pay "slave wages," although millions and millions would gladly migrate to earn one-tenth of present U.S. salaries. But it would be bad business in the long run, and it would not be ethical. "Slave labor" is a hideous phrase. Why, then, is it considered good business and ethical to import slave labor transformed into the products of the underprivileged nations of the world? How can we have a universal family if the rich continue to exchange one hour of their work for ten hours of the work of the poor?

The only answer is that the methods, the mechanisms of international solidarity have not yet been devised. However, the first ingredients are already here: the attitude, the conception, the circumscribed attempts at this new solidarity among countries are already present. "Lend Lease," the "Marshall Plan," "Foreign Aid," the "Alliance for Progress" are all phrases coined in the most progressive of modern nations to identify the embryo of a new policy of solidarity for a unified mankind, just as the terms "Farm Program," "New Deal," and "New Frontier," among others, express the contemporary resolution to make solidarity effective inside a given country of the developed world.

We are holding coffee conferences, tin conferences, communications conferences, and all kinds of meetings in a timid effort to establish justice. No one knows what the best mechanisms will be. But the unintended exploitation of the poor economies by the rich economies will end. In the West, "Imperialism," with its political aims, is dead. "Colonialism," with its economic purposes, is dying. "Free trade," with its unexpected consequences in backwardness and tensions, will die.

Perhaps it will be necessary for a time to establish quotas and minimum prices for the exports of the weak economies. Perhaps a way will be found to finance the destruction of surpluses, and to avoid further unneeded production. Inversely, perhaps subsidies will be applied by the developed nations to reduce the prices of services and capital goods exported to the weak economies. Perhaps foreign investments will be legitimately transferred to the ownership of the host countries. Perhaps, finally, the boldness and the imagination that characterize shooting wars will be applied to the fronts of the Cold War, and, most of all, to the universal battle towards world integration that man is fighting in our time.

ECONOMIC INTEGRATION AND POLITICAL REINTEGRATION

FELIPE HERRERA

President,
Inter-American Development Bank, Chile

INDEPENDENCE AND INTERDEPENDENCE

To study the motives and meaning of world tensions is to analyze and interpret history. Perhaps for this very reason each dawn has been the beginning of a new historic age. But in our times the existence of a vast and far-flung transformation is so evident that for the first time in history it would appear that social developments have the same power of acceleration as scientific advances or technological change.

As a result of various factors, particularly the universal progress in communications, mankind no longer accepts poverty as an inevitable part of life. This change from fatalism to hope, from despair to action, has unleashed a force whose consequences lie beyond our powers of calculation. With the gradual disappearance of imperialism, we are witnessing the end of a system which for more than four centuries welded together the world opened by Spanish and Portuguese navigators to trade and conquest by a Europe more powerful and technologically more advanced. Independent nations emerge or re-emerge from this world to join the international community. Each of these nations brings to the world its decision for self-government and continuing independence, and its demand for a share of well-being.

This progress towards a new world order stirs up almost unbearable tensions. One of the greatest sources of anxiety in our time is precisely the uncertainty concerning the system that will prevail in achieving the brotherhood of all nations.

An increasingly clear perception of joint responsibility and destiny has led to a search for and trial of collective solutions. Thus, the intense preoccupation with problems of regional economic integration that followed World War II has yielded impressive results. Europe is now progressing firmly along these lines. In this connection, I would like to recall here the words of President Kennedy in a speech last July 4 in Philadelphia that strikes a proper note for this day and age:

I will say here and now on this day of independence that the United States will be ready for a Declaration of Interdependence . . . that we will be prepared to discuss with a United Europe the ways and means of forming a concrete Atlantic Partnership—a mutually beneficial partnership between the new union now emerging in Europe and the old American union founded here 175 years ago.

We are becoming familiar with the trend toward the reintegration of nations which throughout recent centuries had severed their ancient ties. Arab nationalism, for example, despite the immediate tensions of the Islamic countries, has become a powerful centripetal force seeking its own political, economic, and philosophical expression. The recently emancipated African nations are also zealously seeking points of cohesion; Pan-Africanism tends to become another interesting, international dynamic force. Now we have the coming economic and political integration of the Malayan peoples. In our opinion, these processes accentuate a "pluralist" trend in international relations.

Latin America, like many other regions, has taken significant steps in the field of collective action. The Inter-American Bank is itself a cooperative Pan American undertaking for the financing of development projects. It also administers the Social Progress

Trust Fund established to implement the Act of Bogotá and the Charter of Punta del Este, both instruments of hemispheric scope. In the more limited field of regional economic integration, the Latin American Free Trade Association, established by the Treaty of Montevideo, is gaining momentum, and Central American economic integration is entering a stage of greater effectiveness with the recent acceptance by Costa Rica of the regional Treaty and its association with the Central American Bank.

However, this action has tended to concern itself exclusively with the economic aspects and, at times, the purely commercial aspects of the process of integration, ignoring the political factors involved. Actually, integration is political as well as economic in both its objectives and its procedures. On the one hand, economic changes to satisfy the requirements of an expanded market can create a need for political unity, although they cannot of themselves bring about such a union. On the other hand, many economic problems can be solved only through political measures. The development and orientation of regional trade, the maintenance of full employment, the regulation of cartels and monopolies, the prevention of depressions and inflation, and the coordination of regional economic plans necessarily require legal provisions, executive decisions, and administrative harmony that are the responsibility of the highest spheres of government.

In this respect, it is helpful to recall certain concepts of Dr. Hallstein, President of the European Commission of the European Economic Community, addressing the Parliamentary Assembly of the three European Communities on March 19, 1958:

We should not forget that the main thing pooled by the Rome Treaty was not the "economies" of our nations—that is to say, the sum total of the decisions and activities of industrialists, workers, bankers, tradesmen, and consumers—but the economic policies of the participating countries. In other words, it is not the citizens who are making a sacrifice to the Community . . . , but the Governments. The merging of the national economies themselves is merely an outcome of this, and in this sense of secondary importance. The significance of our Community lies in political aspects of the institutional setups of our

Community, no less than in the practical regulations relating to the conditions of administration. What is it that we are trying to achieve? We are striving to bring about a transformation of society. We want our citizens, in so far as they regard themselves as political beings, to think of themselves not merely as members of a traditional structure, but as belonging to the great European family.

If Latin America is to recover lost time, it must step up the pace of its economic integration and, to this end, must squarely face up to the need for political integration. Many conditions and circumstances of its geographic, historic, and human situations favor both prospects. Latin America is not a group of nations: it is one great disjointed nation. The historic task of the area, viewed as a unit, is to recover the forward surge of a frustrated process of economic development, rather than undertake a new one.

The Latin American nation is not a fictitious entity. Upon its age-old indigenous heritage, diverse in shape and manner but identical in essence, is the imprint of four centuries of Spanish domination. From Mexico to Cape Horn, it was formed by similar experiences, institutions, cultures and influences. Thus, united in spirit and in power, it rose to claim its independence.

AMERICA DISINTEGRATES

The heroes of our independence were thinking of such a Latin American nation: Padre Hidalgo in Mexico declared himself "Generalíssimo of the Americas," and Belgrano at the Congress of Tucumán spoke of the representatives of the "United Provinces of South America." San Martín and O'Higgins, Santander and Sánchez Carrión, Morazán and Santa Cruz, all advocated the federalist idea. Bolívar, its particular partisan, following the winning of independence, hoped to achieve it at the Congress of Panama. Bolívar failed to achieve his goals because the forces that were to produce or contribute largely to Latin American fragmentation were already at work. Actually, none of the founders of the new nationalities was concerned with strengthening or broadening democratic formulas rooted in colonial institutions. All found inspiration in ideas from the Encyclopedia and adopted the model that had served to constitute modern Europe. The nation-states were born under a concept in which the nation was vague, and, consequently, the state was frail.

I believe that this institutional and ideological Europeanization of the new Latin American countries served partly to affirm their status as independent entities during the period of persistent attempts at reconquest. The diplomatic deterrent of the Monroe Doctrine was not sufficient to keep Europe's fleets away from the American coasts. It was Juárez who had to free Mexico from Maximillian; and it was Chile, Peru, Bolivia, and Ecuador as allies which in 1866 affirmed their independence in the face of latter-day attempts at domination by the Spaniards.

Once independence was achieved, various circumstances conspired to maintain the fragmentation of the Latin American nationality. One of the most serious causes of disintegration following independence, regarded as a decisive factor in the creation of successive independent states, was the extreme difficulty of communications. Even today, even after 150 years of roadbuilding and railroad construction, 90 per cent of inter-American trade is carried by sea. The lack of sufficient land and river routes is still a considerable obstacle to our development.

Communication difficulties had been the same in colonial times, and yet they had failed to dissolve the basic unity. One circumstance, however, radically changed the situation. The colonial economy was not organized to serve the colonies but to serve the metropolis. Consumer economy was a matter for local concern in each province; foreign economy was the concern of the Casa de Contratación of Seville, which, exercising a monopoly from Spain, represented a cohesive factor in the economic life of the Indies.

With independence and freedom of trade secured, the difficulty of communications created insurmountable barriers for unifying an economy that had formerly been mobilized through the metropolis. A Peruvian author explains the breakdown of ties in the following terms: *

According to Spanish policy these separate realms were joined to the principal nucleus—the Crown—but were not united among themselves by any close ties. The Spanish colonial empire functioned in the manner of a solar system but with no relationship between the outlying planets. This is a fact of enormous importance in the history of Spanish America. Independence severed the radii which had connected the parts of that system with its nucleus, the Crown, and naturally the units became absolutely separate and free.

To economic upheaval was soon added the problem of power. The armies massed for the battles of liberation could not easily be disbanded. The old landowners toyed with the notion of returning to the past, while the new native masses wanted to acquire lands, and inept local administration proved incapable of solving the new problems. The early leaders could not have hoped for a more propitious moment. They persisted in thinking in terms of heroic leadership of their troops and glory-bedazzled seduction of the people. Each carved out a state for himself from such land as he could control by force of arms. And so disunity was perpetuated and power-seeking adventurers succeeded each other in turn.

The new economic activities had two alternatives: to restrict themselves to meeting consumer requirements within the former provincial market, or to revolve around four or five basic items. Unprepared and disunited, our countries turned to supplying raw materials to the international market. Fluctuations in the world market for these products became the key to our destinies. Each crisis left its deep impress on the stability of our countries and drove them to a kind of negative nationalism.

Against such a background, the advance towards industrialization was sporadic and artificial. Anti-economic protectionism had

* Victor Andrés Belaunde, *Bolívar y el Pensamiento Político de la Revolución Hispano-Americana*, p. 176.

at times to be justified on nationalistic grounds that served to exacerbate mutual suspicion and distrust. Voices within and without, raised in defense of the interests vested in the continued "balkanization" of Latin America, gained in force and respectability.

The countries turned a deaf ear to each other's needs and drew further apart with each passing day. Each looked to the sea and turned its back upon its neighbors, but the sea led only to Europe. This was the situation during the nineteenth century and up to the first World War.

POLITICAL INTEGRATION

While the more highly developed nations of the world are moving toward unification into large confederations of increasing significance, the ideological, cultural, and economic fragmentation of the countries of Latin America has steadily diminished our capacity for decision-making on the great problems confronting humanity. The small geo-economic areas which characterize most of our structures have tended to minimize the participation of Latin America as an independent and progressive force on the international scene, and to give rise to policies which are incapable of overcoming domestic tensions except through dictatorship and extremism.

For some years past the idea of regional integration has been taking a new and stronger hold upon the minds of many Latin Americans. At Punta del Este, in August 1961, our countries subscribed to the objectives of the Alliance for Progress and for the first time set themselves collective goals of social development and welfare to be attained in the next decade. Several recent international assemblages have recognized the imperative need for a gigantic effort by the region to augment its infrastructure capital, develop its basic industries, and expand its social investments. It has also been recognized that the fragmentation of the Latin American market into a multiplicity of national markets, virtually isolated from each other, poses a serious impediment to development. Conferences have been held on regional markets and experts throughout the hemisphere have striven for formulas of rapprochement. However, the fact remains that, as far as the creation of a Latin American common market is concerned, we are in 1962 repeating formulas which in Europe were first outlined in 1947 or 1948; we are still at the stage of an exchange of expert opinions. It would appear that experts in all fields find it much easier to take action on a hemispheric scale than do political leaders, and that there is no parallelism between the approach of these two groups. Those of our politicians who have supported the ideas of Latin American economists and technicians on our commercial integration should not forget that, in the Old World, the ideas of Briand, Stresemann, Herriot, and Churchill were the cornerstones of contemporary European unity.

I firmly believe it is not premature and utopian to broach at this time the need for working towards the political integration of Latin America. I am convinced that our political integration is a requisite that we cannot ignore.

We might hold that political unity will be the necessary result of the play of forces for economic integration that are now beginning to stir within the hemisphere. However, we have a long road to travel, and all the longer the more we delay in recognizing that economic integration cannot be attained exclusively through strictly economic measures, that economic integration is not in itself enough to assure the progress and welfare of nations, and that every development process entails simultaneous struggles on the fronts of technology, law, education, institutions, and, fundamentally, politics.

Anguished by poverty and trapped by an inferiority complex which is heightened by observation of the progress made in other regions, our nations have lost faith in their own creative capacity. Latin America needs to carry out its political unification not only because it will thus be able to give content and effective form to its economic integration and to the subsequent common prosperity it hopes to achieve, but also because this collective achievement will encourage dynamic spiritual forces which will enable us to consolidate our faith in our own cultural values.

An integrated Latin America is no utopia. The people of this region are seeking forms of common expression in the exercise of their professions, the conduct of their business, the financing and execution of their development programs, and the application of their techniques. At the same time, the popular masses are also seeking common ground. The integration of Latin America will constitute a powerful factor for improved utilization of all our collective capacities that are not being properly channeled today owing to the prevailing factors for disunity.

It is not necessary to dwell on the industrial and technological advantages which would accrue from the integration of our several economic spheres into one great regional market. One of the serious factors limiting the industrialization of Latin America and its prospects for technological absorption is the existence of fragmented markets. The very bases of the Latin American Free Trade Association and the General Treaty for Central American Economic Integration tend to remove such obstacles.

There are other fields in which integration could be promoted on feasible terms. Latin America now holds a very significant volume of monetary reserves. According to recent statistics, by the end of March 1962 Latin American monetary reserves in gold and foreign exchange amounted to 2,615,000,000 dollars. These resources are parceled out among a great many isolated compartments, which detracts from their true significance on the international scale. There are no known technical obstacles to the cooperative and coordinated use of these funds, that is, to the formation of a type of central banking system for the hemisphere. A mechanism of this kind would reinforce the prospects of Latin America as a whole for overcoming short-term financing difficulties. In addition, it could also serve as a multilateral factor in promoting regional trade.

Latin America occupies a decisive position in certain basic items of world trade: 71 per cent of world coffee exports; more than 50 per cent of copper exports; over 33 per cent of petroleum; close to 40 per cent of cocoa; more than 65 per cent of bananas, and an important share in the exports of cotton, wool, tin, and other nonferrous metals. In some of these commodities, particularly coffee, our countries have endeavored to formulate and implement common policies in defense of their markets and prices. Can we not now take joint action with respect to other basic products, in order to prevent discriminatory policies and to improve our trade prospects?

In the past year, following the signing of the Charter of Punta del Este, considerable progress has been made in the preparation of economic development programs by all our countries. Almost all of them now have national agencies responsible for planning and coordinating their own economic policies. Many of them are drafting or executing their own development plans. Certainly credit is due to the inter-American regional agencies for their valuable technical work in the achievement of these objectives. However, we should view such efforts as a preliminary step toward the formulation of an over-all program for Latin American development, within whose framework many existing problems could be solved or mitigated. I refer particularly to the problem of raw materials surpluses on the market and to artificial industrialization efforts.

Latin America is largely dependent on the world outside for transportation and communication facilities. Our countries have attempted to develop their merchant marine fleets and airlines on an individual basis. An interesting exception to this tendency is the GranColombiana merchant fleet, whose efficiency and commercial success are incontestable facts. It is most advisable that Latin America should be able to act jointly or coordinately in these activities requiring heavy investments and broad markets.

The image of Latin America abroad is distorted. Nothing is known of our struggle against poverty; nothing of our Sisyphean labor to achieve monetary stability in the face of declining prices for our export products. If our publicity agencies would organize information on Latin America, we could contribute toward a more accurate understanding of our countries and peoples.

Our countries maintain approximately 650,000 men under arms, and our military expenses amount to the equivalent of 1,400,000,-000 dollars a year. Some countries maintain forces proportionate in size to those of the United States or the Soviet Union. Separately, few of our governments are willing to reduce their armed forces to any appreciable extent. Only the collective disarmament of our countries and a coordinated approach to the task of hemispheric defense will make it possible to overcome many persistent factors of tension and will produce a substantial saving in collective resources that can be usefully applied to accelerate our development.

These are some of the common tasks in which Latin American efforts could multiply the creative capacity of this hemisphere. On all these fronts, as on those relating to juridical systems, health and education, science and international policy, we need political resolution and decision. We have made notable advances during the last fifteen years in exchanges of view among our experts. It is now time to hear the voice of hemispheric political leadership. If we continue to consider Latin American integration strictly as a tariff problem and fail to mobilize our political and social forces, then new international developments toward the interdependence of the great continental states will find us overwhelmed on every hand and bereft of a significant voice even among our own people.

THE NEW BALANCE

The stress we have laid on the need for accelerating the process of Latin American integration primarily through political action does not mean that such action should be construed as a trend toward isolation. In international relations the trend today is toward "pluralism." The best expression of this new scheme is the Atlantic Community; the United States is supporting European integration as a second pillar on which the Community may rest. If we are seeking to strengthen Latin America and to keep it within the family of Western nations, it also seems logical that our countries should be partners and participants in the Western community on terms of functional interdependence analogous to that of the other two partners. The enlistment of Latin America in that undertaking only makes sense if we join as a single unit. In this way, the process of political integration sheds its merely regional perspective and acquires international significance.

Only thus can our nations feel themselves the masters of their own destinies and effective agents in the current process of history. The Alliance for Progress offers the technical solution to our economic, social, and cultural problems; unfortunately, we have failed to create a suitable force for Latin American "motivation." If our nations have conceived of the Alliance for Progress merely as a policy offered by the United States to Latin America, this has been due to the absence of any intimate conviction that we were dealing on a plane of genuine equality. In order that the Latin American peoples may overcome their feelings of frustration vis-à-vis the advanced Western countries, they must be able to act as a unit in their dealings with the United States and Europe.

We repeat that the political and economic integration of the Latin American nations will not only help to overcome tensions among the peoples of the hemisphere, but will also constitute a powerful factor for equilibrium and peace on the international scene. I can think of no more timely observation than the following excerpt from a speech by the French Secretary of State for European Affairs, Maurice Fauvré, concerning the European Common Market:

We are still keeping up the pretense of four great powers. Actually, there are only two—the United States and Russia. Tomorrow there will be a third—China. It is up to you to decide whether or not there can be a fourth—Europe. If you fail to make this choice, you will condemn yourselves to walk backwards into the future.

It is also up to us, the Latin Americans, to march forward into the future and to serve as a new creative and equalizing factor in the interdependent world that is beginning to take shape around us.

A NEW DEAL FOR LATIN AMERICA

CHESTER BOWLES

The President's
Special Representative,
United States

Thirty years after his election to the Presidency of the United States, most Latin Americans still remember Franklin Delano Roosevelt primarily as the author of the Good Neighbor Policy —an effort to end long years of neglect, conflict, and abuse in the relations between our two regions and to establish a new basis for cooperation.

Franklin Roosevelt is less widely remembered in Latin America, however, for the great domestic reforms which he launched in our country—for his bold and hotly debated "New Deal," which sought to bring to the common people of the United States a greater sharing of opportunity, dignity, and justice. Yet I am convinced that the New Deal has special meaning for all of us as we face together the challenge of the Alliance for Progress.

Like the Alliance for Progress, the New Deal represented an effort both to raise our national income and—equally important —to close the gap between the privileged few and the underprivileged millions. It sought to clear away the slums of our North American cities, to create new homes, schools, and hospitals, and to build a solid basis for the small businessman and the farmer.

Above all, it sought to give to all the people of our country a sense of individual participation, a sense of belonging, and a sense of justice.

The New Deal developed a new respect for the rights of labor and minority groups. It created a system of social security to help our parents' generation face old age with fewer concerns and privations. It provided minimum wages so that no man's income could fall below a certain point. It brought new life to our South through such pioneering successes as the Tennessee Valley Authority and the Farm Security Administration. And it developed programs of taxation based directly on each individual's ability to pay: programs that drew from the wealth of the more developed parts of our country to raise the living standards of those areas which had lagged behind.

The New Deal was a program of dynamism and vitality, a period of promise, hope, and brand new concepts for tens of millions of Americans. Through it we learned by trial and error something of the unlimited capacity of a free people to produce a prosperous and well-balanced society. We also learned some important lessons: the dangers of conflict between economic groups, the limitations of governmental action in some fields, the necessity for it in others, and the importance of economic incentives to spur increased effort.

Much of what we learned in those difficult years can assist and inspire us in the present struggle in partnership to create a better life for the people of all of the Americas.

We can also borrow from our experience in fifteen years of international programs of economic assistance, and from the record of many developing nations. As I look back over these years of effort at home and abroad, it strikes me that the greatest single mistake we can make is to assume that economic progress by itself will ensure a happy and stable society.

If we examine the per capita incomes of the twenty Latin American countries and attempt to relate those figures to political stability, we find virtually no relationship between the two:

some of the countries that have the highest per capita income are among the most uneasy and restless. Here is persuasive evidence that, while growth in itself is important, what happens to people in the process of that growth is infinitely more important.

We must clearly establish in our own minds what we are striving to accomplish and why we feel it is important. As part of its contribution to greater freedom and opportunity, the United States is prepared to draw heavily, not only on our experience with the development of economies in many parts of the world, but also on our own financial resources, and on the energies and skills of our people.

Why are we doing this?

Our purpose in joining the Alliance for Progress is not to win the gratitude of Latin American governments or to influence their votes or their attitudes. Experience has taught us that any government whose loyalty can be bought through economic grants is an ally not worth having.

Our objective is to assist in the building of independent nations in which the people are free to choose their own institutions, within the framework of their own cultures, religions, and history. Only through the creation of such societies can peace and freedom be guaranteed for all nations.

As the developing nations shed the political habits and prejudices of the past and achieve this newer sense of independence, they are likely to take the first opportunity to demonstrate their thoroughgoing independence from those who have tried to assist them. There is no reason why we should deplore this or be irritated by it. A strong show of independence is not only the right of every nation; it is often the essential means of expressing a new-found confidence and sense of direction. More than that, such independence is often the first essential step in the building of a solid foundation for *interdependence:* the partnership of free nations that can lead to an increasing willingness to work together toward common objectives of world peace and decency.

Throughout the United States people are deeply interested and excited by the promise of the Alliance for Progress. I do not believe that this interest is a temporary one. If we boldly meet our respective responsibilities, this interest will grow as the development process in Latin America becomes more evident.

However, there is one essential reservation that deserves the greatest emphasis: the willingness of the United States Government and its heavily taxed people to work towards this common future will depend in large measure on the willingness of the countries of Latin America to deal competently, fairly, and vigorously with their own problems. Through free institutions, we are imposing taxes on ourselves not only to provide better schools, hospitals, universities, roads, and housing, but also to create an adequate shield of defense for all free nations. And behind that shield we are investing additional billions to help other nations create the basis for prosperity and individual justice.

But when we see other governments seek to use our assistance as a substitute for funds that might easily be raised from their own privileged people, we become frustrated and critical. When we see great landlords cling to large estates on which hundreds and thousands of people work on a semifeudal basis, we are equally concerned. When we look in vain for evidence of governmental efficiency, teamwork, streamlined administrative techniques, and effective use of national resources in the process of development, our doubts increase. And when we see recipient governments allow their scarce foreign exchange to be used to buy luxuries for the few rather than necessities for the many, we question whether there is an adequate basis for the kind of cooperation that is so essential to what we are striving to achieve.

So let the Alliance for Progress become in fact a New Deal for all the people of Latin America. Let us join together, not only in the plans and the programs, but also in the sacrifices, the hard work, the willingness to face harsh facts, to discard old methods, and to put aside ancient prejudices.

We are living in an era of revolution. The privileged nations of the world, like the privileged individuals in each society, are faced with a decisive choice: to cast off their coats and become participants in this revolution for world betterment, or to sit on the sidelines, anxious and afraid, as history passes them by.

The United States has made its decision. We are participants, prepared to do our share to make this world revolution for human betterment a success.

Are the privileged groups of Latin America prepared to join us in this effort?

II. Internal Tensions and Preconditions for Economic and Social Development

Nationalism

NATIONALISM AND DEVELOPMENT

DANIEL COSÍO VILLEGAS

**Director, El Colegio
de Mexico**

The ideas and the phenomena of nationalism have aroused the interest of a legion of historians, sociologists, political theorists, and philosophers, in Europe and the United States. Their analyses of European nationalism sometimes coincide only to a limited extent with the situations peculiar to Latin America.

There is some relevance in Hans Kohn's observation that in those countries where rule by the people, or the "third force," first came into its own, nationalism was soon reflected in important changes in the economic and political organizations and institutions. In those countries where this process was slower, only the cultural section was affected.

However, misgivings are inevitable concerning Kohn's categorical statement that nationalism is inconceivable without the idea of the sovereignty of the people, and that therefore it cannot antedate the modern state. A study of the efforts of Latin American countries to emancipate themselves reveals that popular sovereignty either does not exist or is so confused that it could hardly be regarded as a determining factor in movements which are undeniably nationalist. Furthermore, it has not yet been possible to speak of the existence of a real and a modern state in any Latin American country.

There is no reason for being distressed because of the difficulty of transplanting to our continent observations and conclusions made for Europe and the United States. Hans Kohn himself admits that there are different categories or types of nationalism, or that each came into being or developed in different parts of the globe. An attempt will be made here to trace the actual origin and salient features of Latin American nationalism.

The romanticists and the Marxists have been most active in painting and repainting the picture of a vast indigenous paradise preceding the discovery and conquest of these lands by the Spanish and Portuguese. This idyllic picture presents, in the foreground, three civilizations—the Mayan, the Aztec, and the Incan —which had achieved true grandeur and had all the stable and complex attributes of a full-fledged society. In the background we find, painted in bucolic shades, poor and primitive indigenous groups who enjoyed the priceless blessing of living in freedom, of feeling themselves masters of their land and capable of developing with their own resources.

In this idyllic picture there are fictitious elements, but there are also aspects which are true, or almost true. No one can doubt the grandeur, complexity, and progressiveness of the Mayan or Incan civilizations. And it can be assumed without grave misgivings that then, as today, even the poor and primitive civilizations preferred isolation and backwardness to subjugation.

Some corrections must, however, be noted. Many anthropologists, archeologists, and historians have observed that even the great indigenous civilizations were in a sorry plight at the end of the fifteenth century. They gave the impression of having reached the utmost limit of their development or, at least, of suffering from growing pains which held them bogged down in a kind of lethargy. The general reason adduced is that their physical and human resources had already produced their best and that the opportunities of replenishment from different races and civilizations then in America were exhausted.

The main flaw in this picture of an indigenous American paradise is that it assumes that the isolation of the Western hemisphere might have been prolonged indefinitely even after the "Age of Discovery" began. It is forgotten that these civilizations lasted until the fifteenth century without the benefit of the active stimulus which, in Europe, was provided by the continuous mixture of races, languages, religions, art, civilizations, and entire cultures. The Marxists and romanticists paint in somber and violent colors because they bewail the destruction of these civilizations by the conquerors. We must examine the nature of their culture in order to explain Europe's domination of America.

The fact that the indigenous societies, both advanced and primitive, were subjugated and to a large extent destroyed, lies at the root of much of the nationalism in which our countries indulge today, particularly those countries whose indigenous past was of importance. Superimposed on this historic fact, there followed, in an attempt to invest nationalism with a certain sublimity, the idealization of the Indian and his feats.

What could the simple fact of discovery have meant to those civilizations? It must have seemed to them at first an irritating impertinence of the utmost magnitude, and later, a dire omen of something very much more serious.

The conquest continued its course of invasion, war, destruction, plunder, and domination. Various circumstances aggravated its destructive and demoralizing effects. Historians agree that its mainsprings were the lust for riches and religious proselytizing.

The lust for riches necessarily led to plunder—wanton in the case of the conqueror, organized and methodical in the case of the state. When plunder ceased to be blatant vandalism, the lust for riches continued to the detriment of the colonies, because the two conquering nations (like all those of Europe) believed that gold was wealth itself or the key to it. Thus the economy imposed by Spain and Portugal was concentrated primarily on the mining of precious metals, with manpower, transport, agriculture, commerce, and finance subject to the requirements of this activity. Political power and sea power, and later the industries of Spain and Portugal, increased with the gold extracted from America, so that the colonies, in addition to supplying gold and silver, were obliged to consume the manufacture of the metropolises without being able to develop themselves industrially. Hence the economic development of the colonies was not a natural process dictated by the requirements of the colonies themselves.

The results of the religious drive were no better. The Indians' own religions were proclaimed false, pagan, and idolatrous; accordingly, the priesthood was abolished, the temples destroyed, and Indian beliefs and practices punished as mortal sin. Some idea can be had of the degree of subjugation which this implied if it is remembered that the indigenous civilizations were, first and foremost, theocratic and military societies. Once their armies were defeated and their religions destroyed, the two great pillars on which they rested collapsed.

Discovery and conquest were followed by "colonization." This stage was reached very swiftly because, when confronted with Western Europe, even the most advanced of the indigenous civilizations proved weak and backward. The American Indian did not know firearms or steel weapons, the horse or the wheel until they were brought by Europeans. Later, Europe brought to America ideological weapons which were destined to become even more destructive than the harquebus and the sword. One of them, whose corrosive power was incalculable, was individualism; it pulverized the collectivist indigenous societies, where the group was everything and the individual merely one of its small parts.

Colonization did not restore any measure of autonomy to the indigenous communities or to the new half-caste groups which were forming. In the political field, for example, during the two or two and a half centuries of colonization, authority was vested exclusively in the Spanish crown. The authority wielded by its representatives in America was only a delegated or secondary authority; it was never vested in the Indian or the half-caste mestizo, or even in the creole, the American-born offspring of Spanish parents.

The aim here is not to draw up a balance sheet of Spanish and Portuguese rule in America. The sole purpose is to emphasize the fact that three centuries of this rule necessarily left on American man and his land an indelible mark of intervention from outside America. They also left the seeds of an ultranationalism.

Such nationalism was apparent not only in the military, political, and moral rebellions which, in 1825, led to the independence of the present Latin American countries, but also in more meaningful facts. So far as I am aware, no outstanding men of the period devoted themselves to a thorough study of the long experience of the Spanish government in America to see whether it did not contain some elements that might be used in the national life of the new countries—for example, a strong central executive authority which would enable the state to embark on economic and social development consistent with its national interests. The individuals and political groups who favored "centralism" always bore a "reactionary" and unprogressive stamp, i.e., they wished to delay the advance towards real independence by retaining the forms of Spanish government, but they had no intention of using elements of that government which might have helped to expedite and guarantee independence.

Far from considering these three centuries in the light of possibly useful patterns, they passionately and blindly rejected the experience because it savored so much of Spain; they adopted the philosophy and political institutions of France, the United States, and even England—the farthest removed from their situation at that time.

This lack of reflection, this immaturity set off a far-reaching process which began with independence and is assuming enormous proportions at the present time. On the one hand, the Latin American looks to the foreigner for solutions to his problems. He studies and compares the thought and political institutions of the more advanced countries; he takes pleasure in learning foreign languages; he enthusiastically joins the great literary, artistic, or philosophical movements of any part of the world; he squanders all his money and displays his best manners to make the foreigner welcome in his home. This process, which has lasted more than a century and a half, has made the Latin American the most adept man on earth at recognizing and enjoying what is foreign, and at copying it and making it his own.

When a foreign idea, a foreign institution, or simply a foreign fashion is transplanted whole, this rarely leads to the best possible results. The dress is too loose or too tight, too long or too short, and we can infer from repeated experiences that though the cloth may come from outside, it is best to give it to a native tailor. The next step is to import wool to make the cloth oneself, then to raise sheep, and finally to shout from the housetops that God Himself dresses in the cloth which the Indians of Tlaxcala have been weaving for centuries.

But the rise of Spanish American nationalism was chiefly due to two other factors. The first is what is commonly called "the hard facts of daily life." For example, all the Latin American countries achieved their independence without the economic resources needed to maintain it, and still less to make it bear fruit. What little money there was belonged to the conquistador or to the Catholic Church, and since the independence movement was directed against both, the money took flight and was hidden.

The government turned to London, which was then the only capital market. Now, a century and a quarter later, the terms on which they got their first loans there seem quite incredible. In

1824, for instance, the government of Mexico issued 5 per cent bonds for £3,200,000 in London. Goldschmidt and Co. bought the bonds at 50 per cent of their nominal value, then it immediately deducted £10,547 for operating cost and £305,496 for amortization and interest in advance. The net result of the operation was that, while really receiving £1,283,957, the government of Mexico acquired an obligation to pay £3,584,000, or nearly three times as much.

This, of course, was not the only case, nor was it the worst. To start the economic motor of a country of 4 million square kilometers and 10 or 12 million inhabitants with a miserable million pounds sterling was frankly impossible. When the first loan was paid up, the terms on which the second was given were far more disadvantageous. But that was not the end of the story. The agreements covering the first loans had been made between a Latin American government and a particular Englishman, but soon the British government—like the French, Spanish, and United States governments—demanded that such agreements should be made between one government and another and the loans be covered by international treaty. Since the largest and surest revenue which Latin America had throughout most of the nineteenth century came from import duties, foreign officials were very soon stationed in the main customs posts of the country concerned, collecting the duty themselves, deducting what was to be paid to the foreign creditor, paying him, and then, last of all, passing on the remainder to the unfortunate Latin American government. And very little was left. In 1861 the payment of the British debts still amounted to 79 per cent of customs revenue in Mexico, and this did not include the amount payable to France and Spain. Mexico was left with exactly 10 per cent.

The process did not stop there. The signing of international treaties which made foreign governments the advocates and the direct representatives of private foreign creditors, and foreign officials who settled down in another country to carry out these agreements, were followed on several occasions by fleets and armies of occupation. Mexico, for example, saw an agreement signed in London on October 31, 1861, under which the three signatory powers—the United Kingdom, France, and Spain— were to send the necessary armies and navies to Mexico to secure their credit; and it saw French armies impose a foreign monarch and wage a general war on the country for six interminable years. When Mexico won the war and decided to shoot the French emperor in order to express its intent to end foreign interference forever, France and Spain, Britain and Austria, Belgium and the United States called it a nation of savages.

The case of Mexico is typical of the tragic course of Latin American relations with the outside world during the first century of their "independent" life. In 1848 Mexico lost more than half its territory to the United States; between 1850 and 1885 local or federal forces of the United States crossed the frontier and penetrated into Mexican territory; in 1914 naval and land forces of the United States occupied the port of Veracruz and set up a military government there; in 1916, 15,000 United States soldiers, under the command of General Pershing, made a deep incursion into Mexican territory. Mexico fought two wars against France, in 1838 and 1862–1867. Britain and Spain blockaded Mexican ports on more than one occasion and even landed troops.

Of course, "reasons" were always given to explain these actions; but the injured country never admitted that there were any legal or moral reasons. The blackest pages of our history are marked by the still blacker hand of the foreign businessmen, the foreign government, the foreign diplomat, and the foreign soldier.

The other fact which revived Latin American nationalism during the last 30 years or so is that the countries which were its traditional models have largely ceased to be so. No country can boast of having solved any of the fundamental human problems of general well-being, peace, equality—in a word, the problem of happiness. Realizing this, and realizing that many of the model countries themselves are now doubtful or disillusioned about many of their own ideas and institutions, Latin Americans have come to believe that, after all, they are not as backward as they had believed or as stupid as others had said.

Apart from this very human tendency to believe that one is growing taller because one's neighbor is growing shorter, there is another nationalism in Latin America which deserves consideration. Old, spontaneous, irrational, and in bad taste, it appears in Latin America as the unity of one Latin American country in the face of another. In each country it is generally believed that that country enjoys all the fruits of Europe and many others to be found only in America. It is thought that, if a tree is particularly fine, this is because it grew in Colombian or in Chilean soil, not because it is an exceptional specimen which, even if it had been planted in the United States, would have grown into a fine tree. The Colombian also believes that the best Spanish is spoken and written in his country, while the Peruvian and the Mexican obstinately claim that distinction for themselves.

The nationalism of the peoples of Spanish America is older and deeper, less verbal, and more a result of bitter historical experiences and of material and human sacrifice than the nationalism of many other underdeveloped peoples. It is well known that the American Indians were discovered by mistake, since Christopher Columbus hoped to reach Asia. Even so, they were not left in peace. They were dominated for three centuries by Spain and Portugal, the first two colonial empires in history, which were less experienced, less alert, and less well informed than such countries as Holland, France, and England in later periods. This domination existed at a time when international law did not claim to be of the nature of a juridical rule, when there were no international organizations. It was also a time when the conquest and domination of a whole continent could be presented to the world under the pious mantle of a "spiritual conquest," designed to win pagan and idolatrous peoples for Catholicism. As if that were not enough, the first fifty or sixty years of independent life of the Latin American nations coincided with the worst, most aggressive, and most shameless period of foreign imperialism, whose favorite victims were these nations.

All this means that Latin American nationalism is of a very unusual kind. It was seldom born from or suckled by faith in its own values, but was born, grew, and flourished as a reaction of protest, suspicion, and even of hatred and contempt for the wrongs done by foreign individuals, companies, and governments. Thus it is understandable that the nationalistic attitude of Latin Americans towards the external aid which is offered to them, and which they themselves seek for their own economic and social development, should be generally negative and irrational.

The Latin American countries have long experience of external aid. The crude and thoughtless stage of nationalism to which we have referred was followed by what has been called "peaceful penetration," which appeared around 1875 or 1880. All those countries owe their first railways, and sometimes all their railways, to foreign capital and technical knowledge, together with their telegraphs, telephones, and maritime communications, their first banking services, the modern exploitations of their deposits of oil and minerals, and even many of their best farming and stock-breeding enterprises. I do not think it is an exaggeration to say that foreign capital and technical knowledge provided everything new and modern, everything belonging to the twentieth century (or at least, the nineteenth) which they had until 1920.

It would be logical to suppose that the Latin American countries should be grateful to foreign capitalism, however large and onerous their debts, and should wish to seek more foreign capital and technology—now more than ever—since the idea of accelerated development is so fashionable. But this is not so; rationally they desire and seek these things, but emotionally and irrationally they fear and resist them.

Why? First, because their previous experience of "peaceful penetration" was far from satisfactory. There are two other main reasons. One was the discovery that the foreign investor's desire for profit seldom coincided with the needs, or even the tastes, of the countries receiving the investment. The other was the discovery that political penetration often follows economic penetration.

The truth of the second observation is clear from the fact that Latin American countries, like all underdeveloped countries, prefer a loan from an international organization, whenever possible, or even from a private company, to a loan from a foreign government. The truth of the first observation is clear from the case of the railways: they were generally built not in order to promote the harmonious internal development of a country but to take from it the raw materials required by foreign industries.

Of course, the situation has changed considerably in the last fifteen or twenty years, but it has changed for the worse as well as for the better. A change for the better is the new understanding between the country giving technical or financial aid and the country receiving it. This is due, in the first place, to the work of the international organizations—the United Nations and its specialized agencies, the regional economic commissions, the Program of Technical Assistance, the Special Fund, the Bank and the International Monetary Fund, the Organization of American States and its program of scholarships, the Inter-American Development Bank. Another important factor has been the almost complete liquidation of political imperialism and a better understanding by the great powers or former imperial nations of the susceptibilities and suspicions of small countries.

Yet the situation has also changed for the worse. Latin American nationalism has never been as fanatical or as blind, and the events which inflamed it have never been as serious as the notorious Cold War. In 1868, a year after the conclusion of the French intervention, a modest French vice-consul made this remark to his superiors: "In Mexico, they think the mere presence of a foreign diplomat is the beginning of armed intervention." This sentence was mere fantasy when it was first uttered but, in the circumstances, it was fully justified. Today it would not be far from the truth in any Latin American country. Here is a parallel: returning from the Conference of Punta del Este, at which the Alliance for Progress was considered, the Secretary of Treasury of one of the "great" countries of Latin America declared solemnly at the airport, "We have not sold our country at Punta del Este."

If there are any conclusions to be drawn from this study, they are:

1. that Latin American nationalism is old and deep and nourished on outrages, robbery, and blood, and that there is the fullest justification for it;

2. that it is wholly or largely expressed negatively in suspicion, contempt, or hatred for foreigners;

3. that in the last twenty years it has reached incredible extremes of emotion and irrationality.

To fight this nationalism, to reduce it to its proper proportions and to convert it into useful forces will be a difficult task, requiring, among other things, great patience and more integrity than is common in governing circles in Latin America or among those who control the chief organs of public opinion.

Economics

THE ROLE OF GOVERNMENT AND FREE ENTERPRISE

MARIO HENRIQUE SIMONSEN

Economist, Brazil

I. ECONOMIC TENSIONS AND SOCIAL DYNAMICS

Economic tensions appear within a society whenever the active aspirations of its individuals regarding the distribution of property and income conflict with each other. This incompatibility results in crippling some of these ambitions and in the consequent discontent of those whose aims have been frustrated. The state of tension, of course, generates the desire for social action. How far this desire is realized depends on the strength and direction of the tensions.

From a pragmatic point of view, the idea of economic tension includes only the disappointment of those aspirations which come to the surface and are transformed into demands. This does not mean that latent aspirations should be disregarded. They play an important part in the generation of future active demands. There is, however, no way of defining them precisely. Although sometimes the accumulation of latent aspirations leads to explosive acts, they often fade like dreams.

The free nations of the modern world, especially the less de-

veloped ones, are exceptionally predisposed to economic tensions
for several reasons. In the first place, there is a growing desire for
progress. Speed of transportation, ease of communication—press,
radio, cinema, and television—have brought before the eyes of
the common people goals of enrichment which are high as compared to their present reality. The widening gap between reality
and desire, combined with the creeping rate of economic development, leads inevitably to a conflict of individual hopes.

Second is the enlargement of the units of economic decision.
The modern world veers more and more from the traditional
patterns of perfect competition. Individuals and small firms no
longer adapt themselves individually to a Walrasian pattern of
salaries, production, and prices, in which the decisions of each
affect the others only infinitesimally. We see gigantic concerns,
associations, and syndicates taking macro-decisions. This does
not necessarily mean an increase in the total of frustrated individual aspirations, but it does mean that the consequences of
this frustration are greater because: (1) many of the demands
which in a system of perfect competition would remain latent,
can now be brought to the surface and transformed into action;
(2) with expansion of the units of decision has come coordination of individual aspirations in the various sectors which take on
more definite direction; and (3) the gains and losses of each unit
of the system are no longer unaffected by the others.

With this rearrangement of economic tensions, pressures for
the redistribution of income are considerably intensified, to the
point that governments succumb to the temptation of inflation.
Although all classes defend themselves tenaciously against any
loss in their nominal income, not all of them react in the same
way regarding the inflationary attrition of their real income.

A third cause of economic tensions is the absence of logical
limits for the degree of interference by the principal unit of
decision—the government. There is no scientific rule to determine universally the best limits of government intervention in
the economic system, even in rather simple cases. For example,

shall the government have or not have the monopoly of public utilities? One can list various factors pro or con, but no objective criterion permits one to conclude what degree of intervention should prevail.

Individual preferences concerning governmental interference in the economic system are not potent, except in the case of minorities for whom political and ideological motivations weigh as much as do material ones. They may assume, for the popular masses, exceptional importance as the expression of their wish for change which results from the frustration of their hopes. Such desires for change appear particularly in underdeveloped countries that remain stagnant, or where the benefits of growth reach only certain privileged groups of the people. Unrestrained desires for change forestall democratic solution, and these countries tend dangerously towards totalitarian regimes in which the police force suppresses such desires.

II. INFLATIONARY TENSIONS

Although the desirable limits of governmental intervention are controversial, one point seems beyond discussion: it is the government's place to play the part of final arbiter in judging the claims of various sectors of the economy.

Confronted with conflicting claims in sharing the communal income, the government has two choices: to accept this incompatibility and give heed only to a coherent subgroup of the claimants, or to accept a multiplicity of demands and thus set loose an inflationary process. It is obviously impossible to satisfy an incompatible array of demands. However, although the claims to participation in the income are thought of in real terms, they are normally formulated in nominal terms, and if one turns to inflation, there is no limit to the growth of a country's nominal income.

It is not surprising that the underdeveloped nations of the free world should be highly predisposed to inflation, because conflicting demands become so insistent. Incidentally, the propensity to inflation usually appears only when the economy has advanced to the stage of preconditions for the take-off, which is generally the time when individual desires begin to transform themselves into demands. This is not a defense of inflation, but only an attempt to explain a visible phenomenon.

The tensions which inflation avoids are replaced by others, no less acute, resulting from the loss in the real income of various groups caused by the general rise of prices. The dynamic effect of these new tensions appears in repeated and disordered distributive movements which could hardly occur in a free economy with stable prices. The lure of inflation promotes new aspirations, and as long as the government does not renounce the attempt to satisfy incompatible aims, the process tends to perpetuate itself.

None of this is a very logical mechanism, unless there should be a deliberate political plan to provoke a redistribution of the communal income. Even so, one could only justify a uni-periodical rise of prices, never a chronic inflation. Popular misunderstanding of the true causes of inflation is notorious, and this facilitates its use by governments. Generally speaking, the layman sees inflation as an ascending process of rising prices due to increased costs, but he does not understand that prices may rise through the pressure of a monetary surplus and increasing demand. Evidence of this incomprehension is the superstition that indirect taxes are inflationary, or that inflation is to a great extent due to the speculation and greed of businessmen. These popular illusions permit a policy of budgetary deficits.

A chronic and violent inflation, in various Latin American countries, causes a series of changes in the distribution of incomes. Elementary textbooks, which assert that in an inflation the losers are those who have a fixed income, do not give the whole picture since, after a certain time, everyone seeks to defend himself against the general rise of prices by readjusting his income. At times some incomes go up, at times they go down. Inflation, however, cannot be reduced to a simple oscillation of the real income of different social groups. The differences in the bargaining power of the various classes create tendential movements within the oscillations. Some of the most characteristic tendencies and the resultant social tensions will be described below.

1. Among employees, certain classes having a higher degree of political organization enjoy considerable advantages over those who are less united. Brazil offers very striking examples. Workmen who earn the minimum wage—and who undeniably constitute a strong political mass—have benefited from inflation. Under the pretext of rising prices, their wages have almost always been given more than proportional adjustments. The table clarifies this point.

INCREASES IN MINIMUM WAGES IN BRAZIL
(STATE OF GUANABARA)

Date	Minimum Salary Cr$	Increase in Minimum Wage	Increase in Cost of Living
Jan. 1952	1,200	—	—
July 1954	2,400	100. %	54.4%
Aug. 1956	3,800	58.3	51.4
Jan. 1959	6,000	57.9	47.8
Oct. 1960	9,600	60.0	70.0
Oct. 1961	13,440	40.0	38.4

Certain classes of employees in politically strategic positions also enjoy considerable advantages in the redistribution of income by inflation. The most striking case in Brazil is that of maritime and port personnel. Today a simple deckhand earns as much as a Navy Commander, and more than a university professor.

Employees of the middle class are usually those whose real income suffers most in the inflationary struggle. Being less united, and under greater pressure from their standard of living, they rarely succeed in having their incomes adjusted to the general rise of prices. There is a certain technocratic group which escapes this crushing process, but the bulk of the middle class tends towards proletarization. A characteristic example in Brazil affects the higher public servants (including military men). Today a public servant of level "O" (that of a university professor) in real terms earns only 45 per cent of what he earned in 1948. This destruction of the salary scale of the middle class is one of the most serious social consequences of chronic inflation.

2. Governments frequently try to fight inflation by attacking its effects. Such a policy, resting on popular incomprehension of the true causes of the process, relies on price controls. Even if such controls sometimes succeed in slowing the rhythm of increase for a short period, over a long period they are systematically self-defeating.

The first victims of the system are usually public utilities which, being natural monopolies, generally have their rates regulated by the government. The practice, in a chronic inflation, is to grant readjustments of rates in certain areas, but proportionally lower than the general rise of prices. A specific case is the legislation regulating electric power rates in Brazil. Such rates are, by law, calculated to cover the cost of production and give the concessionaire 10 per cent on the nominal historical value of the investment. Obviously, in a chronic inflation, 10 per cent will become an absurdly small return on the real capital invested, and the real profit will be even more negligible if we recognize that depreciation is also calculated on the basis of historical cost. This is flagrantly unjust. It is true that this legislation was enacted at a time when the Brazilian economy was not ravaged by inflation; however, the continued existence of such criteria after fifteen years of violent inflation cannot be attributed to mere inertia in the face of changes. In a frank debate the government seemed to agree that remuneration of public utilities on the basis of historical cost is irrational during a chronic inflation; however, the desire to hide the symptoms of the inflationary process prevails. To this one can add the pressure of extreme nationalists, as the concessionaires are usually dominated by foreign capital. The fact that public utilities in underdeveloped countries are generally controlled by foreign capital has been one of the main reasons for denying them realistic rates.

The result of all this is that private capital is not interested in public utilities. A focus of serious incompatibility is thus created between the government and the private sector. The government is obliged to come into these services as a supplementary investor lest grave bottlenecks arise in the economy— the first step toward the socialization of a strategic sector. Here the cycle of illusion in price control completes itself: what the people did not pay in the form of higher rates, they now pay in the form of taxes or inflation. This is socially quite unfair; the disparity between payment and service rendered has caused the withdrawal of national and foreign private resources from financing in this area.

This is not all, however. The government does not come in as a supplemental investor at the exact moment when private enterprise stops being interested in the expansion of public utilities, but only after a considerable lapse of time. During this interregnum substantial disturbances are generated; supply becomes qualitatively and quantitatively deficient. (A typical example is the Brazilian telephone services: about 800,000 lines are installed, an equal number of requests for telephones are not fulfilled, and the quality of service is extremely unsatisfactory.) Private initiative is portrayed to the public as incapable of administering the services, and a favorable atmosphere is created for violent and demagogic expropriation with payment of absurdly low indemnities. The process of nationalization is finally achieved after an intense campaign that demoralizes private enterprise.

3. The attempt to fight inflation by attacking its symptoms also affects the exchange market. As part of the policy of price control, it is customary to maintain overvalued exchange rates, sustained by quantitative controls over imports. A fixed exchange fund cannot be maintained over a long period of inflation, but it can always be readjusted afterwards if expenditures in foreign currency are repressed. Sometimes governments prefer to resort to multiple rates or to a system of highly differentiated customs tariffs and export duties. In any case, inflation seems to tempt underdeveloped countries into taking the road of artificial ex-

change policy.

Generally speaking, the export sectors, which are usually the traditional activities of underdeveloped countries, suffer most under such a policy. The beneficiaries are the importers, who have access to the purchase of foreign currency at artificially low rates. As a rule, certain new industries establish themselves in the country with imported equipment and are especially favored by the government even if they produce at comparative disadvantage. To compensate, such industries are protected by the prohibition of, or by heavy taxation on, imports of similar products of foreign origin. This represents a subsidy to industry which will be discussed further.

4. Obviously, inflation creates severe distortions in the credit market. The first occurs when the process of rising prices begins, not anticipated by lenders or borrowers, and resulting in the well-known gains by debtors at the expense of creditors. In a chronic inflation, of course, the problem cannot be identified with such simplicity since the speculative process is anticipated by everyone. Nevertheless, countless distortions persist.

In countries suffering from chronic inflation there frequently exist legal regulations which limit the nominal interest rate to a level lower than the rhythm of the general rise of prices. This is the case in Brazil where, in spite of an inflation of more than 30 per cent a year, the usury law (often flouted) forbids annual interest of more than 12 per cent. Under these conditions, inflation brings about a negative interest rate in real terms, resulting in the transfer of resources from creditors to debtors, but with one important difference: the transfer is no longer the result of a lack of foresight on the part of the parties concerned, but a legal requirement which amounts to an implied subsidy to the debtor.

Naturally, the expectation of a strong negative real interest rate throws the credit market completely out of balance. Demand increases excessively and remains partly unsatisfied, resulting in the well-known impression (which so greatly intrigues businessmen) of a shortage of money during inflation. Supplies of private funds for loans are converted to bank deposits in current accounts. As sound procedure allows the application of such funds only to short-term loans, the market of private credit for medium- and long-term loans virtually disappears for lack of lenders. Only the government can continue offering such loans on longer terms. Thus it has at its disposal a subtle instrument for the redistribution of property in favor of certain privileged groups, since long-term loans, at interest rates lagging below the inflation, are subsidies which leave no juridical tracks.

In this game the winners are the sectors specially stimulated by the state, such as new industrial activities, great agricultural exploitations, and concerns that have good political connections. The losers are those who would need a loan (without an implicit subsidy) and cannot obtain it due to the exhaustion of the market—namely, traditional industries, small agriculture, and small and medium firms.

The degree of malfunction of the public credit system is considerably narrowed when the interest rate is allowed to be freely determined by the market. Brazil offers an interesting example: the impasse which until three or four years ago persisted in the field of medium-term credit has been practically overcome with the development of credit and financing companies, entities legally authorized to by-pass the usury law. But grave difficulties still exist. The main ingredient of a free interest rate during a violent inflation is the expected rhythm of price increases; the forecasting of the rhythm of inflation is fundamentally precarious when considering a period of more than one or two years. This means that, when a chronic inflation is expected, not even a liberalization of the interest rate can lead the long-term credit market back to normal. The last recourse is the escalator clause; installments would be readjusted in proportion to a predetermined index of prices. The problem of foreseeing the inflationary rhythm thus disappears, but another arises: in the redistribution brought about by inflation, will the borrowers be able to guarantee that their income will keep pace with the average price indexes?

5. Inflation is a perennial source of illusions of profit. The real profit earned by business is, in general, considerably lower than that shown on the income statement. There are three reasons for this: (a) The rate of earnings is based on a profit expressed in currency of present purchasing power, divided by a capital recorded in currency of past purchasing power. (b) Part of the profit retained by firms is only implied provision for depreciation. However, the stated depreciation reserves, which are normally calculated on the nominal value of equipment and installations (in some cases, as in Brazil, imposed by law), become absolutely incapable of covering the necessary replacement of fixed assets at the new higher price level. (c) A portion of the retained profits (which is considerable when working capital is financed with the concern's own funds) is intended for the replacement of inventories—the prices, due to inflation, having risen. Thus the gains are illusive, for their reinvestment adds nothing to the real worth of the concern.

Because of these three kinds of illusion of profitability, many firms present accounts showing profits varying from 25 to 30 per cent a year when, in reality, they are losing capital while imagining they are distributing dividends. The illusions of profit created by inflation are profoundly pernicious to private initiative. They not only hamper the action of the management, but they are too technical to be understood by people in general. High nominal profits are always considered as a symptom of abuse of economic power, even if real profits are negligible. They create a propitious atmosphere for repeated attacks on private enterprise, including the charge of nonexistent monopolies and the fostering of a belief that the chief cause of inflation is business greed.

(6) One of the principal components of subversion of the economic system by inflation is the decline of correlation between productive effort and enrichment. Immense fortunes have been accumulated in the hands of a so-called "New Class," although

their holders have offered no significant contribution to the development of the country either by means of their capital, their work, or their inventive capacity. There are entrepreneurs who obtain the shelter of governmental credit, being granted long-term loans at negative real interest rates. There are speculators who play with marked cards and who anticipate the sudden leaps of prices which are subject to state control. There are intermediaries who, at the height of inflation of demand, cleverly enter the market and grasp for themselves the difference between the prices that consumers are able to pay and the prices at which the producers are willing to sell.

The appearance of the New Class has sometimes the advantage of breaking the rock-like immobility of a traditional society formed by layers of classes which cannot communicate with each other. It is, however, one of the worst ways of activating a society. The people develop the idea that being clever is more advantageous than working. Meanwhile, the facility with which the New Class accumulates fortunes inclines it toward luxury consumption. This generates dangerous social tensions because of the obvious contrast between the prosperity of the few and the misery of the many.

III. UNBALANCED GROWTH

Many underdeveloped countries of the Free World, which are trying to raise their standard of living, tend toward unbalanced growth. From the angle of production, this disequilibrium takes on three main forms: (1) the non-use of export potentials; (2) the inversion of priority criteria; and (3) the repeated occurrence of bottlenecks. This disequilibrium rarely springs up spontaneously but is nearly always the result of government interference in fields occupied by private enterprise. It is not characteristic of market economies, nor of totally planned systems, but of the mixed ones.

1. The first form arises from the fact that a neglected potential of exports coexists along with industries producing for the in-

ternal market under conditions of comparative disadvantage. This type of disequilibrium is usually the consequence of a strongly protectionist customs policy, or of an overvaluation of exchange rates linked to the prohibition of those import goods that have national equivalents; or it is the corollary of a system of multiple exchange rates.

There is nothing new in stating that many countries insist upon introducing and expanding industrial sectors which are uneconomic or in a position of comparative disadvantage. The motivations, however, deserve some comment.

Industrialization is a necessary condition for the growth of most underdeveloped areas. The export possibilities of products in which these countries have a comparative advantage—nearly always primary products—grow very slowly because of the inelasticity of demand for food products, growing technological economies in the use of industrial raw materials, and the development of synthetic substitutes for some of them. Economic growth through exclusive international specialization is obviously impossible in this case; instead, we have goods produced through domestic industrialization substituted for imports. What was comparatively disadvantageous in a static sense is no longer so from a dynamic point of view. It must be noted, however, that some of these limited possibilities of export are not being utilized by many underdeveloped countries. This certainly demands an explanation.

One must first observe that the degree of satisfaction of popular aspirations cannot be gauged merely by the availability of goods and services. Offer an underdeveloped people two alternatives leading to exactly the same quantity of available goods— the first involving the export of primary goods with a subsequent import of industrial manufactures, and the second involving the national production of these goods—and popular preference will choose the latter. There seems to exist a psychological ingredient in the aspirations of a people which one might call the "fascination of industry." This is pure nationalism, for which people seem willing to pay a price in the form of renouncing a certain quantity of goods and services. One can argue that this is irrational, but one must admit that theories which ignore this ingredient are more irrational.

Evaluation of comparative advantages should, therefore, take the fascination of industry into account. It is not easy to turn this new ingredient into figures, but even if it were possible, we should have to start with the fact that nonutilized potentials of comparatively advantageous exports exist.

There are three explanations (not justifications) for this fact. In the first place, it may be a result of the attempt to fight inflation through its effects. Facing a continuous rise of prices, the government probably would choose a policy of overvaluing exchange. Consequently, some of the export possibilities are not utilized, which creates the need for accelerating unduly the process of import substitution. As a result, we have the introduction of industries with flagrantly disadvantageous comparative costs.

A second explanation is that nationalists shrink from increasing the export of primary products, which they consider a vestige of colonialism. This attitude, emotionally distorted as it is, has been largely responsible for foregoing the advantageous possibilities of sales to foreign countries.

A third explanation, more political, concerns a popular evaluation of the economic effectiveness of governments. This evaluation is based on two components: one, rational, is the degree to which pre-existent aspirations (including psychological ingredients, such as the fascination of industry) are satisfied; another, irrational, is the impact caused by the advertising of the government's achievements. This second component would not exist if people could estimate the alternative cost of these achievements. Obviously they cannot. In an underdeveloped country, the introduction of new industrial sectors creates a much greater advertising impact in favor of the government than does the expansion of traditional export sectors.

2. This same illusory and popular evaluation of the economic

efficiency of governments explains the second form of disequilibrium in the growth of underdeveloped nations: the inversion of priority criteria. The investments most stimulated are those which make a deeper impression on public opinion. The development boom concentrates on spectacular industries, on building great highways, while traditional industries—agronomy, cattle raising, mining, and investments in education are neglected. The building of Brasilia, the opening of the Belem-Brasilia highway, and the incentives to the motor-car industry (extremely useful to the country, but one which should not have received such great stimuli) are characteristic examples. The enthusiasm for spectacular development frequently reaches such a point that the two sectors which cover the immediate needs of a people, namely, food and housing, are also neglected. At this point the system then loses its popularity, giving rise to greater tensions in distribution.

3. The third disequilibrium in the growth of underdeveloped nations is the repeated occurrence of bottlenecks. These arise from the scarcity of certain natural resources, the potential limitation of the capacity to export, the monopolistic structures of production, and the policy of price control during inflation. Propaganda criteria of priority also have the same effect, since complementary investments are not always able to arouse public opinion. A curious example lies in the Brazilian programs of electrification: investment in the distribution of facilities has been neglected, while investment in power generation plants, which have great advertising effect, is promoted.

Distortions in the productive process bring about important imbalances in distribution. The nonutilization of export possibilities, with a corresponding stimulation of industries which are comparatively disadvantageous in dynamic terms, results in deterioration in the terms of trade in traditional economic sectors. At the same time, a kind of "New Industrial Class" appears (frequently made up of old members of the traditional sectors, who have taken advantage of the opportunities offered by the policy of import substitution). This class is not much interested in improving productivity, but is basically concerned with obtaining governmental subsidies and protecting itself against foreign competition by means of prohibitive customs tariffs.

Industries of great advertising potential usually succeed well in this shift. The new industrial class, benefiting from the narrow internal dimensions of the market, the internal scarcity of capital, and the savings in cost due to greater units of manufacture, frequently attains monopolistic positions, which seem to be accepted with excessive benevolence when held by national "impresarios."

IV. Nationalistic Tensions

The expression "nationalism," as it is understood today in underdeveloped countries includes a variety of factors which vary in importance from country to country. Generally speaking, nationalists are preoccupied with exalting the sentiment of national cohesion, preaching social reforms and changes in the distribution of income, an aversion to foreign capital, a reaction against the export of primary products, susceptibility to the fascination of industry, a tolerance towards monopolies of the new industrial class, a disbelief in the proper functioning of market mechanisms, the acceptance of a high degree of state interference in the economy, a tolerance of inflation and of attempts to fight it through price control, and, above all, a great propensity to dogmatism. The area of agreement is, however, more qualitative than quantitative. There are great divergencies among nationalists as to the desirable degree of state intervention, the acceptable amount of foreign capital, and the tolerable rhythm of inflation. Moreover, nationalists are seldom logical when passing from premises to conclusions. A number of nationalistic leaders in Brazil revolt against the incessant rise in the cost of living but preach, as a remedy, increases in subsidies, reductions of taxes and expansions of credit, and sometimes even raises in salaries; or they propose economic programs which are equivalent to a simultaneous increase in the propensities to consume and to save. Nationalism has been seducing eminent intellectuals who are nearly always blind to economic theory. It is not easy to regard nationalism as logical.

In a superficial attempt at classification, one can point out at least eight types of nationalism: authentic, phantasmagoric, xenophobic, monopolistic, opportunistic, socialistic, Marxian, and coerced.

Authentic nationalism, an exaltation of the consciousness of national interest and a reaction against everything opposing it, has been one of the greatest propulsive powers in the development of nations. It is capable both of breaking up the hardened structure of a traditional society reconciled to colonial exploitation, and of giving the population strength to endure the sacrifices of growth. Most of all, it represents the excessive growth of sentiment in relation to reason. But sentiment and reason here move in the same direction, invigorating each other cumulatively.

Two spurious subproducts derive from authentic nationalism, phantasmagoric and xenophobic nationalisms. The first has the same purity of motive but errs in point of time: it rebels against colonialism after colonialism ceases to exist. In its consequences, it greatly resembles xenophobic nationalism which, instead of promoting national interests, engages exclusively in opposing foreign interests.

The worst form of impure nationalism is monopolistic nationalism. This is fostered in underdeveloped countries by so-called "progressive industrial groups," which benefit from the fascination of industry and the tolerance towards indigenous monopolies that nationalists defend. Their motivation is restricted to immediate material interests. They cling to nationalism in order to secure their monopolistic positions through prohibitive customs tariffs, and through the creation of obstacles to the entrance of foreign capital which might compete with them. Their horizons are narrow, and they defend their immediate interests while endangering those of longer range. Other types of nationalists tolerate indigenous monopolies provisionally and temporarily, since, over a longer period of time, these tend to create socialistic reactions in which monopolists are the first to be affected.

In the hands of unscrupulous politicians, phantasmagoric or delusive nationalism also distracts the people's attention from the real causes of underdevelopment and from inflation when it exists. This is a matter of finding scapegoats; the most ingenious device is to import them from abroad. Such political use of phantasmagoric nationalism may be called "opportunistic nationalism."

It is no novelty that socialists in general, and Marxists in particular, should see in nationalism the ideal vehicle and ally for the achievement of their aims. In the first phase, this alliance aims at removing colonial intrusion, real or imaginary. Then the structure of the state is fortified, and socialization is preached as a natural response to the weakness of national capital and its propensity to monopoly. There is no doubt that Marxists, even when greatly in the minority, have a special skill in taking over the command of nationalistic fronts. In the first place, in a movement characterized by emotional imbalance—an excess of sentiment in relation to reason—they, more than others, keep a cool head. In the second place, while most nationalists unite for the immediate objective of fighting, Marxists offer a solution after the fight which is predestined to seduce weary emotions, for it is the antithesis of the order which prevailed before. Look at the example of Cuba.

The word nationalism has a special power of coercion. Even when the nonexistence of colonial maneuvers reduces authentic nationalism to a moderate attitude, there are few people who could dare rise against it. Marxian leadership is especially skillful in coercing opponents by accusing them of betraying the fatherland in the service of foreign nations. Thus they frequently succeed in subjecting divided majorities to a process of "coerced nationalism."

Nationalism acts like a double-edged knife in an underdeveloped country. In its authentic manifestations it undeniably

propels growth and maintains social order. In its spurious devia-
tions, however, it wastes opportunities for progress and aggravates
internal tensions.

The first of these concerns the rejection of foreign capital.
Underdeveloped countries cannot disdain the collaboration of
such capital and, in a great number of cases, this collaboration
has been historically advantageous. A pragmatic attitude cannot
ignore the three reasons which make such collaboration potentially desirable: the need for increasing the investment rate
(an influx of foreign capital is the only means of increasing this
rate without reducing the consumption rate); the chance to improve the relation of capital to volume of production through
importing technology; and the need for expanding the import
capacity.

Genuine nationalism would handle foreign capital so as to ex-
tract from it the greatest advantage for the country's economy.
This treatment would not always be identical, but would be based
on an objective analysis of facts. Spurious nationalism, remember-
ing colonialism and its remittance of profits, simply repels foreign
capital *a priori*. A typical manifestation of this was the approval
by the Brazilian House of Deputies (December 1961) of the
famous Celso Brant bill which, among other things, limited the
remittance of profits to 10 per cent a year based on the historical
nominal value (*in cruzeiros*) of the invested capital. Marxian,
phantasmagoric, coerced, and opportunistic nationalism came together in support of the bill.

A second wasting effect of spurious nationalism consists in the
nonutilization of all export possibilities in primary products. We
have already pointed out that in most underdeveloped countries
there really are natural barriers to the export of these products,
and that international specialization will rarely be a definite route
to growth. Nationalistic dogmatism, however, anticipates a halt
in the growth of exports while they still offer dynamic comparative advantages. This means the premature abandonment of a

field where the scarce growth factors could still be applied with increased productivity.

A third disturbing effect of spurious nationalism is its irrational attitude toward the dilemma of consumption versus saving. Every nationalist passionately preaches the doctrine of development. As it is not his habit to appeal for foreign capital or for an improvement in the productivity of capital, one assumes that an increase in the saving rate is implicit. At the same time, nationalists usually lead advanced distributivist movements, preaching social reforms and accepting with extreme benevolence the tradition of a paternalistic state which distributes jobs without demanding work. The problem would be solved if elimination of the conspicuous consumption of the rich could produce an immediate increase in the saving rate and in popular distribution. Unfortunately, statistics prove the contrary. The superfluous consumption of the richer classes, however desirable its repression, represents but an insignificant portion of the national income. And the only way of increasing the consumption rate of the others is to increase production and reduce the rate of saving. Nationalists seem not to perceive that they frequently try to distribute income where it does not exist.

Another tendency of spurious nationalism is the acceptance, and often the defense, of chronic inflationary processes. The motivations vary. One may be a distribution-development irrationality which tries simultaneously to increase the consumption and the saving rates; another may be a Marxian snare to aggravate popular discontent and lead the country into chaos; a third may be a socialist artifice to lead certain sectors to nationalization by means of price control; a fourth may be a monopolistic interest aiming to obtain subsidies through credits with repressed interest rates. Many nationalists rebel against the continued rise in the cost of living but prescribe remedies still more inflationary. Nationalism in underdeveloped countries has been one of the main forces in preserving chronic inflationary pressures.

V. CONCLUSION

The question of how to reconcile, within a democratic regime, the internal tensions which spring up in underdeveloped nations desiring to grow, constitutes one of the great challenges to politicians and social scientists in the Free World. There is *a priori* no assurance of success. It will depend primarily on the rate at which each country succeeds in raising its income per capita while maintaining a reasonable balance in distribution. The way is arduous. Underdeveloped countries have against them not only their low capacity for investment and high capacity for demographic explosion, but also certain irrational patterns of behavior. Dogmatic prejudices, inflation, and political illusions spoil the opportunities for development. Only an insistent effort to enlighten public opinion will eliminate this resistance. Noneconomic motivations should not be slighted. A real feeling of national cohesion, free from phantasmagoric visions or xenophobic complexes, will help the people to endure with patience the sacrifices demanded by development. Finally, informed help from the outside, wisely distributed between development projects and social investment, may stabilize the course of underdeveloped countries toward democratic growth.

LEGISLATION FOR
ECONOMIC DEVELOPMENT

VICTOR L. URQUIDI

*Economist, author, and
lecturer, Mexico*

At Punta del Este, in August 1961, representatives of nineteen Latin American governments and of the United States recommended that long-range, well-planned programs of economic and social development should be adopted and carried out by each Latin American country. These programs, involving a higher rate of investment, are to be instrumental in raising the per capita product by at least 2.5 per cent annually over a ten-year period, as well as in achieving better income distribution and extending the benefits of economic progress to the bulk of the population through improvements in education, health, land tenure, and other areas. Economic development is conceived as diversification of output, reduced dependence on exports of only a few primary products, a rational process of industrialization (including capital goods industries), higher productivity in agriculture, and better transportation, storage, and distribution. In addition, reasonable domestic price stability is to be pursued, as well as protection from fluctuations in external prices of basic products. National development is to be undertaken with the aim, also, of promoting economic integration in Latin America through an eventual common market.

To help carry out the ten-year development programs, the Alliance for Progress envisages external support on an unprecedented scale of no less than 20 billion dollars, largely in the form of long-term loans from international financial agencies and United States public sources. Such external financing is designed to supplement an increasing mobilization of domestic resources, to be achieved partly through tax reform.

It is doubtful that such a multiplicity of objectives, requiring at the same time a judicious marshaling and an efficient utilization of resources, could be attained without full-scale planning. Yet the Punta del Este Charter is not very specific on this point. It mentions "systems" for the preparation, implementation, and periodic revision of the development programs. It also enumerates the main elements such a program may involve: adoption of mutually consistent targets and determination of priorities, measures to increase public and private investment, estimates of the domestic and foreign exchange cost of the various projects and of the program as a whole, evaluation of available resources, relationship to the balance of payments, fiscal and monetary policy, and a suitable administrative machinery for execution of the program. It is thus left to each country to choose and establish its "system" in the light of its own problems, its institutions, and its interpretation of what a development program means.

So far, a number of Latin American countries—some even before Punta del Este—have set up central planning bodies. These agencies are usually responsible for the technical preparation of the investment and financing programs and for translating them into capital expenditure allocations in the central budget and those of other government entities. However, in a number of cases, implementation has been held up due to inadequacy of the programs themselves, lack of a suitable mechanism to put them into operation, uncertainty regarding foreign financing, or unforeseen political events.

Other Latin American countries have in effect been carrying out fairly well integrated development programs without having established a centralized or even a coordinated planning mechanism. In a sense, this indicates that development cannot wait for over-all planning. Even when basic development needs have been roughly identified and policies for key sectors have been worked out, some countries have been reluctant to adopt a formal planning system, or have limited this process to sectors such as power or transport.

Apart from the practical difficulties deriving from the lack of data and of suitably trained personnel, the relatively limited extent of economic and social planning so far in Latin America seems to be due mainly to a belief that planning is not necessary for development. There are also widespread misconceptions regarding the scope and method of planning (an erroneous identification with collectivist planning), and there is perhaps a deep-seated mistrust on the part of political leaders who fear that they may lose power to economic experts whose judgment on broader questions of national policy they doubt. It would be realistic to assume that these conditions will not change very rapidly, and that an "education for planning" will for some time have to play an important role in modifying them.

Meanwhile, "programs" have to be drawn up under the Alliance for Progress, no less than for purely domestic purposes. Few people in Latin America believe that living standards and productive capacity could be raised—in the face of a 2.5 to 3 per cent annual population increase—by allowing the economy to drift. Thus a "development policy," whether or not it is expressed in the quantitative terms of a plan or a program, is today a generally accepted part of public and private national aims. At what point a "development policy" can be transformed into a "development program," or at least into a series of programs in key sectors, is a question that must largely be answered by the political scientist or the politician. The economist can at best point to the advantages of a program, and to the cost of not having one, and recommend a suitable method of planning. He can also indicate the lines along which piecemeal development policies should be carried out, and he can suggest the type of legislation that might be required to enable the policies to be implemented.

At any given moment in this process of trying to establish a clearly defined development policy and, if possible, a coherent program or plan, there is a body of existing legislation that has to be taken into account. Its origin may sometimes be obscure (this is frequently the case with tax legislation), or it may be the result of some short-term need. Most tax laws have been written to enable the government to obtain revenues, without sufficient regard to their economic effects. A good deal of legislation affecting foreign exchange transactions has been of the emergency type and frequently self-defeating. Legislation on foreign investments, though often related to exchange control, has had primarily a political content. Social security, enacted to pursue a definite welfare purpose, has rarely been devised to serve also, through its accumulation of savings, as an instrument in financing economic development. Labor legislation has in some cases run ahead of economic reality and has failed to achieve its aims.

On the other hand, existing legislation may represent a survival of nineteenth century economic liberalism or even of the pre-independence economic framework, or a contradictory mixture of both. Nineteenth century freedom of enterprise as established in most constitutions, together with the enactment of laws granting an individual or a corporation exclusive rights to produce, import, or transport something (in other words, creating a private legal monopoly), is a combination that is difficult to understand, but is found in some countries. Whatever its particular merits, it is certainly not a good legal basis for economic development.

Minimum wages, land reform, or an income tax have not gained a strong foothold in countries where the social structure has produced governments content with short-term objectives or believing that the free working of market forces produces the best results. The absence of suitable banking and financial legislation (and even of a central bank) can only be explained in terms of an inapplicable and unrealistic economic ideology. The same can be said for the lack of agrarian legislation, or the piecemeal approach to industrial development that prevails in many countries.

If a Latin American country should succeed in appraising its development problems and in firmly adopting some sort of rational long-range program, one of the first steps to be taken would be to revise critically all economic legislation, beginning with constitutional provisions, in order to determine its compatibility with a development policy or a program. Many basic legal concepts would have to come under review, since, fundamentally, a development program is usually devised to achieve a desired allocation of investment, specific targets in the growth of productive capacity and output, and a redistribution of income and wealth in favor of the underprivileged. Legislation for development thus involves an individual's right to dispose of property and income, and his right to pursue an economic activity or enterprise of his own choice.

To implement a development policy, the main areas of necessary legislation—and the implicit need for reviewing and revising existing legislation—can perhaps usefully be identified by taking as a vantage point that of the economist concerned specifically with development as a whole. The following discussion will attempt to indicate legislative needs in terms of the economic objectives to be pursued.

Briefly, programed development requires a suitable governmental organization and a specific planning mechanism, the purpose of which should be to achieve: (1) a higher ratio of investment to national product; (2) a pattern of public and private investment that may enable output to be raised more rapidly than in the past and, if possible, beyond a basic minimum so as to allow for increases in per capita consumption and a strengthening of the balance of payments; (3) a more productive and rational use of physical resources and the raising of productivity; (4) an improvement in skills through education and training, and a fuller utilization and better allocation of manpower; (5) a pattern of expenditure on consumption that may avoid waste, bolster domestic output, save foreign exchange, and improve standards of health and welfare; (6) greater fluidity in the flow of personal, business, and public savings into the desired areas of investment, through taxation, financial intermediaries, and otherwise; and (7) an advantageous and effective use of foreign exchange resources and of supplementary external investment funds.

1, 2, 3. The first requirement is for a government to establish a clearly defined and adequately staffed technical body fully responsible for analyzing, on a continuous and full-time basis, the long-term trends and structural changes in the economy, and for preparing short, medium, and long-range projections of the economy as a whole and of its sectors which may serve as a general framework for development policy decisions. Such a body should have authority to obtain the best available information from all public and private sources (this may involve overcoming some legal taboos) and should be treated by the executive branch as its economic development general staff.

Policy decisions should be taken by the Executive at the ministerial or cabinet level, preferably through a council or committee composed of the principal ministers or secretaries concerned with development and including the head of the central bank, the development corporation, and any other agency of similar importance.

The actual formulation of the public investment program and its financing should be made by each government department and every significant autonomous agency, under the guidance and supervision of a programing committee composed of representatives of the budget office (or Treasury), the development projections staff, the central bank, and the development corporation. Similar committees, involving representatives of specified ministries (agriculture, industry, etc.) can be set up to review the investment plans or programs of the main private sectors. Suitable subcommittees, advisory groups (in which private sector representatives ought to take part), and working groups should function when necessary.

Final adoption of the over-all investment and financial program should be made by the ministerial committee on the basis of proposals and recommendations submitted by the development projections staff and the programing committees. Implementation of the program should be supervised by the same committees with a view to making recommendations to the Executive for further action, or for modifications if necessary. Presentation of the development program or plan as a whole to the legislative branch, where appropriate, should be made by the Executive through the minister of the Treasury in connection with authorization of the budget.

The above mechanisms may be regarded as a minimum in government organization for development. It is important to realize, however, that what is involved is not the setting up of a few more official bodies to deal with new functions, but a complete centralization of the strategy and over-all formulation of the development program and its financing under the highest authority, while its detailed formulation and its operations should be decentralized and, where suitable, regionalized. Thus, unless some traditional legislation is modified to make room for the central development programing function over and above ordinary ministerial or departmental functions, and unless legal and constitutional relations between federal or central and state or provincial governments are changed to fit the concept of centralized programing with regionalized execution, it is doubtful that much could be accomplished in the effort to intensify economic and social development as envisaged by the Alliance for Progress.

Now, even assuming that the organizational problem is not ideally solved, the main areas of development legislation that should be reviewed in any case, in accordance with the purposes of development programing or policy enumerated before, may be stated as follows:

To achieve a higher ratio of investment to product requires the adoption of an over-all investment target based on an expected relationship between the growth in investment and the growth of output. Aggregate required investment has to be allocated by activity, with each divided between the public and the private sector. Hence some basic decisions are necessary (whatever the projections and the desired goals) regarding the extent and type of public investment in each activity (e.g., agriculture, industry, power, transport), the proportion of public to total investment, and the allocation of financial resources. But given the decisions on public investment, and assuming that the necessary legislation is enacted authorizing the state to undertake investment in fields not previously considered appropriate (e.g., electric power, steel, chemicals) and that the financial resources are assured, there remains the critical question of creating conditions conducive to the growth of private investment in accordance with the targets set up. It is not enough for a government to proclaim the need for private investment. A whole series of legal provisions and administrative policies should, as a consistent whole, attempt to induce the desired volume of private investment.

In manufacturing and mining, as well as utilities, aside from questions of the general political atmosphere or the state of short-term economic uncertainty, the problem revolves around the adequacy of tax incentives, rates of profits taxation, labor legislation, social security contributions, tariff protection and import controls, equitable treatment of foreign private capital, utility rates, and, where such is the case, special legislation regulating the integration and expansion of an industrial branch through both publicly and privately owned plants. It is obvious that failings in any one type of measure, the adoption of contradictory legislation, or the application of mutually inconsistent operational policies will result in delays in private industrial investment and a falling short of desired targets.

Unfortunately, tariffs and import controls are too often handled by Latin American governments under particular pressures instead of under broad policy lines. Tax-exemption laws have operated on a first-come first-served basis instead of as part of an industrial development plan. Certain incentive features of tax laws, such as special or accelerated depreciation allowances, have hardly been made use of or have been offered but sparingly. Taxation of profits is often inequitable to the small and medium-sized business, or as between equal-size enterprises that are variously affected by inadequate or inefficient tax administration measures. Foreign capital especially has been subjected to ambiguous policies—being wanted and at the same time not wanted—and in most countries foreign investors would like to know where they stood as to permissible fields of investment, extent of local capital participation required, treatment of exchange transfer of profits, and security of investment.

To promote agricultural development, there is usually a limit to what public investment can do directly beyond providing public irrigation and river regulation schemes, roads, experimental stations, power, and long-term credit facilities for permanent improvements. But agricultural output and investment in private hands are extremely dependent on government policies on farm prices, taxation, foreign trade, rural wages, marketing and storage services, and so on. Only a set of mutually consistent policies can raise farm productivity, help to solve problems of domestic foodstuffs and raw materials supply, and alleviate balance of payments pressures.

The basic question Latin America faces today is that of land reform, understood not in the limited sense of redistribution of large holdings among the rural population, but of redistribution plus fuller and better use of land, improved farm methods and higher productivity, and retention of earnings in the hands of the rural mass itself, which is a vast potential market for manufacturing growth. Indeed, agrarian reform is increasingly accepted as a requisite for agricultural development, since the land-tenure structure prevailing in most Latin American countries favors the use of a fraction of the available farmland and tends to keep peasant incomes at the subsistence level.

With the exception of Mexico, Bolivia, Cuba (in its own way), and, recently and limitedly, Venezuela and Colombia, the agrarian economy is essentially an area of free enterprise, free acquisition and accumulation of land, unfettered use or non-use of land, and gross social injustice. Agrarian legislation today must not stop at the breaking up of large estates, whether through expropriation, purchase, or taxation. It should envisage the organization and productive improvement of agriculture at all levels and the raising of the skills and culture of the peasant and the farm laborer; all this will require the establishment of agricultural credit media, cooperative marketing organizations, suitable price policies, and related measures.

Investment in the expansion of the power and transport sectors, apart from direct public investment, is determined in large part by rate regulation; here again, policy and legislation are not always consistent with the development programs. Most frequently, the holding down of rates as a subsidy to the consumer or a stimulant to business has resulted in a serious lag in investment and thus in a negative contribution to development, compounded by the deteriorating financial position of state-owned power and transport enterprises. The fuel sector has posed special problems of its own, connected with the predominance of foreign investment in petroleum in some countries and the reluctance or refusal to accept foreign capital in others. It is for each country to enact the legislation that suits its own decision on the subject, once an appraisal of its needs and prospects has been carried out nationally.

4. It is becoming fashionable to speak of improvements in the quality and skills of manpower, through education and training, as a form of investment. The projection of manpower needs, hinging on economic projections in general, requires gazing much further into the future than a ten-year program of public and private investment. At any given moment the bulk of the employed labor force is adult and beyond the influence of educational reform, apart from special adult education programs and industrial training or retraining schemes. It it therefore difficult to trans-

late the manpower needs of, say, twenty years hence into the educational and training programs of today, except in gross quantitative terms—raising school attendance generally and making secondary education universal—and on the assumption that an orientation away from purely academic and towards technical trades and careers and scientific pursuits is clearly desirable.

Yet this alone would require in most Latin American countries a thorough reappraisal of the educational systems, of industrial legislation, parts of labor and employment legislation, the social security regimes, and the general welfare policies affecting the ability of families to keep their children in school. As the recent Santiago Conference on Education and Development showed, these problems are far from being understood by economists and much less by educators. Educational planning, hardly existent in Latin America, is not even envisaged as a key part of over-all economic development programs. Hence, the latter are not covering one of the most potentially productive types of investment for development.

5. A development policy should aim obviously at raising consumption, which is the ultimate purpose of an economic system. The often stated dilemma between higher consumption and larger investment is in practice a false one in Latin America, since it is not generally borne out by experience. Nevertheless, a development program must envisage measures to adapt the pattern of consumption to structural needs and to balance of payments requirements.

Granted that in Latin America it will be considered desirable to allow freedom of consumers' choice within broad limits and also to maintain a largely free price system, certain forms of consumption can be encouraged and others discouraged as a means of facilitating investment and development generally. One means of bolstering private consumption lies in the provision of free or subsidized educational, health, sanitation, and welfare services, as well as housing, to the lower income groups. If financed largely out of taxation and social security contributions (and provided the tax system is progressive), such programs are redistributive and should enable the urban and rural mass to grow into a stronger market force favoring industrial and agricultural expansion.

Here are important implications for tax policy. There will be a need to reform the tax structure, particularly through the adoption and extension of full progressive personal income taxation, the establishment of taxes on capital gains and possibly on net wealth, the alleviation of indirect taxes, including local taxes, on basic commodities, and the creation of special purchase taxes on goods and services consumed by the higher income groups. The aim should be to discourage luxury consumption (including imports) and divert resources, through taxation, to the implementation of governmental, educational, and other social programs. The corollary in this field is, of course, not to set rates of taxation that would discourage saving or reduce investment incentives.

The insistence on tax reform under the Alliance for Progress is quite justified. The Latin American tax structure and its administration are inadequate to exert a desirable influence on the pattern of consumption, furnish governments with sufficient current revenues, or encourage enough investment. With some exceptions, tax legislation continues to be a composite of piecemeal measures that are ineffective, unjust, and inefficiently administered.

6. Taxation is related also to the whole question of a desirable use and flow of savings in a development program, as a counterpart to the investment objectives. A great deal of attention is usually paid to the effects of taxation and other measures on personal and business savings, but not enough to their importance in the formation of public savings, that is, in creating a surplus of current income over current expenditure in the public sector. Even when the "public sector" is sufficiently well defined in Latin America to include, besides government, the autonomous agencies, social security funds, state enterprises, and sundry commissions, boards, and institutes, it is rarely possible to have an

adequate integrated financial statement covering all sources of income and expenditure and indicating clearly the amount of savings (as defined above) generated in each of the divisions and entities of the sector.

Usually, in Latin America, the public sector as a whole runs a capital investment deficit, requiring the transfer to it of savings from the private sector or from other countries. However, in some cases the public sector runs a current deficit, the private and external sectors have to finance, out of their surplus, part of the public sector's consumption expenditures. This situation, in so far as domestic financing is concerned, is usually associated with inflationary expansion through central bank operations ("printing of currency"). It should therefore be an immediate aim of financial policy to avoid a current account deficit in the public sector. This will require both reduction of less urgent central government expenditures (e.g., on military equipment and certain subsidies) and, generally, increases in revenues. It will also involve economies in current expenditures of autonomous agencies and government enterprises and, where applicable, increases in their current income through adjustment of rates and prices in order to generate sufficient net earnings. It will in many cases be necessary to raise the rate of contributions to social security funds, in order to maintain their liquidity and provide the public sector with resources that may temporarily finance investments of the central government, or of public corporations.

Even more important, the effort should go further in creating a current surplus in the public sector that could be used to finance a considerable part of public investment. Such a surplus exists in many Latin American countries, but either it is not large enough or it has been dwindling due to the rise in current expenditures, the inelasticity of the tax systems, and the fixity of utility rates.

For a well-ordered development program in which the public sector is to carry a large share of total investment, it is essential that savings generated in the public sector should cover at least one-half to two-thirds of the required financing, since external funds cannot usually be obtained to finance more than about one-third of the public investment projects, and the domestic capital market and the banking system cannot, without inflationary consequences, absorb internal government debt issues beyond narrow limits.

In fact, the key to much of the foreign borrowing required for public investment projects lies in the need to increase domestic public financial resources to the point where a sizable public saving becomes available. Thus tax reform and improvement in the finances of government entities and corporations are vitally important. If tax reform should have desirable distributive effects, as well as resulting in considerable revenue, and can be devised so as to stimulate private investment, it may become one of the most powerful tools of economic development in Latin America. If the necessary measures are taken, also, to integrate the finances of the whole of the public sector, to increase net earnings of government autonomous agencies, and to allow transferability of savings within the public sector to meet priority investment needs, a significant step will have been taken toward the adoption of a financial plan consistent with a development program as a whole. Much remains to be done in these respects.

To obtain a higher rate of over-all investment also requires, for the private sector, a better use of private savings. Most private savings normally consist in retained earnings and depreciation allowances of business enterprises. It is assumed also that a considerable proportion of private gross investment, in manufacturing, power, transport, distribution, and the like, is financed in Latin America out of business savings. Nevertheless, there is need for greater fluidity in the use of savings, both through financial intermediaries, including investment banks, and through the securities market. An increase in such savings could be achieved with the help of better business practices and of fiscal incentives. Also, there is need for making the securities market more accessible to the small individual saver, and for a greater choice of forms of investment suited to the savings structure. Few of the banking systems in Latin America are sufficiently integrated, or tailored to assets that could serve as effective alternatives to the traditionally-liquid foreign exchange or bullion holdings, or the traditionally-secure real estate holdings and short-term commercial and speculative claims. In short, the banking and financial systems are not yet making a substantial contribution to economic development.

7. The role of external borrowing and direct foreign investment in Latin America's economic development is essentially to release domestic resources that can then be diverted to forms of expenditure not amenable to foreign or international financing. Provided a development program is being carried out that implies a higher rate of investment and a more efficient over-all effort, external financing will permit growth and capital formation to take place without sacrificing basic consumption. External aid is also a necessary supplement to current foreign exchange earnings; it enables the developing country to generate an import surplus—in other words, to increase the available supply of goods and services beyond the limits of current output.

It is therefore necessary that the best possible use be made both of current foreign exchange earnings and of capital borrowing, including direct foreign investment. Current earnings need to be economized to provide for essential imports over nonessential purchases, and to make it possible to limit borrowing to the maximum compatible with the future exchange-earning capacity out of which debt service is to be met. This is also the reason, from a balance of payments point of view, why external credit should be used judiciously.

The implications of these principles are important, for although in recent years much use has been made in Latin America of foreign capital, and different forms of exchange rationing (or, alternatively, of restricting imports by means of tariffs and controls) have been adopted, it is doubtful that most governments have been able to formulate and implement a general plan for the use of external financing. This does not necessarily mean control of transactions, but the execution of a consistent policy, particularly within the public sector. The indiscriminate resort to foreign short-term credit for medium and long-term development projects, and the uncontrolled accumulation of current account indebtedness, with the consequent immediate burden on payments possibilities, are witness to the absence of an integrated financial policy of the sort that should match the total development effort. This, too, is an area where there is need for a careful reappraisal of existing legislation and regulation covering foreign exchange transactions, the use of external credit, and the exchange operations of direct foreign investment.

Legislation is only an instrument with which to carry out policy, and it may be changed accordingly. If legislation concerning economic matters is inadequate, the fault—aside from juridical blocks—must lie with the policy itself, with the definition of the ends and the means. It may also occur that the legislative process is inappropriate, or that those who write the laws—rarely economic experts—are not fully competent. The right policy decisions must be the determining factor. Latin America faces a huge challenge. It is to be hoped that comprehensive development programs and policies will increasingly be undertaken, and that the necessary legislation will be adopted with appropriate urgency.

Education

PROBLEMS OF EDUCATION
IN LATIN AMERICA

GALO PLAZA

*Former President
of Ecuador*

Within our hemisphere, education has played a major role in developing a free and prosperous society in North America. What must happen in Latin America if education is to fulfill a similar role? If we compare the major traits and trends of education in Latin America and in the United States, we will find differences that stem from our varying historical backgrounds.

DIFFERENCES

Although both our cultures have their roots in Europe, the divergences in scale of values and philosophy of life have created wide differences in the conception and the purpose of education.

The semifeudal, absolute system of government in Spain and Portugal, in which Church and State were closely united, was transplanted by the Spaniards and the Portuguese to their colonies in America, and Catholicism was imposed as the only religion. The English colonists in the North had fled from religious persecution in Europe and organized their new communities on the basis of freedom and tolerance. They were governed, for the most part, under charters which were really democratic constitutions. In Latin America, colonial despotism bred military dictatorships.

The northern part of the hemisphere benefited greatly from the full impact of the Reformation and the industrial revolution, which served to extend education to the masses as a means for improving their conditions of life. In Latin America the political and social environment produced a system of selective aristocratic education, dominated by the Church, for the purpose of preparing for service to the Crown and the Church. In the North, education was influenced by the scientific achievements in Germany and England and acquired an element of social responsibility, while in Latin America, French culture, which was most highly regarded and which emphasized culture for culture's sake, became the dominant influence.

Today these differences are not so clear cut because cross-currents of influence are flowing in both directions. A distinguished Chilean educator, Irma Salas, has ably stated some of the differences between Latin America and the United States, thus:

(a) Education in the United States is democratic in purpose, while education in Latin America has been, and to a large extent still is, aristocratic in purpose.

(b) Education in Latin America is characterized by centralization of control, in contrast to the local control characteristic of North American education. While in the United States education is a community enterprise, responsive to the interests and needs of the people, in Latin America it is a state enterprise, imposed on the people.

(c) Education in Latin America, in general, follows a pattern of uniformity, in contrast to the variety which characterizes North American education.

(d) The Latin American secondary school, like the French lycée, imparts general education and prepares for the university, while North American education is more concerned with usefulness, with preparation for practical life.

(e) The administration of the schools in the United States is unified

for all grades and branches. The superintendent of schools will
have under his administration all public schools—elementary,
secondary, or vocational—in his city. In Latin America, the different branches of education—elementary, secondary, and professional—are usually administered separately. Therefore, the artic-
ulation, correlation, continuity, and unity of the school system
are greatly impaired.

Advocates of the Latin American philosophy of education find
fault with the United States system for being pragmatic, ma-
terialistic, and utilitarian, without sufficient interest in the appreciation of the higher values of the spirit; while critics from
the North find our system humanistic, purely cultural, highly
impractical, and remote in time and space.

In certain quarters of Latin America it is argued that our mentality, used to the humanistic theory of life, does not yield readily
to pragmatism; that an education aimed at answering only practical questions does not fit well with the Latin American tradition.

These arguments for resisting change, stemming from dangerous generalizations, could hardly stand up under careful analysis. But the fact that such views are expressed is proof of differences of conceptions, deeply tied in with cultural traditions, that
should be reorientated for the benefit of all concerned.

PRIMARY EDUCATION

That elementary education should be universal, that all children, whatever their sex, color, creed, or social status, should have
access to free primary education, is written into every constitution in Latin America. Unfortunately, this principle has not always been carried into full practice.

Our countries, with limited resources, have had to serve many
other vital needs of the people as well. Consequently public education has suffered from all kinds of limitations, and what it has
accomplished is a tribute to all those dedicated to the cause, from
the administrators down to the teachers, many of whom in rural
areas carry out their missions under conditions that border on

the heroic.

Private schools, mostly run by the Catholic Church, have helped the state carry this grave responsibility. Unfortunately, not enough has been done or could be done, and an alarming percentage of children of school age are deprived of the privileges of education.

If the quantity of schools is insufficient, the quality of education also needs improvement. Although new ideas are already influencing methods and programs of study, traditional ideas still prevail, particularly in rural areas, where the student takes dictation or copies from the blackboard and memorizes his lessons, day in and day out, with little opportunity to develop his creative talents or to learn the important characteristics of his home and community environment. Physical facilities are usually meager. The relationship between teacher and pupil is quite formal, and not much recognition is given to the different abilities and interests of the developing child as he moves from infancy to adulthood. Many children go no further than the third or fourth grade.

The very future of Latin America is at stake on this issue. Governments are increasing their budgets for education; successful methods from abroad are being studied and converted into terms of national realities. The school is becoming more and more a living part of the community. But if we are to lower substantially the menacing statistical figures for illiteracy, we will have to treat the problem on an emergency basis. Quality will have to be sacrificed for the sake of quantity. At this point, more schools are more urgently needed than better schools. A policy of enough schools for all children rather than improved schools for some children is the present answer to our problem.

SECONDARY EDUCATION

Secondary education is by far the weakest link in our school system. This goes back to colonial times, when it was almost exclusively in the hands of the church and designed for a selected minority. After the wars of independence the French concept prevailed. The aim of secondary education was to develop an intellectual élite, capable of appreciating the arts, letters, and sciences. Its task was to select and train the best minds for positions of leadership in social, economic, and public life. It imparted general education, with a heavy emphasis on classical subjects and little attention to applied sciences and vocational subjects. Its goal was to prepare for the universities.

Economic development and industrialization, during the last two decades, are slowly helping Latin America to break away from traditional practices and methods. Leaders in education realize that the task now is to bring education to an entire heterogeneous population, which must be trained for living and educated for life in a democracy. Necessity demands that secondary education should stimulate vocations and offer a terminal course for those not going to universities. It should develop the personality, not just train the mind or impart knowledge.

Programs of studies are being continuously revised in the search for improvement, but the results have not always been encouraging. The pull of tradition, in some cases, has been too great. Traditionally, the secondary school has been conserved as a uniform structure, with the same requirements for all students. The concept of its aims is not sufficiently clear to satisfy the needs of the student or of society.

ADULT EDUCATION

As a consequence of the inadequate coverage of the school age population, adult illiteracy is a major problem in Latin America. Even those who have had some schooling need additional training to be effective in their jobs. A very small fraction of the labor force possesses the education necessary to operate a modern economy. The rapid rate of change in underdeveloped countries, and the time lag before new programs for universal primary education and extensive secondary education begin to pay off in terms of a trained adult labor force, demand special measures to raise the educational level of the existing labor force.

VOCATIONAL EDUCATION

Vocational education in Latin America has been neglected, being viewed as a poor alternative for academic secondary education. Industrial and commercial training is given in schools that are completely separated from the academic high schools. Vocational education has yet to become an integral part of the total educational picture and will remain a weak link in the educational system until it becomes articulated with other levels and types of education.

HIGHER EDUCATION

At least a score of universities in Latin America are older than Harvard. The University of Santo Tomás de Aquino in the Dominican Republic was founded in 1538, a century earlier than Harvard; Mexico, Lima, Quito, Santiago, Sucre, and Córdova had universities before any such institutions were founded in the English colonies to the north. The universities reflected the mentalities prevailing at those times. The teaching was academic and abstract, although in a few instances enlightened educators, with ideas far ahead of their times, introduced the studies of mathematics and natural sciences. All these schools were church-controlled and dominated.

The birth of the republics brought about the nationalization of many institutions of higher learning and the church lost its absolute hold on higher education. The struggle against the crown and clerical power continued against tyranny and all forms of oppression. The universities became politically and intellectually autonomous, a status which they have always defended and protected with great zeal. They are proud of their spirit of liberalism, their record of resistance to dictatorships and continued concern with social reform. All this makes for a politically charged atmosphere on the campus, but it has not contributed to the improvement of academic standards. The students in their struggle to protect the university from the political instability surrounding it have achieved the opposite effect by bringing politics into the classroom.

However, the university tends to remain apart from the community it must serve. Higher education is still the prerogative of an élite, although it is no longer restricted to those privileged by birth, by social status, or by wealth. The fact that tuitions are very low and in some cases nonexistent, and that higher education is available to students from the lower economic sectors, does not mean that those nonprivileged students have brought the university closer to the people. These students simply join the élite.

Because of grossly inadequate budgets and administrative organization, of part-time professors whose main source of income and interest is outside the university, and of excessive student influence and control, the universities in Latin America as a whole are not prepared to play the role they must in shaping the future of the continent. The students are not learning the necessary intellectual and moral discipline that would equip them to assume in the future the responsibilities of managing the more complex socio-economic structure necessary to meet the urgent demands of the people of Latin America.

Many of the changes that must take place are of an organizational nature. There is an incredible waste by dispersion or duplication of already very limited resources. In many cases there are separate laboratories and staff in each school or division to teach the same subject. For instance, most universities offer the same courses in inorganic chemistry in the schools of medicine, engineering, and agriculture.

In most institutions a student who changes his plans cannot transfer grades earned in one faculty or school to another. He has to start all over again. This anachronism contributes to that plague of Latin American universities, the perennial or professional student.

Because of financial limitations, not only professors, but students as well, in many instances, are dedicating only part of their time to the university. Professors must seek other sources of income, and students, working on the side, attend classes in the early mornings and evenings during their off hours.

The University of Concepción in Chile has taken a great step forward to correct these weaknesses by creating four departments for the basic sciences: physics, chemistry, biology, and mathematics, where all students can go for their science requirements. This has brought about a notable upgrading of the standards of education. The UNESCO meeting in Paris in 1958 was so impressed that it recommended the "Concepción Plan" as a pilot project for university education in Latin America.

Other institutions of higher learning have escaped the pull of tradition and are making remarkable progress—for example, the Institute of Technology and Higher Education at Monterrey, Mexico, the Medical School at the Universidad del Valle, in Cali, Colombia, and the new University of Brasilia.

Unfortunately, many more serious situations need correcting. The venerable University of San Marcos, Lima, has been a chronic victim of political strife which has interfered with academic activities to an alarming degree. The students at the Universidad de Caracas, located on a splendid campus that could compare favorably with some of the finest in the United States, has been on strike for half the school year.

However, in spite of these problems, some universities of Latin America have managed to make remarkable strides in keeping abreast of the demands of modern education, and their influence is felt in the economic, political, and social life of their communities.

The most important objective now is to put the university at the service of the community. Our institutions of higher learning should be capable of offering a liberal and practical education to all who can benefit from it. They should broaden their curricula to prepare students for the multiple demands of modern society. Basic and applied research should be an integral part of university work, and through extension, the university should disseminate useful knowledge for practical living to the entire population.

The training for leadership to improve technology and to achieve economic development should be done in the universities. Much of the research designed to yield results directly applicable to the problems and conditions should be carried out there. Ways of transmitting accumulated knowledge to the people and translating it into action should be developed at local institutions. Unfortunately, because of limited resources, many universities in Latin America are not providing sufficient training in enough technologic fields, nor are they conducting enough research aimed at faster development. We urgently need well-trained personnel, research facilities, and laboratories, as well as efficient organization.

THE SCOPE OF THE PROBLEM

It is dangerous to generalize for the whole of Latin America with a population over 119 million people which, if present rates of population growth are maintained, will have a population by the turn of the century of between 500 and 600 million, or nearly twice the combined population of the United States and Canada at that date.

It was reported at the Conference on Education and Social Development, sponsored by several regional organizations at Santiago, Chile, last March, that 40 per cent of the children of school age in Latin America are not in school; that only 17 out of 100 children who enter school finish their primary education; and that only 4 per cent of the young people of university age reach the universities. The Conference estimated that 34 billion dollars will be needed to correct the situation by 1970 and recommended the use of 4 per cent of the gross national income of each country, as well as 15 per cent of all Alliance for Progress funds, on education.

A recent study by a group of prominent United States educators agreed on six fields of action that we consider most urgent:

1. The development and improvement of science in educational programs.
2. Aid for programs in agricultural and industrial education.
3. The selection of books for translation, publication, and distribution, and the granting of subsidies for the writing of textbooks in Spanish and Portuguese.
4. The encouragement of research programs related to regional needs.
5. The establishment of cooperative programs among universities in the United States and Latin America.
6. Increase in fellowships and research grants for Latin American schools.

The educational system in Latin America is a source of tensions. The high school graduate who is unable to continue his education and is unprepared to earn his living after twelve years of schooling is understandably a frustrated individual. The great majority of institutions of higher learning are not yet prepared to offer the kind of education that the times require. In Latin America we are not only failing to make the best use of our natural resources, we are also neglecting our human resources. If we are to upgrade living standards for large segments of the population, trained personnel in many and diversified disciplines is indispensable. Education is our bottleneck in molding the future for Latin America. A bridge, a road, a school can be built in half the normally required time if we have at our disposal twice the amount of funds. But there is no such shortcut to education, because the human mind is able to absorb just so much knowledge at a time. Whatever we manage to accomplish in the socio-economic field depends on what is done to gear education to progress.

EDUCATION FOR LATIN AMERICA

LUIS B. PRIETO F.

President of the Senate,
Venezuela

Latin America is usually considered as a geographic unit and a
community of peoples who inherited a culture and an historical
background which shaped its political structure, its social evolution, its virtues and defects. While it is true that there are common features that identify our countries, there are also characteristics that differentiate us. The similarities and differences
of our peoples demand varying standards.

If education is to be a social process, its structure and orientation must be determined by the aspirations and the ideals of the
people. While it conserves values contributed by tradition, education is also an effective instrument for promoting progress. Our
education must be progressive in the sense of an education for
economic and social development, capable of procuring ample
production not for the profit of a few but for greater social
benefit. The competent producer and the discriminating consumer are essential objectives of education for peoples in the
process of development. Education to this end serves the purposes of individual and social improvement and enables man to
be useful to himself by serving others.

Our scholastic organization had its beginnings in the Spanish
royal commissions, and under the sponsorship of the missionaries,

who tried to convert the Indians in order to get them to help in the exploitation of the continent, which could not be accomplished without slaves. Latin American schools from their beginning were for the service of the privileged who could pay for education. This created a parasitic intellectual class living at the expense of those who worked on the farms or in the mines.

After independence, anti-democratic regimes continued the inherited educational system. Although the liberal revolution, triumphant in all countries of Latin America in the middle of the nineteenth century, established the principle of free and compulsory education, these ideals remain unfulfilled. Even now, 32 per cent of children of school age are without schools. The average education span of our citizens covers 2.2 years, while for the United States it is 9 years, for Japan 7.2 years, and for Puerto Rico 4.5 years. Illiteracy prevails among 40 per cent of the adult population, and only 17 per cent of the children who commence primary education complete it. Children without schools need half a million teachers; those receiving education are taught by teachers of whom 40 per cent hold no degree.

We have remained captives of a literary humanism. When the continent needed expert labor and technicians, we were turning out lawyers to settle suits among landowners, clergymen, and poets. While industrialization forged ahead in Europe and the United States, we were fomenting civil wars. We lived a pastoral life, and in the shadow of the large coffee, cocoa, and rubber plantations, or working in the mines, the mass of the people went their ancient way. At the same time they continued to cherish their desires for liberty, culture, and an easing of misery. Tensions have been accentuated between the country and the city, between possessors and dispossessed, between the cultured and those lacking culture, between the people and their rulers. These tensions become aggressive and destructive because in the pursuit of liberty men also seek escape from insecurity.

PRIMARY EDUCATION

Primary education has specific tasks to fulfill in Latin America, as in all underdeveloped countries. Education in our continent must become a means to attain security and freedom, and to foster habits of cooperation in a free world. It must be compulsory and free, designed to give man an understanding of his environment and to train him for productive work. It should awaken community spirit, through which the pupil learns by cooperation with others that he is a member of a larger nucleus from which he receives benefits and to which he has obligations. It must also foster respect for the principles of coexistence, which is the law of the community.

To see the urban and the rural school as two different forms of education is false. In the city as in the country, the ends are the same: to form capable and productive citizens having a democratic spirit, respectful of the rights of others and defending their own rights. Schools and workshops should be everywhere consecrated to fostering the national spirit and the responsibility of the citizen of a democratic country. In place of a school for the classes, we should establish a national school for the masses.

For us, agrarian reform is the point of departure in an integral process of transformation, of economic and social growth. The land in the hands of the peasant who works it becomes a means of increasing income per capita, so that a redistribution of national income is possible. It is of no avail to place instruments of production in the hands of men who cannot use them effectively. With workers who are incompetent to produce, land reform can even mean that the national income may drop. Hence agrarian reform must be supported by education for the peasant.

The American rural school must also provide labor sources for the city; it must "de-ruralize" the countryside. The man from the country who comes to the city to look for work suffers from his lack of training to cope with the new work and situations. Education would facilitate the change.

A complete primary education would enable man to make even more headway in this changing world. Rural schools must become agencies for social change. Little by little, the country is becoming urban; in developed countries there are few notable differences between country and city, and signs of rapid de-ruralization are visible even in Venezuela, Cuba, Argentina, and Uruguay—signs that will multiply as industrialization grows and agricultural mechanization increases.

Gunnar Myrdal points out that "the determined zest for learning" is an element of major importance in national development. "Like any educational reform of value," continues Myrdal, "this will indisputably introduce a new complex of tensions in a backward country, and will strengthen all the other factors that change the customs of a stagnant community." *

In Latin America this zest for learning is growing. The Conference on Education and Economic Development that took place in Chile found that from 1957 to 1960 the enrollment in primary schools increased by 23 per cent, while the increase in children of school age in the same period was only 8.5 per cent. The number in secondary schools increased 37 per cent, and that in universities by 14 per cent. The increase is particularly evident in Cuba, Honduras, and Venezuela. In the latter, illiteracy dropped from 56 per cent to 26 per cent in the last four years, and it is hoped to eradicate it in the next five years; children of school age for this year of 1962 are almost all in school, though a high percentage of drop-outs persists.

SECONDARY EDUCATION

In almost all Latin American countries, secondary education embraces the traditional course preparatory to university studies, and studies leading to professions. The professional type, also called vocational, can be a final stage of study for adolescents; it

* Gunnar Myrdal, *Solidarity or Disintegration*, Fondo de Cultura Economica, Mexico, 1956.

enables them to enter a profession or trade in which they begin to work productively. This educational level, however, is decidedly backward in Latin America.

The groups which complete their primary school represent a very low percentage of adolescents. Out of a total of 19,643,000 adolescents (15 to 19 years old), 3,361,000 adolescents or 17 per cent are enrolled in high schools. Only 22 per cent of those enrolled finish their studies. Generally over 70 per cent of the enrolled take only the first general cycle, and the small proportion of those who take professional studies at this level has slight relationship to the productive needs of our countries. Bolivia has 84 per cent high school students as compared to 1.4 per cent technical students; Costa Rica has 79 per cent high school students as against 2 per cent technical students; and Venezuela has 66 per cent high school students as compared to 9.3 per cent technical students. Studies leading to commerce, as contrasted with production, have increased. Honduras has 30 per cent students of commerce, Colombia 15 per cent, Costa Rica 15 per cent, and Venezuela 11 per cent. Countries such as ours have a great lack of technicians in the field of agriculture. In Brazil, .5 per cent of the pupils in the cycle study agriculture and cattle, and .2 per cent in Venezuela. The situation is more or less similar in other countries.

The traditional secondary school has suffered from an excessive intellectualism inherited from French and English schools, a survival which is dangerous to our economic and social development. Reform at this level of study is urgent, but extremely difficult, because for secondary teachers reform would necessitate a new learning process.

The application of new techniques and training creates in the pupils a new mentality. The problem of underdevelopment is aggravated because the people lack the urge to work and to produce as much as development demands; this lack is found not only among illiterates but in the men in charge of developing the national conscience and guiding cultural and social improvement.

What is needed is a new understanding of education, within a new environment and with new tasks. It is a matter of applying what is called "democratic humanism," the tasks of which we define as follows:

1. To educate man to the full extent of his physical and moral potentialities as a positive factor in the communities;
2. To equip him for the defense of a democratic system within which the essential civil and political rights of individuals are enforced and guaranteed; and
3. To equip him for productive work through techniques required for technical development in this period.

The extension of secondary-school opportunities to the majority of adolescents is not a luxury. The ideal would be to continue primary education in a unified school for five or six years, at the end of which the adolescent could enter productive life or higher technical education. This implies a school with a minimum of eleven years of study, entirely free, as in Venezuela and some other countries of the continent. The educational structure would thus eliminate discrimination and would put an end to the struggle between primary and secondary schools. It would not merely call for the reform of a cycle of studies, but would reorganize the whole educative process in a single school of eleven years, where secondary education would appear as a natural sequence in the process of moving from childhood to adolescence.

Secondary even more than primary education must envisage the training and conditioning of the producer and consumer which increasing industrialization demands. With them comes an increasing democratization.

HIGHER EDUCATION

Higher education in our continent has been limited to universities, the structure of which originated in the Middle Ages. The Latin American university is not the dynamic institution that our epoch demands. Universities have been fighting for reform from the beginning of the century, but this reform was too much concerned with politics, and too little with technical and scientific aspects.

Autonomy for the university was interpreted as a form of self-government in which professors and pupils share responsibilities, as did such communities in the Middle Ages. This desire for segregation lessened the influence of the universities, which engaged in belfry battles to obtain more independence from the state and more participation of students and professors in their administration.

This situation impedes development by failing to train personnel qualified to influence the planning and implementation of development programs. At the university level, preparation for careers in the literary field and for professions with great tradition predominates: Medicine, Law, Civil Engineering, and Pedagogy. In Central America, in Venezuela and other countries, pupils of secondary schools also prefer traditional professions because of the prestige that they enjoy. On the other hand, Mechanical Engineering, Electrical and Chemical Engineering, Agronomy, Veterinary Science, and other studies more necessary for economic development have few followers; in many universities of the continent they are not even offered. It could be alleged that the fault lies not entirely with the university, but with the school systems which do not provide adequate counseling service to advise young men where they can find secure employment and greater success. But it also underlines the need to link the processes of professional education with development plans.

Administrative autonomy does not present as many difficulties as autonomy in teaching, since the latter must deal with other parts of the educational cycle and with correlation of the curricula, as well as with the number and quality of its graduates in relation to the needs for development. Hence the university should share in the elaboration of development plans and adjust itself to their obligations—obligations which are outside the orbit of its autonomy.

Absolute autonomy of the university has become a barrier to

reform and progress, for it seeks to detach the university from contemporary basic problems. The autonomy of the university can no longer be honestly sustained.

THE EDUCATION OF ADULTS

In a world which changes rapidly, men ought to be in a constant attitude of adaptability and learning in order to be able to act in newly created situations. A new machine, a new invention, presupposes new abilities in those who handle them. The education of adults for this constant readaptation implies in-service training of the type that private enterprises include in the normal training of their leaders.

But there is another kind of adult education with greater social and economic scope. This is the training of large masses who have had no chance to acquire any kind of education—the literary and technical illiterate.

Statistics indicate adult illiteracy of 40 per cent, not including those who once learned to read and write and then forgot it, or those who can only scribble their name. In Venezuela, the Shoup Mission carried out an extensive investigation which revealed the poor production and low wages of the illiterate, intimating that education guarantees better means of subsistence.

The teaching of reading and writing sometimes brings spectacular results. But adult education is not only a matter of teaching how to read and write; these are instruments that the peasant may not need immediately, and therefore he may not appreciate their value. What is important is the creation of new habits and attitudes that help to improve the communities, to make better use of natural resources, and to apply new techniques of cultivation. Furthermore, the promotion of new attitudes encourages the illiterate to send their children to school in order that they in turn shall not be illiterate.

Elementary technical training is also important. Economic development demands qualified laborers for both country and city. Establishments organized with the collaboration of entrepreneurs for in-service training of laborers and employees and for the technical training of apprentices have already been functioning, for example, SENAI and SENAC in Brazil, SENA * in Colombia, and INCE in Venezuela.

The law that created the National Institute of Educational Cooperation (INCE) in Venezuela involves the cooperation of managers with the state and the workers, and it considers the contribution of entrepreneurs as a duty which derives from the relations of the enterprises with their workers.

Where there are no technical schools, this form of in-service training renders invaluable benefits. For this reason it was approved in the Sixth Inter-American Conference on Education, convened in Washington in 1958, as a prerequisite of development and its adequate planning.

Karl Mannheim warned that it is not possible to repair a train while in motion, but necessity obliges the peoples in development processes to repair defects and to overcome deficiencies while in progress. They cannot wait for the schools to prepare expert workers for development, and they seize whatever is available and train them in service.

In Venezuela a Foundation for Municipal Development has been started, and the organizations in charge of adult education have a system of schools where adults can complete their primary education and acquire easy techniques to improve their working and living conditions.

Within ten or more years, given the present rate of increase, all children in Latin America will have primary schooling. The problem of illiteracy will be conquered, provided an understanding of the need of education awakens in the people. That is the purpose of adult education: to make the population aware of the value of culture, how it leads them to improve and helps others to improve.

* SENAI, National Center of Industrial Apprenticeship; SENAC, National Center of Commercial Apprenticeship; SENA, National Center of Apprenticeship.

Labor

THE LABOR MOVEMENT AND ECONOMIC DEVELOPMENT

LUIS ALBERTO MONGE

Labor Leader, Member
Legislative Assembly,
Costa Rica

Certain principles, though elementary, are none the less important in dealing with the Latin American labor movement and the economic development programs.

1. Labor unions, however they are regarded, are an inevitable factor in contemporary society. Their weight will be felt more and more, in the economic, social, cultural, and political life of Latin America.

2. Opposition of management and other groups cannot eliminate the labor movement, but it can so affect the activities of workers as to hinder the cooperation which is indispensable to the success of democratic institutions and development programs.

3. Few Latin American governments have taken seriously the need for formulating economic development programs. Where they exist, such plans pay little heed to social and human factors. The labor movement is given no share in the information and operation.

178

4. Economic underdevelopment impedes the growth of labor organizations, yet such underdevelopment cannot be overcome without deep changes in the social and economic structure, which requires the help of strong unions and cooperatives. This becomes a vicious circle.

5. Weak unions, and those under totalitarian or demagogic influence or controlled by foreign interests, cannot offer constructive support to economic development programs. Therefore, workers and management, governors and governed share a common need to strengthen independent, responsible, and democratic unions.

6. Structural changes and the strengthening of responsible unionism depend not only on factors within Latin America but also on international factors such as exchange relationships between "poor countries" and "rich countries." Solutions to problems based on factors outside the Latin American sphere should be coordinated with policies laid down by such suitable international workers' organizations as the Inter-American Regional Workers Organization, the International Confederation of Free Trade Unions, and the International Federation of Christian Trade Unions, as well as the International Labor Organization of the United Nations.

THE LATIN AMERICAN LABOR MOVEMENT

It would be more correct to speak of the Latin American labor movement in the plural. The structure, program, achievements, and history of Latin American unions vary greatly from country to country and from one region to another. Certain industrial centers have unions of some importance, while in the agricultural areas these are practically nonexistent. This is very serious because a large part of the working population (57 per cent) is engaged in agriculture, and live in very bad conditions in which the unions have been unable to force any change.

Latin American labor unionism—with some exceptions—is weak intrinsically and is subject to internal dissensions and Communistic and demagogic tendencies. It has not the strength to force the necessary structural changes for rapid economic development. It needs the intervention of political factors to help in the task, because political factors based on economic interests impede the changes so insistently demanded.

Statistics on the membership of the Latin American unions are imperfect and incomplete. However, an article by Dr. Robert J. Alexander, published in the Venezuelan publication *Politica,** indicates how greatly membership in labor unions varies.

LABOR UNION MEMBERSHIP

Argentina	2,500,000
Bolivia	100,000
Brazil	1,000,000
Colombia	150,000
Costa Rica	25,000
Cuba	800,000
Chile	300,000
Ecuador	75,000
El Salvador	25,000
Guatemala	15,000
Honduras	25,000
Mexico	1,000,000
Panama	15,000
Peru	200,000
Uruguay	75,000
Venezuela	250,000
TOTAL	6,555,000

If the economically active population is calculated at 64 millions, hardly 10 per cent is unionized; the strength of this small minority is further lessened by the demagogic and Communistic groups included and by the fact that the upper echelons of the unions are blessed by few able people familiar with the technical, administrative, social, and political problems of economic development.

The anti-union attitude of some governments and certain management circles, revealed in their refusal to allow the unions to participate in economic planning, may seem justified by these bit-

* No. 16, June–July 1961.

ter truths. This in no way diminishes the gravity of the error. The unions and their leaders cannot make a positive contribution while they remain ignorant of and excluded from experience in the policy and planning bodies.

In some countries, however, it cannot be denied that union movements have achieved a certain strength and influence in economic planning. Despite marked differences in the movements, there are similarities in doctrine and especially in the common challenges that every honest and democratic union must face if the union movement is to play its part in the present and the future of our peoples. Its success in meeting these challenges depends not only on the movement itself, but also on mutual understanding of and action with the healthy democratic political forces of the continent. At the present moment this cooperation and understanding leave much to be desired.

The main challenges facing honest political and union forces are:

1. The grave economic and social situation characteristic of underdeveloped countries.
2. The minority forces that believe it is possible to ride out the disturbing economic and social situation, maintaining their privileges to the detriment of the majority.
3. The minority forces, such as the Communists, that offer false solutions of a violent and totalitarian nature.
4. The imperative need to achieve just and equitable understanding between rich countries and poor countries.

First Challenge: Grave Economic and Social Conditions

A few statistics indicate the explosive nature of certain economic and social factors.

The rate of population increase, 2.5 per cent, is high, while the rise in per capita production is low. In 1955 and 1956 the rise in per capita productivity was, respectively, 3.6 per cent and 1.8 per cent, and in 1958 and 1959 it was 1.3 per cent and 0.3 per cent, respectively.

It is estimated that Latin America will have some 303 million inhabitants by 1975 and that 42 million more jobs will have to be found than were required in 1960. The urban population, 53.6 million in 1945, rose to 76.4 million in 1955. The rate of industrialization was lower than that of urbanization.

Approximately 100 million of the 192 million population of the twenty Latin American republics are illiterate, although one billion dollars are presently spent on education services. Some 15 million children are without schools; to provide these children with schooling 1,500 million dollars would have to be spent on 500,000 schoolrooms, and the running costs would amount to 600 million dollars per year.

The number of qualified engineers and technicians and the amount of skilled labor available must be doubled, tripled, and even quadrupled. Our own higher education and technical institutes cannot meet this demand,* and we turn in part to Russia. Some 8,000 students from Latin America and Africa are following courses of study in the higher education and technical institutes of the USSR. The "Patrice Lumumba University," opened in Moscow a few years ago, offered 500 scholarships to students from Asia, Africa, and Latin America, and 130 Latin Americans are presently studying there.†

Fifty per cent of our population is undernourished. There are 54 doctors for 100,000 inhabitants, while in the United States the proportion is 135 to 100,000.

The housing shortage is alarming. Millions of Latin Americans are homeless or live in poor, unhealthy, and most primitive conditions.

Latin American armies perform no economic function; rather, they withdraw labor from production. They represent no real defense in case of war, but nevertheless consume 1,000 million dollars annually. In many countries they have served to destroy democratic institutions and repress the people's demand for justice.

* *International Labor Review*, Vol. LXIV, Nos. 1–2, July–August 1961, Geneva, Switzerland.
† Research Institute of the Friedrich Ebert-Bonn Foundation.

As for Latin American agriculture, its anachronistic and uneconomic structure may be summarized as follows: concentration of the largest and best lands in few hands (latifundium) on the one hand, partition of the small properties (minifundium) on the other hand, with low productivity in both cases.

About 1.4 per cent of the number of estates are in holdings of more than 1,000 hectares each, but they represent 65 per cent of the total farming land. Eight per cent of the estates are in holdings of 100 to 1,000 hectares, and these represent another 22 per cent of the land. Thus 9.4 per cent of the estates hold 87 per cent of the farming lands. The remaining 13 per cent of the land is in holdings of less than 100 hectares, but the majority of these (72.6 per cent of the number of estates) are in holdings of less than 20 hectares each.

Thanks to unjust taxation systems, the lower income groups are obliged to meet a high percentage of the fiscal expenses. The privileged minority groups have managed to guide fiscal policy along indirect taxation lines, largely to escape direct taxation. Some figures will provide an idea of the seriousness of this problem.

PERCENTAGES OF DIRECT AND INDIRECT TAXES IN SOME
LATIN AMERICAN COUNTRIES *

Country	Direct taxes % of total	Indirect taxes % of total
Argentina	48	52
Brazil	25	75
Colombia	45	55
Costa Rica	28	72
Chile	56	44
Ecuador	21	79
El Salvador	39	61
Guatemala	27	73
Honduras	24	76
Mexico	47	53
Nicaragua	13	87
Peru	34	66
Venezuela	58	42

* United Nations, *Economic Survey of Latin America.* New York, 1957, p. 138.

These conditions create an enormous task for those interested in saving democracy in Latin America. This task cannot be successfully accomplished by the unions alone, but the unions should be able to influence a trend towards overcoming such inequities. Industrial and farm workers, organized in unions and suitable cooperatives, the middle classes and enlightened management must find common ground to meet the extraordinary challenge of Latin American social and economic conditions.

Second Challenges: Minorities Resisting Change

Privileged minority groups, which we call oligarchies, have dominated the Latin American economic and political scene for more than a century. They control most of the available wealth. Since the beginning of the century they have lost all sense of the changes affecting Latin America, and they do not realize the extraordinary nature of the threats that face them. In the awakening of our peoples and their demands for justice, they see only Russian Communism instead of a reaction against their own failures as a ruling class. They do not understand that the fact that the Communists make the most of present circumstances to forward Russian imperialism does not invalidate the justice of popular demands for better conditions.

Naturally they do not accept the structural changes that are indispensable for rapid and healthy economic growth. When demands are made for agrarian reform and for formulae that will provide a more solid and democratic basis for private property, they insist that the very principle of private property is in danger. Some go so far as to say that industrialization is not good because it draws the peasants away from the land, or makes them demand higher agricultural wages. Others accept industrialization but insist on repeating the mistakes of industrial processes in other lands and earlier decades. They do not want larger groups of small and medium savers to participate in business ownership, and they resist measures designed to protect the interests of the worker and the consumer.

The attitude of the oligarchs toward the Alliance for Progress is contradictory and harmful. They want money from Washington because they labor under the delusion that money itself will be oil on the troubled waters of Latin American demands. However, they prefer not to acknowledge the flight of their own capital to Swiss banks and to other investments outside Latin America. It is estimated that in the last ten years the Latin American oligarchs have withdrawn 10 billion dollars from the production process. Ironically, this is precisely the amount of external aid envisaged in the Alliance for Progress for the next ten years.*

The social and economic reforms recommended by the Alliance for Progress are either accepted and then deprived of their content, or resisted, as being the result of American ignorance of the Latin American state of affairs. Earlier, however, when American political and financial forces supported the privileges of the oligarchs, no one questioned their understanding of Latin American affairs.

The Alliance for Progress has accepted, at least in theory, the need to set the prices of Latin America's main export products at a just level. Unions, management, governments, all agree that this is fundamental to our swift and peaceful economic development. But then the uncomfortable question arises: better prices and stabilization for what, and for whom? A fairer exchange relationship finds moral justification in a general improvement in living conditions of the broad mass of Latin Americans. Actually, however, most of the profits from Latin American exports are monopolized by minority groups. Consequently, unless substantial changes are made in the way these earnings are distributed, the net result of price stabilization will only be to deepen the gulf already existing between rich and poor.

The following figures from the *International Labor Review,* published by the International Labor Organization at Geneva, Switzerland, bear witness to these problems:

* The figure more commonly used is $20 billion for the next twenty years.

In Venezuela half the total wealth is in the hands of 12% of the families; in Chile a third of the national wealth is controlled by 5% of the population; in Colombia, 1953 figures show that 41% of the national income was received by 5% of the population; in Mexico, in 1957, 16% of the population received 56.5% of the total income; while in Brazil, 63% of the wealth went to 17% of the population.

Without the abolition of oligarchical influence in Latin American governments, and unless the oligarchs realize that non-violent economic and social changes are in their own long-term interests, there will be no chance for the emergence of a strong union movement, able to play an effective role in economic development and immune to totalitarian and demagogic tendencies.

Third Challenge: Minority Forces Offering Totalitarian Solutions

The Leninist-Stalinist-Khruschevian "socialist construction" has become a huge form of state capitalism. The Soviet Union today is an aggressive military, political, and economic power. Communist imperialism has made Latin America one of its principal battlefields, and billions of dollars are spent on operations there every year. Up to the present moment the measures used to arrest this threat have been totally inadequate. To entrust the saving of Latin America from totalitarianism primarily to hysterical anti-Communist campaigns is a mistake that can precipitate us into the gulf sooner than we imagine. Educational measures must be strengthened, especially in training political and union leaders, and a positive campaign waged against the economic and social ills that are the scourge of the Latin American masses and that make them a prey to Communist propaganda.

If the battle is defined in terms of the oligarchical circles versus the Communist forces, the Communists will surely win the day, and there will be no hope for Latin America. Realistically, we must accept the fact that poverty and lack of social justice in Latin America work in favor of Communist strategy. We must also admit that Communist tactics have been logical and frequently successful.

The Communists have supported oligarchical groups, especially when directed by demagogic elements, in their fight against the unions and the genuinely democratic parties. Within the context of the struggle for power in Latin America, this alliance is logical. The oligarchies reason that the Communists are a minority group with very little chance of wresting the power from their hands. On the other hand, they feel threatened by the unions and the democratic parties which may obtain sufficient popular support to win control. The Communists, in turn, feel that since the oligarchies are not their main opponents and do not now enjoy much prestige as a ruling class, the longer they stay in power the easier it will be to bring about the Communist revolution. Consequently, the Communists do not consider the oligarchs to be an impediment to their strategy for taking over Latin America. This explains why the two opposite groups have so often joined forces against responsible unions and democratic elements. However, the fate of Cuba may have made some oligarchs realize the dangerously suicidal nature of this criminal alliance.

Failure to bring about improvements, despair in the face of injustice, and repression of what they consider to be just aspirations have produced a widespread state of frustration among the Latin American masses. This has brought forth a new kind of frustrated and psychopathic leader who, in spite of or perhaps because of being psychologically unbalanced, has a kind of attraction for the masses. A megalomaniac, and spectacularly histrionic, he does not lead but is carried along by the worst passions that underlie the Latin American political scene. He is a sign of what might be called political schizophrenia.

The Communists find this type of leader ideal for their present tactics, and we may be sure that they have discovered at least one of them in every country. The results can be seen in Cuba, and there is no reason why such characters should not be equally successful in Peru, Venezuela, and other countries.

The war against the challenge of Communism and totalitarian regimes in general must be waged simultaneously on three fronts:

1. Overcome the oligarchical resistance to those structural changes which will encourage the abolition of the prevailing poverty and injustice.
2. Begin an intense and thorough doctrinal and ethical training for Latin American political and labor leaders.
3. Wage a determined fight against the causes of the widespread frustration of the Latin American masses and the resultant isolation of their leaders.

Fourth Challenge: Relations Between Rich Nations and Poor Nations

There is a spiritual link between all countries that consider the ideas of freedom and dignity to be essential. Yet forces opposed to a regime of liberty and justice have developed within these nations.

We should not deceive ourselves by hiding the very real antagonisms between the underdeveloped "poor" countries and the industrialized "rich" countries of the West. The cultural link is there, but it weakens in the face of contradictions affecting the relationships between these countries. The present relationships are far from just. Understanding and readjustment are both urgent and necessary.

The rate of investment in Latin American countries must be greatly increased if important structural changes and a fast rhythm of development are to be achieved. Such additional resources must be supplied by non-Latin American nations, especially the United States.

Up to now, direct private investment has been considered the best solution. It is our honest opinion, however, that the benefits accruing from this type of investment, at the present stage of Latin American underdevelopment, are at best relative.

In 1956 the United States directly invested 7,408 million dollars in Latin America. It would be interesting to know how much has left the continent since then in the form of interest and dividends from those particular investments; only then could we know whether it was truly beneficial to our countries.

Experience seems to show that direct investment has not been coordinated with healthy and harmonious economic planning for development and has even meant a considerable drawing off of Latin American wealth. A radical change in the relationship between our countries and private investors is urgently required; otherwise, far from helping, the private investor sometimes actually prejudices our development.

All the loans, donations, and direct investments that industrialized countries may contribute to Latin America will never compensate for the catastrophic effects of the unjust exchange relationship presently affecting our economies. All of the good ideas of the Alliance for Progress are condemned to failure unless a solution can be found to this problem, which can be summed up in the phrase, "we buy dear and sell cheap."

Owing to the constant deterioration in exchange prices, Latin America received 1,700 million dollars less in 1959 than would have been expected at stable prices. What kind of aid can make up for this annual loss?

Optimistically supposing that individual efforts to overcome oligarchical resistance to structural changes and to prevent the penetration of Communist imperialism could be crowned with success, there is still no possibility of serious economic development programs for rapid growth unless a plan for a more just relationship between strong and weak countries can be found— a plan by which the rich nations can help the poor nations to strengthen themselves. And only on the basis of such a plan can democracy summon up enough strength to defeat totalitarianism.

TRAINING OF UNION AND POLITICAL LEADERS

To summarize, economic growth will not be possible unless democratic unions and political forces successfully respond to these four challenges; and the quality of the response will largely depend on the type of political and union leader we produce.

In the fight for democratic survival there are certain responsibilities that fall directly on the unions and the parties: the firm statement of ethical and doctrinal principles; efficiency of union and political action; the establishment of good relations founded on mutual respect between union and party; and adequate political and union training.

These tasks have not been performed satisfactorily. We must make up for lost time if we are to carry through our economic development programs and save our democratic institutions.

Communist-controlled countries have long been in a position to train hundreds of Latin American union and political leaders every year. We democrats must not be satisfied with the small number we are now training at home. Apart from certain isolated efforts of a few parties and universities, training for political leadership in Latin America has been almost completely neglected. However, the work begun two years ago by the Inter-American Institute of Political Education in Costa Rica, sponsored by various democratic parties and institutions, is an encouraging sign.

Among labor unions, the national centers have been making very worthy efforts in favor of workers' education. The international labor entities have also been dedicating more attention to education. UNESCO and ILO have taken steps in this direction, and the Institute for Labor Relations of the University of Puerto Rico has been making a valuable contribution.

Two new institutes have recently been founded which, although arriving late on the scene, are better late than never. These are the Inter-American Institute for Advanced Labor Union Studies in Mexico, sponsored by the Inter-American Regional Workers Organization, and the American Institute for the Development of a Free Labor Union Movement in Washington, D.C., sponsored by the United States labor movement and the Alliance for Progress. But all this is only a "drop in the bucket." Together we must redouble our efforts in this vital field of political and union education for Latin American leadership.

The Church

NOTES ON THE CATHOLIC CHURCH AND DEVELOPMENT

EDUARDO FREI MONTALVA

Senator, Chile

In the following notes, we are referring to the Church as an historical phenomenon and a sociological factor of great importance in Latin America, not as a religious phenomenon. One of the difficulties in approaching this subject is that generalizations are often misleading because there are substantial differences among the different nations of the Southern Hemisphere.

I. Direct Historical Influence of the Church
on the Economic Situation

The Church has had a directly favorable economic influence on the history of Latin America. The following might be mentioned among its principal effects:

1. The economic experience of the villages of Indian converts in Paraguay, organized directly by the Jesuits, which were mainly concerned with the promotion of production marketing.

2. The organization of technical farming on large estates belonging to the Church or to certain religious communities. In some cases, there was also elementary industrial processing (copper

smelting in Chile).

3. The development of certain industrial and vocational specialties among the members of the religious communities (watchmakers, apothecaries).

The Church also had an unfavorable influence on the economic situation in these respects:

1. Investment tended to be channeled into economically unproductive projects (construction of large and expensive buildings for exclusively religious purposes).

2. Growing social rigidity and immobility of capital as the power of the religious institutions to acquire the ownership of land and real estate grew continuously.

The influence of the Church on the economic situation tended, however, to decrease, particularly after the independence of Latin America. This was mainly due to a decline in its ability to determine the course of economic development and to a decrease in the human resources available to it exclusively (people employed only in the service of the Church), and hence fewer possibilities of assigning its members to strictly technical work.

In spite of the weakening of its direct influence on the economic situation, the Church still carries weight in Latin America because it retains a certain control over some economic sectors, but more particularly because it can wield influence through its own activities.

1. Its favorable influence is illustrated by the case of a Bishop of Talca who, in the midst of discussions on land reform, carried out, in one of his farms, a specific reform which had far-reaching consequences.

2. One unfavorable aspect is the continuing tendency on the part of certain groups to erect unproductive monuments.

II. DIRECT HISTORICAL INFLUENCE OF THE CHURCH ON THE SOCIAL SITUATION

Social development has a twofold connection with economic development, and is at the same time its cause and effect. It is the effect in the sense that unless economic development is social and humane there is no point in promoting it; it is not true development. And it is the cause in the sense that it has a decisive, although often indirect, influence on economic development. To encourage social, political, and, in general, human development is, in the long run, to encourage economic development; to obstruct social and political development is to obstruct economic development.

There have been historic instances in which the Church has taken a stand directly in connection with problems of social development:

1. The defense of certain sectors of the population whose human rights were being seriously violated was resolutely taken up by Father Las Casas and an entire highly influential group in the sixteenth century Church.

2. The work done by the Jesuits in founding the villages of Indian converts in Paraguay involved the establishment of a social order and justice as well as a certain measure of political autonomy, which made it possible to protect the inhabitants against more specific groups that were in closer contact with them than the Crown.

3. For centuries education in all its facets was the virtually exclusive responsibility of the Church.

On the other hand, the direct influence of the Church was in some aspects unfavorable to social and political change because:

1. It supported the predominant social structures.

2. It defended the political regime in power during the colonial era, with all the abuses of the metropolitan power and restrictions on international trade. These two facts must be judged against the historical background and ideas of the times, and not in the light of present-day developments.

There is, however, especially in this century, a strong tendency to increase the direct social influence of the Church on Latin American society through lay movements and trends which, while not clerical or direct instruments of the Church, depend on the

Church for the contribution they make in the matter of doctrine and often for their establishment and continued existence. These include the following:

1. Political groups of Christian persuasion, with reservations as to their being nonclerical and independent of the Church hierarchy, and as to the variety of the religious beliefs held by their members.

2. Trade-union movements of Christian persuasion, most of which are at present grouped in the Latin American Confederation of Christian Trade Unions, with the same reservations as in the case of political parties.

3. National unions of Christian entrepreneurs which, with the same reservations, endeavor to instill an attitude of greater dedication to economic and human progress than prevails in unions participating in productive enterprise (USEC in Chile, ACDE in Argentina).

4. The research and technical institutes forming part of the educational system of the Church in Latin America.

5. The mass or adult education campaigns launched and maintained by the Church in various countries (Sutatenza, Institute of Popular Education, etc.).

6. Bodies such as the Rural Education Institute in Chile which, by concentrating on the general education of the rural inhabitants, are an important factor in the country worker's development.

7. Institutions such as Techo in Chile, whose main purpose is to develop the productive and entrepreneurial skills of the inhabitants of workers' districts.

8. Cooperatives, mutual associations, and vocational organizations in almost all the Latin American countries.

9. University students.

10. A new and vigorous approach in all branches of education, accompanied by the modernization of study methods and more intensive social training.

11. The example of many priests and bishops who have abandoned traditional methods and cooperate directly with town and

rural workers.

Each of the above depends, of course, on the conditions prevailing in the country selected for this analysis. Nevertheless, there is also a direct social influence which is unfavorable to economic development, as reflected in the following:

1. A tendency to preserve the *status quo*, very common among the economically powerful Catholic groups.

2. Bewilderment as regards economic and social problems, together with a marked conservative bias at certain levels of the Church hierarchy and the Latin American clergy, or the clergy working in Latin America.

III. INDIRECT INFLUENCE OF THE CHURCH
ON ECONOMIC DEVELOPMENT

Apart from the influence which the Church exercises on the economic situation through direct action in the social sector, it has another indirect influence on specifically economic affairs, namely, the influence which any code of ethics has on human attitudes and on the scale of values and social institutions which condition them.

Economic development is indirectly conditioned by the economic system as a whole. Behind the complicated system of economic relations there is always human decision, based on human motivations, highly dependent on a scale of values and a network of institutions which sanction the motivations and the decisions to which they lead.

If we summarize such favorable (necessary) human attitudes, we shall finally come to determine what we might term the "ethos" of economic development, in the sense in which Max Weber spoke of the "ethos" of capitalist development, the "spirit of capitalism." Any system of beliefs, with its respective code of morality, which is favorable to such an ethos will be favorable to economic development, and any religious system unfavorable to the ethos of development will be unfavorable to economic development.

Obviously the interest here lies not so much in the principles as in the vivid reality of the religious system. In other words, if we call "religious ethos" that system of human attitudes advocated by a given religious system, the important thing is not so much the theoretical religious ethos as the practical religious ethos of such a religious system.

There is one tremendous difficulty involved in identifying the practical ethos and in studying the true behavior of the Latin American masses and the extent to which it is attributable to the practical religious ethos of the Catholic Church. Suffice it to recall the still inconclusive argument raised by Max Weber's essay on the practical religious ethos of the ascetic branches of the Protestant movement. We could hardly expect the sociologists to provide us with further information, in this connection, on the actual situation in Latin America. But, so long as they fail to do so, we shall have either to give up the attempt to deal with the over-all problem of the practical ethos of the Catholic Church or to adopt a more limited approach. Since we wish to cast some light on this problem, we decided to choose the more limited approach, which consists in using, for purposes of comparison with the ethos of development, not the practical but the theoretical religious ethos. This is justified not only by the present impossibility of investigating the practical ethos but also by the fact that the theoretical ethos leaves its mark in some form on the practical ethos. However ineffective or abstract the principles of an ethical system may be, some vestige of its influence will always be found in the practical ethos, or, to speak more modestly, if we wish to avoid taking causation for granted, let us refer to the fact that to some extent there is a correspondence, or at least no inconsistency, between the theoretical ethos and the practical ethos.

Let us therefore take the theoretical religious ethos of the Catholic Church in Latin America as one of the components (it might be the main one, but we could not prove this) of the practical ethos of the Catholics. Having gone thus far, we can define the sense in which we may speak of the indirect influence of the Catholic Church on the economic development of Latin America. The problem would be reduced to the following question: to what extent are the ethical principles of the Catholic Church consistent with what the development ethos should be for Latin America?

The only way of making a comparison is to specify the nature of the terms to be compared. We must therefore begin by defining: (a) the ethos of Latin American development, and (b) the theoretical religious ethos of the Catholic Church in Latin America.

(a) Without going into an exhaustive list of the human attitudes required for economic development, we can mention some of those which seem most fundamental:

1. Acceptance of social and economic change.

2. Interest in the productive process itself, or in its result: material goods and services.

3. Concern with insuring, or the desire to insure, that human beings can satisfy their most essential material needs.

4. The conviction that man has power to change his environment.

5. The spirit to inquire into and rationalize the processes of production and of the other aspects of life.

6. The allocation of resources in accordance with their productive capacity rather than for personal material considerations.

7. Concern for future consumption and production in relation to present levels.

8. A more equitable evaluation of the different types of occupation or of goods in order to avoid the exclusion of some which, although necessary, are neglected because they lack social prestige.

(b) There is one version of the theoretical ethos of Catholic theology which we consider to be a deviation but which, at one time, was passed on to the Latin American Catholic by what we might call the Spanish stream of spirituality, which is inconsistent with some of the features of the development ethos. This version is characterized by the following:

1. The presentation of existing social and economic structures as the will of God, as authorized by divine authority, and therefore the condemnation of any more or less radical change.

2. Disinterest in material goods, an almost exclusive concentration on the life to come, and indifference to present life.

3. Resignation to one's own and other people's misery or want, and emphasis on the necessary imperfection of social organisms as a consequence of original sin.

4. Fatalism as regards man's ability to control and transform his environment—leaving everything "in God's hands."

5. Emphasis on the goodness of intention, and disregard of practical effectiveness and the functional value of good intentions.

6. Charity, taken to mean "favoring" certain peoples because of their needs or personal links with them.

7. Emphasis on the cultural, spiritual, and Christian humanistic values, and contempt for more material occupations.

However, another version of the theoretical ethos of Catholic theology underlies the lay Christian institutions to which we referred above. This derives mainly from the Franco-Belgian Christian theology and philosophy, which seems to us to be clearly favorable to the development ethos and which has obviously been strengthened by the teaching of the popes and by the encyclical *Mater et Magistra*. This version of the Catholic ethos is characterized by the following:

1. A favorable attitude toward change, since Christian morality is a morality of specific replies to specific problems, which are always different, and thus requires a dynamism that continuously adapts the Christian reply to the problems of existence.

2. A concern with present life, in which the future life has a stake, and a concern which also extends to the material and the physical.

3. Resignation only to the inevitable, but a bitter struggle to adapt existence and its structures in order to improve them, i.e., to make them consistent with a life of union, harmony, and love.

4. The conviction that to leave things "in God's hands" does not imply renouncing personal responsibility or a slackening in the effort to achieve change, but only a cautious uncertainty concerning the success of endeavor and its real effectiveness in view of the congenital limitation of knowledge and technique, which are always susceptible of improvement.

5. The inadequacy of good intention by itself. It is particularly important for the Christian to be effective in his action, because his object is not to make use of his neighbor in order to show an ineffective good disposition but to love him in endeavoring to satisfy his needs.

6. Charity directed towards people and potentially towards all mankind and the common good; this excludes all nepotism or personal considerations in the allocation of productive resources. One loves one's neighbor more by assigning the posts, in enterprises producing goods or services, to the most competent people than by assigning them to those who need them most or are most thankful for them.

7. Deeply respectful consideration for all the range of human activities, including the economic activities of manual worker, employee, businessman, and moneylender. All are contributors to the common good, or can become so, and the handling of money does not in itself degrade anyone. It is possible to establish a genuine "spirituality of economic development," or a Christian mystique of the various functions of the productive process.

IV. FUTURE PROSPECTS

Historically speaking, the first of the trends outlined and simplified above was prevalent in the course of the last century. In the last twenty years there has been a very favorable development which has enabled the new attitude to exercise a progressive influence. There is evidence of a continuous and accelerated development and spread of the lay movements of Christian persuasion which are strengthening its humanistic position. This development might be characterized by the following features:

1. Recognition of the fact that we live in a pluralist society and therefore respect the diversity of religious and political beliefs.

2. The affirmation of democracy and rejection of all dictatorships and totalitarian forms.

3. The resolute will to carry out reforms, and support for the cause of the people and their desire for justice.

4. The conviction that planning is required if there is to be economic development and thus higher levels of living.

To the extent that the main teaching of the Catholic Church favors these tendencies, it may be said that the religious ethos is promoting the economic ethos. For this reason, in our opinion, the influence of the Catholic Church, which is favorable in some aspects, will become an increasingly important factor in the economic development of Latin America.

III. Latin America and the European Common Market

LATIN AMERICA IN A DEVELOPING WORLD

GERMÁN ARCINIEGAS

Ambassador to Italy,
Colombia

Integrated by the Common Market, Europe comes on stage to herald a change of scene in a world where the historical drama of our times seemed for a while to be dominated exclusively by two leading characters: the United States and Soviet Russia. Europe, united or federated, acquires the stature of something like a great empire, which cannot fail to exert a more effective influence than mere votes in the United Nations.

In the last few months, Russia has come to realize that what really blocks its imperialistic ambitions is the appearance of a united Europe held together by the Common Market. With the conversion into a European miracle of what has amounted to a partial miracle in the individual cases of Germany, Italy, and other European nations, a wall of interests will be raised that can withstand the formidable pressure of wealth and industry, military force and revolutionary virus available to the Communist world.

This Common Market is not a new idea. The United States is a common market that began with the thirteen colonies of old and now has spread to fifty states. At the same time, Latin America, for reasons arising from its geography, history, races, and resources, split up into a score of islands of sovereign home markets, creating not only anarchy, but the weaknesses that, taken together, furnish a measure of its problems in this second half of the twentieth century.

Russia has succeeded in building up an undeniable reserve of power around the hard core of international Communism, and on the same basis—a common market. Its formula for unity is the reaffirmation of an old Muscovite tradition from the days of Saint Petersburg, when despotic rule guillotined all opposition. The subjugation of Hungary and the whole of the imperialistic colonial plan engineered by Moscow are the vigorous thrusts of an iron will that openly defines itself as a dictatorship. Russia's ambition is to make the common market it dominates the greatest of all.

Meanwhile the Africans, clearly perceiving the extent to which Europe is willing to allow them to make use of Common Market facilities, have drawn up their own charter of Punta del Este, and applied to the nations of the Common Market for credits amounting to 1,200 million dollars—480 million of which they have already received. This starts a sort of Kennedy plan for the Africans themselves.

To achieve the basis of the European Common Market, the member nations have had to give up a good deal of their proud tradition of independence. Watching the development of this process and seeing Europe's struggles to unify itself, Latin Americans will recall a similar approach in 1810 when we erased every frontier and launched a war in common to emerge from the colonial way of living. One hundred and fifty years ago, a Colombian in Mexico was a Mexican, a Venezuelan in Peru was a Peruvian, and an Argentine in Chile was a Chilean. We were all fellow citizens. As soon as the reason for striving in common disappeared, however, we separated and lost the strength of those years in which a great European empire was overthrown in our America. Today, European integration is an example we would do well to heed.

Taking North, South, and Central America as a whole, there are many more inhabitants of European extraction there than in Western Europe. We are now close to four hundred million Americans who might well call ourselves a New Europe. London is still the city with the largest English-speaking population—it has half a million more inhabitants than New York—but London has existed for more than twenty centuries and New York less than three. Madrid has barely two million inhabitants, as compared with Mexico City and Buenos Aires, each with five million. Thus, the great Spanish-language capitals are to be found in Spanish America, and the same thing occurs with Portuguese. Lisbon has 794,000 inhabitants, while Brazil's São Paulo has 3,417,000 and Rio de Janeiro almost three million. To judge by the number of persons of Italian descent in Buenos Aires, this city might well be called New Rome.

The Europeans who made the trip to America brought with them the best of the Old World; they were men of industry with a spirit of adventure, of daring and faith, of creative imagination and heroic endurance in the struggle for existence. Experiences in a new land with men of every race have changed their conduct. The European in America was led to democracy as an original system of government; he proclaimed republics and declared himself independent. Only a few individuals, a mere handful of families, remained aloof in traditions of privileges, hierarchies, and titles that are foreign to the reality of America. The immense majority came out in favor of the republic and continues to stand up for it; in favor of freedom and continues to uphold it; in favor of social justice and continues to defend it from the now archaic system of privileges.

Europeans accord a certain superiority to the United States, for its fabulous wealth—multiplied, rather than accumulated, in less than two centuries. They are less appreciative of its culture. And yet, in the culture of the United States, there are political values and democratic affirmations so great and so manifold that they amount to one of the most amazing positive contributions to universal thought.

Latin America is the most ambitious, the most far-reaching experiment, and the only one that has been successful in engaging the peoples, races, individuals varying in blood and color, of three continents to live together without exterminating each other and, finally, without discrimination. It has suffered from revolutions, from anarchy and instability that at certain times have given it a barbaric appearance. In the pursuit of the idea of a free democratic republic we have run through a hundred small revolutions in a century and a half, and these relatively minor revolts have been grim samples of our most picturesque and deplorable vices. But it is not to be imagined that the introduction of democracy into Europe was obtained with less difficulty or bloodshed. The burden we have borne in the shape of the poor Indian, the manacled Negro, and the proud white man, left us by the colony, is closely paralleled in European history.

Today the whole world is an underdeveloped world. Institutions do not progress as fast as science and technology. On the other hand, very prosperous regions or cities enjoy all the advantages of civilization and yet suffer from evils that manifestly retard their progress. The poverty of Latin America is not identical with that of other great sectors of the planet. Nevertheless, since there is a wide difference of standards between the townsman and the countryman, the social conflict is all the more acute.

Agrarian reform is a matter of the utmost urgency. The cities of Latin America have progressed to a point where they enjoy more comfort, and services not inferior to those found in European cities. They display a luxury that is really monstrous compared with the poverty of the surrounding districts. Industry now thrives from Mexico to Chile and Argentina to an extent that rivals the activity in the industrial zones of the United States in the last century and the beginning of this one. With its exorbitant expansion, Latin American capital is yielding a rate of interest far higher than any investments in other parts of the world. What is considered the problem of underdevelopment consists in extending to a wider zone the development that is concentrated in the cities. A search must be made for formulae of common welfare. The underdevelopment is as serious as the massive development, and from the human viewpoint it is advisable to refer the concept to social groups rather than to countries.

Bogotá has leaped from a population of 120,000 in 1910 to one of about 1,360,000 today.* There live the very wealthy and the very poor. The city offers such great attractions that it has become a kind of frustration. The problem of Bogotá, which is akin to that of every one of the Latin American capitals, consists in directing development in such a way that, for a radius of at least sixty miles around the city, life should be made pleasanter for the country worker.

In the last century, illiteracy may have been blissful ignorance of things that did not matter. Now it is the bitter sensation of being left behind in the evolutionary backwash of the world. Even the circumstance of being in the immediate neighborhood of the United States tends to sharpen the sting of this widespread feeling of inferiority. While subdevelopment may formerly have been a factor of repose and peace in large zones of the continent, it has now become a time bomb that may explode at any moment.

Conditions in Asia, Africa, and Latin America are very different, and it is oversimplification to lump together regions varying widely from one continent to the next. But there is one difference between Africa and Latin America that demands direct discussion.

When they began to glimpse Africa's advance toward independence, the European countries set about strengthening the traditional colonial economic links in such a way as to adapt them to the advent of freedom. A framework of Euro-African

* Latest estimate published by ECLA (Economic Commission for Latin America).

rapprochement was constructed, designed to protect the interests of the former colonizers. Ever since the Marshall Plan, much of the money sent by the United States to further the reconstruction of Europe was siphoned off to refresh the soils of Africa. The first schemes to revitalize the economy of the so-called Black Continent were developed on the basis of introducing and intensifying the planting of the very tropical products that form the basis of Latin American exports. For the time being, the low cost of labor in Africa insured excellent returns to whomever was connected with this operation, an operation that in the long run would shift an appreciable percentage of the cost of African emancipation to the shoulders of the Latin Americans. No thought was given to the possibility of future conflict between the economies of Africa and Latin America. Unwittingly, the United States contributed to this situation by favoring these schemes. The Latin Americans themselves showed a lack of foresight in approving with their votes the plans of technical assistance that FAO * was preparing to promote coffee planting in Africa.

France conditioned its entry into the Common Market by discrimination in favor of the African products. Latin American ambassadors have been obliged to strive energetically with the Market to insure that the coffee and bananas shipped to Europe by Latin America should not suffer from the most-favored-nation treatment which the Common Market was anxious to grant to Africa. It was absurd to promote new coffee plantations when the world market for this commodity was saturated to a point where millions of tons were destroyed to keep prices on a level high enough to pay the subsistence wages essential to the Latin American worker. Today this problem of the surpluses, unwisely aggravated, is being brought home to the Africans, who are the first to deplore an initial blunder that cannot fairly be laid at their door.

An understanding that would allow planning for two complementary economies would have a better effect. It is to the

* Food and Agriculture Organization.

interests of Africa and Latin America to try to set up a round-table conference to interrupt what have been up until now one-sided discussions between Europe and Africa.

To unite Latin America, to adjust it as the United States, Russia, and Europe are adjusting themselves, is essential for its very survival, and for strengthening the forces defending democracy, freedom, and social justice based on the dignity of man. These aspirations are common to the whole world. They are not easy to express all over the world, but they are aspirations that constitute the underlying theme of our history and the *raison d'être* of our independent life. To achieve Latin American unity, it is indispensable to devise a plan to control poverty and ignorance, to raise the standard of living of the common man, and to promote industrial development without accentuating the differences between the peasant and the worker.

Such a plan requires a financial basis if it is to be workable. This was the purpose of the agreements of Punta del Este, the first plan of so wide a scope presented to all of the nations. It remains in the hands of Latin America to see that full benefit is obtained therefrom. If Latin America, through the Kennedy plan, is to keep and accentuate its own historical personality, it must emphasize the spirit of solidarity displayed by the republics involved in this outstandingly generous undertaking. For obvious reasons, the Kennedy plan, an instrument of Latin American integration, and the Common Market, an instrument of European integration, are bearing the brunt of the Russian offensive.

For Latin American unity, however, purely economic foundations are not enough. The prosperity of a country may have quite different prospects according to its political management. Parties that attain power operate in one of two ways: they establish as essential conditions of their government a respect for the dignity of man, the right to doubt, to discuss, to dissent, or else they subject the whole process to the despotic rule of a dictatorship that reduces it to a referendum on the conduct of the dictator.

Politics in Latin America have been deeply affected in the last thirty years by causes extraneous to its own initiative. Earlier, Europe exported immigrants to Latin America and stimulated the movements of emancipation with revolutionary ideas concerning the social contract and the rights of man. But in the last few years it has supplied the Western Hemisphere, and Latin America in particular, with communicable diseases: Nazism, Fascism, Falangism, and Communism. At the root of the movements that have affected American life most deeply lie these ideologies which are radically opposed to the free, unprejudiced spirit of a land where humanity has successfully striven for its freedom in order to overthrow absolutism.

Inasmuch as the appeal of totalitarianism consists in easy solutions and in satisfaction for those seeking power through violence, it also alters the quality of political parties. In Latin America, the exaggerated strengthening of the armed forces threatens to turn republics into countries occupied by their own armies. This is the first continent in which international war has been eliminated by a convention that makes it impossible for one country successfully to proceed against another. From the point of view of international security, our countries could get along quite well with an adequate police force. There is no sense whatever in a display of modern weapons, huge navies and air forces, or armies with hundreds of thousands of soldiers.

It was an unpardonable error on the part of the United States to stimulate the growth of Latin American armies, armies that could serve only to aggravate domestic problems and disturb the even flow of civilian life which is so necessary to democratic security. These armies, contrary to the constitutional principles of each country, have assumed the function of arbiters of electoral processes, political debates, and popular decisions. In every constitution the intention was to alienate the armed forces from politics. Now these forces form their own political party. The armies were brought into being to guard the Constitution; now they turn against the Constitution. Select groups of officers make heroic efforts to prevent this deflection of the army from its natural purposes. Unfortunately, the moral order of the civilian world is being undermined by the penetration of anti-democratic doctrines among officers on the general staff, together with the excessive power of certain armies with time on their hands and an arsenal overburdened with modern weapons.

Such, then, viewed through the mist of their difficulties, are the prospects that darken the future of Latin America. The difficulties could be readily overcome, and we would have no need to fear the prospects if a sense of strong unity and an elementary instinct of self-defense were at hand to correct a series of artificial situations that have nothing to do with the formidable moral reserves which are available. From the days of the conquest, Cortes, Quesada, Orellana, Cuauhtemoc, and Lautaro have set the stage for unarmed men to surpass the stature of the traditional hero. When the desire for independence induced man to struggle against nature, there was no mountain of ice, or untrod forest, or desert that could turn back an army without weapons, spurred on by a craving for freedom. The imagination is fired by the naked troops of Bolívar, riding out from the Llanos with water rippling at the bellies of their horses, to meet the trained European armies in wait to destroy them.

These are enough to show the terms on which the Latin Americans have fought and won. Nor are such examples confined to the heroic periods of our history. In recent years our women thronged the streets to overthrow tyrants with snatches of song, and before them the armed troops fell back, surrendered, despite their modern rifles and submachine guns. So long as the caliber of Latin America is not crushed to the level of the lowest, these two hundred millions who are industrializing their cities, who are about to bring justice to the countryside, who are striving to build schools and roads and clean villages, will play the role of people who do not depend on the peoples of other countries.

What is essential is to hold fast to an attitude of unwavering confidence and mutual solidarity. We must not flee from one yoke to shoulder another, nor bind ourselves to other land than our own, nor believe that all our misfortunes come from abroad. They come rather from our willingness to accept them, to act as cards that others play to rake in the blue chips of their own winnings. From a Latin America that behaves with dignity and coalesces into one solid group, advantages will accrue to the whole Free World. This is the mission which is entrusted to the rising generation.

EUROPEAN INTEGRATION AND THE DECLINE OF NATIONALISM

FRANÇOIS FONTAINE

**Director, Bureau d'information
des Communautés Européennes**

MAX KOHNSTAMM

**Director, Institut de la Communauté
Européenne pour les Études Universitaires**

Nowadays an accusing finger is pointed at nationalism in some parts of the world while it is championed in others. In one place it is regarded as a barrier, in another as a stimulus to development. Economists who critize it in Germany and moralists who condemn it in France may approve it in Guinea or find it legitimate in Algeria.

At this time of widely varying sociological trends in the world, no blanket judgment can be made. It is, however, possible to view nationalism in one of its most dramatic crises, and to describe its rapid decline in Western Europe today.

Theories about the formation of nations and the role they play are legion. Was there nationalism in Athens at the time of Pericles, in England under Cromwell, in France under Napoleon? We have every reason to believe that there was. By transposing a spontaneous national feeling into the field of ideology, the political philosophers made of it a very powerful political instrument, capable of being exported, of existing even before the reality of the nation itself, and of giving rise to the nation itself.

To maintain nations, or to create new ones, became the role of this militant doctrine which seeks acceptance as the revealed truth—a doctrine difficult to discuss without glancing at its metaphysical side. The least one can do is make a choice between two hypotheses: the nation is an end in itself, or the nation is tending to be left behind by current events.

When we say that the nation is tending to be left behind by current events, we are not making a value judgment. We allow that nationalism was good for our peoples at a certain stage of their intellectual and technical growth, and that it still is good for certain developing countries. But we believe that its creative impact in history decreases and changes direction when it has fulfilled its main function, which is to provide a framework and protection for societies in the early periods of technical growth. A time comes when national dynamism, bound within frontiers and struggling with its rivals, ceases to set energy free and destroys its own substance. In the twentieth century this remarkably diversified form of organization has lost resilience, and its capacity to adapt has been strained to the utmost.

To survive, nationalism must make big concessions to the community spirit. The economic, technical, and military interdependence of the world today is unavoidable, and nationalists no longer have any choice save to sacrifice progress or sacrifice principles. But this choice is itself a trap. Countries which seek to keep their sovereignty intact at the cost of their development will only succeed in increasing their economic and military dependence on foreign powers.

To evade this difficulty, certain governments conceal *de facto* concessions to international solidarity behind nationalist attitudes. Others endeavor to transpose nationalist doctrine into the new forms of international life. It is likely that the retreat will gather pace and that the countries of Western Europe will have to abandon piecemeal first the actual fact and soon the principle itself of national sovereignty. Whether they will attempt to reestablish it at the level of the unified whole which they are going to set up remains to be seen.

That question deserves the greatest attention. On the capacity Europeans show to bring about their unification without recourse to old nationalist habits will depend the fate of the national principle in the West. The current experiment of the Six may be the beginning of a new form of relationship between peoples. It is from this angle that we shall examine the origin and development of the European Community.

Whatever the relative importance of economic or psychological factors in causing wars, it is undeniable that nationalism was at the root of the three great conflicts which laid Europe waste between 1870 and 1945. Mutual intolerance between nations, or economic difficulties which it was hoped to solve by force—these sources of strain stemmed from the selfish and exclusive concept of the national interest.

It was only after the 1914–1918 war that people began to think that God was not with the nationalists after all, since He allowed those who had invoked his name loudest to go to the wall and failed to protect the others from disaster. The internationalist doctrines which until then had found favor only among a few dreamers forced themselves on the attention of the realists. The League of Nations was set up. Its existence implied that there could be a common interest and a collective feeling between former enemies. It is very instructive to reread the great Briand plan of 1931, in which all the basic principles of today's European Community are set out, and in which the very expression "common market" is used. The project seemed too bold, yet it involved no derogation of national sovereignty.

It is not the failure of the Briand plan which gives us the measure of this period; it is the fact that it was even thought possible at that time to reconcile the principle of absolute sovereignty with the principle of federation. Efforts based on this contradiction were doomed to failure.

The responsibility for the misunderstandings which led to the last great world conflict must be borne less by the excesses of nationalism than by the mistakes of internationalism, which had good intentions but insufficient methods. The League of Nations was bound to engender dangerous illusions, since the veto inevitably put a stop to any useful undertaking. Events have shown that in practice negotiators are tied by instructions from their governments, and however great their good will they can make no concessions. Wherever joint solutions infringe on a sovereign right, they come hard up against the unanimity rule. This was the obstacle that had to be tackled if a genuine international organization was to be achieved. Opinion was not yet ready.

The notion of national sovereignty was for a long time correctly assessed as providing a better safeguard for the political, economic, and military interests of a people than the federal or community principle. Freedom to make alliances and to revoke agreements was in harmony with a pessimistic and cynical view of international equilibrium, itself based on the belief that wealth and power were kept or lost through force. The old notion of an economy based on plunder had not disappeared in 1939, and it was still believed that a country could attain wealth by ruining its neighbors.

Internationalism has grown from the fact, realized by a few farseeing spirits, that modern wars were likely to lay the victor as low as the vanquished, that peace is the safest means of avoiding ruin. But it has not led to a higher order of things, since the political doctrines of nonaggression lacked an element of dynamism which only the economic expansionist doctrines were to bring.

The determination of the League's backers to establish a static international order crumbled when in 1939 yet another gamble was made on conquest. This temptation will continue to be a factor in world politics as long as the possession of wealth remains an attribute of a nation. Peace is never quite secure when access to the natural resources essential to a country's economy and defense is not guaranteed. No commercial agreement and no alliance affords the absolute certainty of external supply, which all national economies need in order to create and keep alive their industries. No system of free exchange will seem so sound that our separate countries can commit their productive framework irrevocably along the road of interdependence. Here nationalist misgivings are justified. A good government must strive to control, more or less directly and aggressively, the foreign markets from which its economy draws supplies and in which it sells its products.

Let us now imagine that one of these good governments proposes that instead of seeking out several solutions to that particular problem, we change the problem itself; that with one's close neighbors, as a beginning, we should drop the notions of foreign markets, trade treaties, bargaining, dumping, threats of trade reprisals, and that the idea of a common pool open to all without distinction of nationality should take their place. Economic conflicts, which are the main reason and the very means for waging wars between these countries, would at once disappear.

This is what happened in 1950 when the French government suggested the idea of the European Coal and Steel Community. Such a proposal attacked the very roots of nationalism: there would no longer be any valid motive for one country to destroy another for the possession of coal and steel. The Schuman Plan was therefore more than a symbol; it damped world conflagrations at the source. It forged unbreakable links, and offered an enormous field for experiment.

Today the European Coal and Steel Community is carrying forward its task in the areas covered by these two great basic industries, but its prestige has been eclipsed by that of the Common Market. It remains, however, the boldest undertaking—for which European statesmen have assumed the most daunting political responsibilities in modern times.

In the present European revolution, the stress is on the constructive side. The aim is not to forbid war but to make it useless by replacing a state of discord with a situation in which interests are common to all. Abolishing customs barriers is not enough;

common policies are also instituted. Nationalism is not destroyed; it is left by the wayside. That is why the Schuman Plan raised such high hopes in 1950, when Europeans were beginning once more to be suspicious of all the schemes proposed for the establishment of peace.

The famous declaration of May 9, 1950, stated:

> The contribution which an organized and living Europe can bring to civilization is indispensable to the maintenance of peaceful relations. . . . Europe will not be made all at once, or according to a single, general plan: it will be built through concrete achievements, which first create a *de facto* solidarity.

These words assume extraordinary aptness. Today we can see that there is an organized and living Europe, living *because* it is organized.

But this organization began modestly, and it began pragmatically. The secret of its success must be its originality. It had seemed necessary to establish *de facto* solidarity first of all for three reasons: (1) if it succeeded it would secure the beginnings of an economic merger; (2) it would serve as a model; and (3) it would give rise to the minimum of ideological squabbling since it was to be introduced at a practical level.

The great idea of Jean Monnet, the father of the European Community, is that if men are to be changed, you must begin by changing the framework within which they act. To attack nationalism as such is worse than useless. But if the national framework can be widened and the national institutions—in particular the economic institutions—can be superseded, the ideology of nationalism will have lost its *raison d'être*.

What has been the success of this pragmatic onslaught on nationalism? There were two difficulties it might encounter. First, it was feared that it would not be equal to the task of allaying the great disquiet of the nations. Between the end—world peace—and the means—a coal and steel pool, the disparity was at first sight too wide. Second, the economic approach to the problem was in danger of arousing opposition in the sectors chosen for the experiment. This is what happened, and between 1950 and 1954 the power with which industrial nationalism resisted was substantial.

Some have felt that this form of nationalism was by far the most dangerous. It contained all the others and made use of them. It will be extremely interesting to study in detail the means it used in an attempt to bring to nought the European venture. We shall content ourselves here with the question of why and how industry, which is today the motive force behind unification, served ten years ago to slow it down.

The disadvantages of nationalism had for more than fifty years dogged the coal industry, and particularly the steel industry. They had coped with these disadvantages by secret methods. The establishment of cartels was a response to the need to curb the impact of commercial war between nations. The ironmasters had implemented, on their own account, the diplomats' system of political alliances, and they had added a certain degree of supranationality, since they accepted restrictions on sovereignty in the choice of merchandise produced and of markets, as well as arbitration by international corporate tribunals. But this was a frail structure. Solely defensive and self-centered, its total lack of legal standing put it out of action the moment that strain on the market became excessive.

The Coal and Steel Community tackled the same business difficulties by an approach opposite to that adopted by the cartels. Market control was put in the hands of democratic institutions, independent of private interests and of national governments. The governments had taken the initiative, prepared the documents transferring sovereignty, and requested the parliaments to approve them. In this way the Treaty of Paris, setting up the High Authority (the executive body), the European Parliament, the Court of Justice, and the Council of Ministers, was ratified.

Throughout this system, the Community interest is the sole consideration. It finds expression in the High Authority, the Parliament, and the Court—all composed of independent men of

several nationalities. The national interest finds expression in the
Council of Ministers. Here, as in any body politic, private interest
is subordinated to that of society as a whole.

It is not surprising that industrialists should have felt that this
loss of power over the political conduct of their own affairs consti-
tuted a threat. To defend their cause, they invoked, not the principle of free enterprise (not questioned by the Community), but
that of national sovereignty. They found little support in European opinion as long as they defended the maintenance of existing
situations in the business field—customs and quota protection,
double pricing, bilateral agreements—even when they linked these
practices with notions of national power and security. It was obvious that the myth of national boundaries, like that of national
ownership of resources, had lost its validity in Europe. In contrast,
the prospect of the common ownership and management of the
wealth of six countries was welcomed, despite the campaigns
waged by industry among the general public.

These campaigns became decisive when the development of the
European edifice led to the project for a European army based on
the same principle of the integration of separate forces. This
brought to the surface the deeper stratum of nationalist resistance,
and gave the measure of its solidity. The problem was dramatic
only in France, the only European country having a large national
army which would have had to dissolve itself into the Defense
Community. The alliance of the extreme left and the extreme
right made possible a wide appeal to patriotic sentiment, and in
the French Parliament in 1954 powerful lobbies succeeded in
bringing the venture to a halt. Public feeling was not adequately
prepared for such a ruthless break with national traditions; when
the problem was presented in emotional terms, with its consequences highly dramatized, the country divided. With the affirmation: "The European army is the end of the history of France,"
the powerful forces of conservatism brought the scales down on
their side.

But the failure of the European Defense Community was not so serious as to jeopardize the Coal and Steel Community, not only because this Community was based on an irrevocable treaty, but also because it had already created a new set of circumstances. Here was additional proof of the wisdom of the method based on *de facto* solidarity in practical things. Industrialists soon tired of a negative attitude; they decided to adapt themselves and to exploit the opportunities offered by a wider market and more severe competition.

If we did not remember this change of heart, it would be difficult to explain the ease with which the idea of a new European start, this time on the economic plane, was accepted after defeat on the doctrinal plane. The Common Market was the natural outcome of ECSC; it is organizing a total merger of the economies of six countries. EURATOM is developing their joint power in the peaceful use of atomic energy.

Both these new communities dealt decisive blows to the principle of national sovereignty. The complete and final abolition of frontiers, the free movement of all products, the freedom to exercise any activity, and also the common organizations—all to be effective within a few years—did not seem mortal dangers for the souls of our peoples. Private interests, after a short resistance, have dovetailed into the system; though they all strive to turn it to their own advantage, they are agreed that it is profitable and there is no going back on it. Nationalism has been obliged to accept much of this new European concept. It is now concentrating on defending the political forms of national sovereignty. But there too it understands that economic policy determines a great deal of social, military, and foreign policy. It is fair to say that in Europe there are virtually no open enemies of the new Europe left. Disagreement now concerns only constitutional methods: confederation or federation, and a timetable.

How can we explain this retreat, in less than twelve years, of one of the most powerful ideologies to have molded the European continent for several centuries? Has there been a genuine change in public feeling, or will nationalism resume the offensive if the forces fighting against it relax their pressure?

Surveys carried out recently in the European Community, particularly among young people, show that there is no longer any rational or emotional basis for a return to nationalist doctrines. The fact that the great problems of today cannot be settled within a purely national framework is accepted by the great majority. Cultural exchanges are developing rapidly. Generations which have seen war seem to have overcome their differences. The younger have no principles on which they are hostile or suspicious with regard to their neighbors.

It is not easy to say whether these attitudes developed before or after the European Community was set up—whether they were a prerequisite or the outcome. It is reasonable to suppose that they would not have developed so fast if a bold and tangible undertaking had not encouraged them, if they had not been able to hold fast to a concept of organization.

But this new concept would not have resisted the nationalist forces of inertia and the temptations of historical habit if circumstances had not been created from which there would be no retreat. This is the profound originality of the Community. Alliances can be called into question, coalitions can be dissolved, but what has been physically merged cannot be broken up. The indissolubility of the Common Market rests less on agreements than on the fact that the common undertakings and the division of labor make any backward step impossible. The dynamic force of economic integration must not make us forget that the basis of the Community is institutional. Europe's greatest risk lies in the excessive confidence we are tempted to put in "the nature of things." If the institutions did not take great care, "things" would cease to be "European" and yet could not again become national, so the system would be one of unorganized free trade. But it is an illusion to believe that free trade can work lastingly without a common authority administering rules with which the countries concerned agree beforehand to comply.

Without this discipline there is no free trade; there is only the interplay of commerce between the nations—profitable or unprofitable, bound by agreements or beset by conflict, depending on the advantages they find. Nowadays everybody admits that discipline is essential. The original contribution of the Community is that it is based on institutions as strong and exacting as the political institutions that have enabled societies to develop.

What place have these new institutions in Western Europe? What chance have they of surviving, of setting up and maintaining the claim of right that has been the success of national institutions? These are the focal points of the debate that is exercising European minds today. Everybody agrees that the Community should now take political form. Some believe that the competence of the economic institutions based on a federal model—Executive, Parliament, Court of Justice—can be extended into the political sphere. Others think that, politics being of a special nature, something new must be created.

The most controversial question is whether the same measure of integration that was possible on the economic plane is desirable on the political plane. Is the political organization of Europe to be a mere alliance, a confederation, or a federation?

For their last stand the nationalists have chosen the ground of political cooperation. They intend to retain sovereign rights in matters of diplomacy and defense for the nation. Obviously, these rights are still national, and it would be difficult to decide that they should cease to be national overnight. But they are gradually being curtailed and will probably disappear in time. It is this probability and the question of how long it will take the nationalists are contesting so forcibly.

These elements reduced, the debate loses its importance, and the outline appears of a feasible political system that could take its place beside the existing economic system in Europe once the latter is consolidated. Experience will show how fast and how far the forms of economic union can be adapted to political union.

Whether this political organization will be set back if Great Britain joins is a serious question. But if we assume that the European Community will have political substance, we may certainly ask whether it might not eventually take the shape of a nation, transferring the sovereignty complex of the older nations onto the continental plane.

The Common Market has been suspected of setting up an autonomous economic power working only to its own advantage. The mutual benefits agreed on by the countries bound by the Treaty of Rome, their unity of action, and, above all, the success of their experiment give rise to serious doubts in the rest of the world. The establishment of a single tariff on the frontiers of the Community has given some substance to this anxiety.

The new Europe must assert its originality. As a customs union it must have an external tariff. As an economic union it must have a common policy. As a union of states—confederation or federation—it must have its own foreign policy and perhaps a common defense policy. But the resolve has been taken to do all this in the interest of the Free World, and it would be a contradiction of its own aims of peace and progress for the Community to be prejudicial to the development of friendly peoples.

The external tariff is low; it has even been cut since the beginning. Further reductions are to be made in the application of GATT * regulations with which the Common Market is in agreement. The greatest attention is paid to comments from any country that might consider itself an injured party—whether in the course of negotiations such as those with Great Britain, or those enabling European countries to become associates; whether in the form of the association of African States, or in negotiations that will certainly be carried on with the United States and with Latin America. There is an infinite variety of forms of association, involving reductions or the abolition of duties, market guarantees, contributions to development, and so on.

The Community is open to anyone who subscribes to its economic and political aims and accepts its rules. These facilities are obviously of interest only to European countries, whose geography

* General Agreement on Tariffs and Trade.

and history naturally fit them for the creation of a federation. For other countries, no type of agreement is impossible.

This might not be enough to reassure those countries that have found in the nations of Europe the medium-sized powers that they needed as partners. If Europe in its turn becomes a great power or constitutes a bloc, will it not also start to throw its weight about, and will the smaller countries not be still more isolated? This fear is making itself felt in the newly independent nations, which are uneasy about the risks of European neo-colonialism.

We do not find these theoretical anxieties in the men who have had the opportunity of watching the Communities at work. There is no trace of imperialist spirit in the challenge of unifying Europe. To give more weight to this assurance, we quote the words of the man who has always put the impress of his thought and action on the European Community. In May of this year, Jean Monnet said in London, at a decisive point in the development of British policy:

This system is quite different from the old forms of inter-governmental cooperation . . . that we all know by experience do not prevent nations from going divergent ways.

It leads to a completely changed approach to common action. In the past, the nations felt no irrevocable commitment. Their responsibility was strictly to themselves, not to any common interest. They had to rely on themselves alone. Relations took the form of domination if one country was much stronger than the others, or of the trading of advantages if there was a balance of power between them. This balance was necessarily unstable and the concessions made in an agreement one year could always be retracted the next.

But in the European Community, common rules applied by joint institutions give each a responsibility for the effective working of the community as a whole. This leads the nations within the disciplines of the Community to seek a solution to the problems themselves, instead of trading temporary advantages. It is this method which has caused a silent revolution in men's attitudes.

So, Europe has overcome the attitude of domination which ruled state policies for so many centuries. This is a fact of world importance.

It is obvious that countries and peoples who are overcoming this state of mind between themselves will bring the same mentality to their relations with others, outside Europe.

The new method of action developed in Europe replaces the efforts at domination of nation states by a constant process of collective adaptation to new conditions, a chain reaction, a ferment where one change induces another.

Similarly, problems are arising that only Europe and the United States together have the resources to deal with. The need to develop policies of sustained growth, which in large part depend on maintaining international monetary stability, is one example. Increasing the aid of the West to the underdeveloped areas on a large scale is another. Separately, the European nations have inevitably taken divergent views of aid policies. But tomorrow, the nations of Europe by acting together can make a decisive contribution.

In my mind one impression predominates. It is this: unity in Europe does not create a new kind of great power; it is a method for introducing change in Europe and consequently in the world.

European unity is the most important event in the West since the war, not because it is a new great power, but because the new institutional method it introduces is permanently modifying relations between nations and men. Human nature does not change, but when nations and men accept the same rules and the same institutions to make sure that they are applied, their behavior towards each other changes. This is the process of civilization itself.

EUROPE AND THE DEVELOPMENT OF LATIN AMERICA

EGIDIO ORTONA

*Director-General for
Economic Affairs,
Italian Foreign Ministry*

The American continent entered the scene of history barely four centuries ago, but in this brief span of time it has boldly carved out for itself a strong place in the world. The people of America were able to do this because the early settlers were heirs to an ancient civilization. But then, was the New World nothing but an offshoot of European civilization? Whoever would answer "yes" would pervert history. Over centuries there has been a continuous and alternating movement, from Europe to the Americas and back again, of centers of radiation and of energy.

As early as the end of the eighteenth century the New World contributed modifying influences to the economic and social pattern of European societies. Europe's industrial revolution, the very foundation of the modern world, was achieved in the context of world-wide trade, which supplied Europe with the raw materials she needed and which enabled her to send her own growing output of manufactures to growing populations throughout the world. In turn, massive overseas investment, with European entrepreneurship and labor skills, exercised decisive influence on the development of the Latin American countries, especially on basic infrastructures such as railways, port installations, electric power generation and distribution, and inland waterways.

In the postwar years, Latin America's spurt of economic expansion has not been matched by the necessary structural and social reforms. Fluctuations in the prices of primary commodities hit the Latin American economies just at the precarious moment of their take-off. This slowing of economic growth has created a sense of frustration throughout the Latin American continent, with repercussions which are most evident among the young generation and which dangerously feed extreme propaganda and demagogic revulsions.

Europeans have looked with deep interest at the Charter of Punta del Este, which reaffirms the importance of man's determination to help himself. We know, through the experience of the Marshall Plan, the psychological importance of self-help in any program of aid. But we also know that, however much self-help remains the primary element, it cannot become fully effective without outside assistance. We are aware of the need to meet the challenge which has been with us ever since the Bogotá Conference; the challenge to do more together with the United States in every field—trade, investment, and technical aid—to help the economic development of Latin America in a framework of cooperation resting not on charity, but on reason and common interests.

At present the United States and the European Economic Community, including Great Britain, encompass between them the mightiest production potential now in existence; together, they account for 90 per cent of the Free World's industrial production and for about two-thirds of world trade. Given a more intense economic cooperation, they ought to be in a position to foster the development of the countries of the Latin American continent, with which ethnic, spiritual, and economic ties have been long since established.

The West has already begun to face up to the implications of a world-wide concept of development. The Organization for Economic Cooperation and Development is taking the first steps toward the coordination of the economic foreign policies of its member countries and has worked out new machinery to step up aid to underdeveloped areas. In recent meetings in Paris it created *ad hoc* groups to study the problems of aid to certain areas, including Latin America.

The European Economic Community attracts particular attention. Over the last ten years, the countries of the Community have had the highest growth rate in the world, and it is not unreasonable to expect them to exceed the OECD estimate of a 50 per cent increase in national income between 1960 and 1970.

The Treaty of Rome says, in Article 110, that it is one of the Community purposes to contribute to the harmonious development of world trade, to the gradual elimination of restrictions, to international exchange and the reduction of tariff barriers. That this principle, which involves specialization of production, expansion of consumption, and growing trade with third countries, has been upheld is proved by the statistics of the EEC's trade with the rest of the world. A glance at these data will show a steady expansion of both exports and imports, and in particular of imports from Latin American countries. Moreover, the extraordinary increase of the consumption rate of Common Market countries in recent years leads one to an optimistic view of the possibility of increasing the cooperation between them and the developing countries.

The common agricultural policy is meant fundamentally to achieve the integration of a basic economic sector in the member countries which thus far has presented striking structural differences and has, in each country, been more or less sealed off from equivalent sectors in the other countries. The aim is to bring about, through reasonable provisions and a gradual process of reconversion, a satisfactory and well-established level of production, income, and competition in the world market. If this is achieved, it should not forcibly reduce imports from third countries because it would be offset by expansion of consumption in the wake of general economic growth and higher standards of living in the Common Market countries. In agriculture, as in other sectors, the ultimate effect of the EEC should not be a decrease of trade with the outside world.

As regards the preferential treatment accorded by the EEC to the tropical products of associate members overseas, it must be remembered that in the current negotiations for a new pattern of association with formerly dependent territories, the Community has gone a fair way toward solutions which take adequate account of the interests and expectations of other developing countries that export tropical products. A first step in this direction is the acceptance by the overseas associate members of the principle of a reduction of the Common Market's joint external tariff for certain products of particular interest to third countries. As a result, the EEC Council decided, with the general concurrence of the overseas associate members, to reduce the common external tariff on coffee and cocoa by 40 per cent the next year. These two commodities are, of course, among the major exportable resources of many Latin American countries.

During the transitional period ahead, the preferential treatment granted to African countries will place these in an advantageous position. But one must not overlook the fact that they were already enjoying a preferential situation with France, and that the provisions to be decided in their favor will be only of a temporary character.

The preferential system of the new pattern of association with the EEC should be viewed as just one stage in a long-term development in the areas of agricultural and tropical products. The ultimate aim is to arrive at international agreements to organize on a world scale the production and trade of raw materials and other commodities of interest to all developing countries. That is where the EEC, having already proved to be an important center of attraction, can become a positive element also for the Latin American countries.

The presence in the world of the EEC and the association with it of former dependencies will serve as a catalyst for efforts in the direction of world agreements pertaining to those agricultural and tropical products which are at the core of Latin American economies. In other words, the EEC is offering to the friendly countries a policy of intense cooperation in areas particularly important, and all interested nations should respond.

The Commission of the EEC has recently been engaged in thorough studies concerning the improved relations to be established with the countries of Latin America. The main points being examined pertain to the organization of international trade in primary commodities; aid in the expansion of Latin American industrial exports; special facilities to ease capital goods imports for Latin American countries; measures to promote direct investment in Latin America; coordination of technical aid to be rendered by Common Market countries; institutional contacts between the Common Market and Latin America.

It is, of course, true that any increase of the ties between Europe and Latin America is bound to encounter a number of delicate and complex problems and that it would be a mistake to underestimate the difficulties which stand in the way of satisfactory solutions. But, given good will and constructiveness of purposes, we can look forward with hopeful prospects. In today's world, countries have been gradually tending towards regional economic groupings. The EEC is an eloquent example, and Latin America itself has been steadily moving in the same direction in recent years.

We must avoid the sealing off of regional groupings as independent units, but must take advantage of the dynamics inherent in them to bring about a more intense reciprocal intercourse. All the elements of a higher degree of cooperation exist: on one side, the prosperity and the willingness of the EEC to look beyond its boundaries; on the other side, the power of attraction which the EEC has already exercised and which could strengthen the already existing traditional ties between Latin America and Europe.

SUMMARY OF DISCUSSIONS: EVOLUTION OR EXPLOSION?

REYNOLD E. CARLSON

Latin America, as a continent and in its various national units, is in the midst of a difficult transition, so difficult that it may spark revolutions. Latin America is at no single crossroad, faced with a simple decision which would send it down one path or another. Its progress is the more complicated passage in time from the nineteenth century to the latter half of the twentieth, amid a widespread demand that this be achieved overnight.

In more precise terms, the countries are moving from a traditionally agrarian, hierarchical, and oligarchical society to one which is urban, industrial, and, hopefully, democratic. This transition creates tensions which in turn create cross-tensions. Would the process of change be orderly and evolutionary, with enough flexibility to accommodate the stresses and the strains being generated? What about traditional institutions? Would the existing educational system, the military establishment, the church, the present arrangements of economic and political power slow the process? Or could those institutions be adapted so as to speed up the process rather than serving as a drag on it? Would their rigidities create barriers and lead to explosions? And what about their effect on economic and political relations with the outside world?

At the same time, what about the validity and the effect of economic and political concepts, of devices such as nationalism, statism, inflation, Soviet Communism, North American democracy?

The background papers published in this volume were designed to provide factual knowledge regarding the attitudes, institutions, policies and aspirations which are acting and interacting on the growth and development of Latin America, as well as opinions on how to deal constructively with all these factors. Against that setting, the participants plunged into warm debate, probing and dissecting the political, economic, and social realities of Latin America today. In three separate seminars the discussions covered the main topics of the Conference: (A) Tensions Between Nations, (B) Tensions Within Nations, and (C) Preconditions for Economic and Social Development. Each participant chose the seminar he wished to attend. Final plenary sessions reviewed the reports of the seminars with further stimulating reactions.

There was some overlapping in the discussion, since many topics, the Alliance for Progress, for example, were bound to be treated in more than one seminar. But because of the differing angles of vision there was no actual duplication. The Conferences organized by the Council on World Tensions are designed to expose different points of view, to stimulate further thought and study, and to suggest lines of constructive action rather than to attempt to force a consensus of opinion. Hence, no recommendations, but plenty of suggestions emerged. Obviously any summary must be greatly condensed and cannot possibly convey the flavor as well as the substance of the meetings. Many interesting comments and important arguments are, perforce, omitted. Some of the ideas are far from new, but the fact that they were reiterated by this thoughtful group gives them added weight.

Many participants regretted that time was lacking to deal with a number of troubling factors such as the population problem, or the role of the press in heightening arguments between and within countries rather than in helping to resolve them. Others deplored the lack of opportunity to explore adequately the cultural factors as aids or hindrances in development, the psychological importance of cultural advancement; the value, in international relations, of cultural achievements as a source of national pride and a basis for mutual respect and cooperation. Too little time could be devoted to relations of Latin America with Europe, Asia, and Africa.

The following summaries of the three seminars attempt to give the essence of the discussions and the points of controversy which arose, and to demonstrate how they point the way to an understanding of Latin America's problems and place in the world.

SEMINAR A—TENSIONS BETWEEN NATIONS

Seminar A had as its joint Chairmen Roberto de Oliveira Campos, Ambassador of Brazil to the United States, and Lincoln Gordon, Ambassador of the United States to Brazil. It started with a detailed examination of nationalism, including an attempt to decide whether its values were negative or positive. An analysis of its various types revealed more facets than historians who have dealt with this subject exhaustively have ever uncovered. Nationalism appeared as a spectrum, its values ranging from the positive one of unifying and mobilizing a country for development and enlisting the imagination of its peoples, to the negative one which can lead to totalitarianism of the Hitler type. There followed a discussion of the Alliance for Progress, its merits and difficulties, possible alternative forms of organization which might offer improvements, and the place of Latin America in a pluralistic world —a somewhat obscure phrase which gained vividness if compared with a bipolar scheme in which relationships run merely north and south.

Within this three-part framework, it was not only inevitable but also healthy that much of the discussion should concern tensions existing between Latin America and the United States. A short review of nationalism in the Northern Hemisphere, and of tensions between Canada and the United States, yielded the interesting observation that while foreign investment in Canada is largely from the United States and 75 to 80 per cent of certain industries in Canada are controlled by the United States, this does not overly worry the Canadians. On the contrary, Canada accepts the responsibility for keeping the corporations in order and under control, while profiting from their presence within her borders.

As for Central America, it was stated at the outset that although the five countries, being small, take their national entities seriously, they are also serious about some form of integration which will give them a viable working association and establish a personality in the world's esteem. "Nationalism," it was said, "is an ailment of the big countries."

The examples of small European countries—Switzerland, Belgium, and Denmark—were offered in support of this assertion. Latin American nationalism was, however, discussed partly in terms of Brazil, Chile, and Mexico, all sizable, and also in rather abstract terms as though there were a Latin American form as such, permeating the whole continent. It was noticeable that tensions between individual countries in Latin America, which at times have been feverish, were left, by general agreement, quiescent on the agenda.

Nationalism in Spanish America was described as having its roots in the characteristics of three periods: the Spanish invasion of the continent, when Spain had barely emerged from long Moorish wars and was by no means integrated; the early nineteenth century, when the newly independent ex-colonials lived mentally in Europe while maintaining residences in Spanish America; and the later period when their leaders did their utmost to nourish the idea that the only real good was European. Only after World War I did Latin America, in reaction against this long bondage, begin to cultivate its own cultural values and seek its own political expressions.

This description brought out a Brazilian declaration that the sources of nationalism in this country were very different, in keeping with the difference in the histories of the Spanish and the Portuguese colonies, and that nationalism in Brazil dated only from the nineteenth century and was a phenomenon of the spirit. The ensuing discussion began to distinguish between types of nationalism in various southern countries, describing it, in part, as a reaction against geographic mutilation, armed intervention, financial overlordship, and other evidences of acute tensions between individual nations.

The importance of distinguishing between types was stressed in terms both of understanding and of action. Various participants mentioned the impact on Latin America of the Fascist nationalism which arose after World War I, the neonationalism which is at times identified with reformist tendencies, a tactical nationalism which Communists exploit, and a "phantasmagoric nationalism" which has a totem character and is more of the emotions than of the mind. All of these, as well as a nationalism invoked to create an historic figure, sway various parts of the population and can be made political tools.

The dangers which could be created by combining various types of nationalism were illustrated by a statement that, despite the great economic progress in Mexico (a progress which began to slow in 1956), the mystique of the revolution still holds, and some groups of students there are clamoring for a new revolution. Whether this desire is due to the slowing of economic improvement and the recent drop in exports, or stems from an endemic love for the tradition of revolution as a cure-all, was not clear, but it contains a threat at a difficult moment.

The lively consideration of economic nationalism which followed, brought out many familiar charges against North American policies and activities, or the lack of them, and the psychological advantage of using Yankees as whipping boys became clear, if unexpressed. At the same time, facts, as well as emotions began to emerge. It was, for example, stated that foreign investment in Brazil has dropped sharply since the passage by the Chamber of Deputies in December 1961 of a bill to limit profit remittances, although the bill will apparently be greatly modified. Work "in the pipeline" will probably continue until 1964, when the sharpness of the drop may make itself felt. An objection was raised that

Latin America might not yet be ready for foreign investment on any terms but its own, or be a fertile place for it from an outside point of view, but individual countries are still exploring ways and means of managing it to their satisfaction. At the same time, there were deep doubts that the Latin countries with their expanding populations could find the way to live without such investments, even if heavy sacrifices were invoked and conceded.

A proposal was made that the desirable goal be nationalism in aims, internationalization of means, and supranationalism in markets. This would recognize the need for foreign capital and technology if development is to be accelerated without totalitarian leadership. Supranationalism in markets would simply recognize that large-scale production demands large markets. The practicality of this proposal seemed somewhat in doubt, and a final stone was thrown at the argued values of nationalism by calling it "anachronous." Nevertheless, although appearing obsolete in the European continent and impractical for the smaller countries that need regional integration, it was recognized as having a very powerful emotional appeal, and a unifying value, especially in the larger developing countries.

The problems created by the Alliance for Progress were debated with no less fervor and interest, but with an enhanced degree of reality and of specific example. The consensus of opinion reflected a somewhat cautious approval of the Alliance, while voicing considerable criticism of its format and operation.

The Alliance was said to have been "over-sold" and to have aroused hopes of impossibly quick results when it was proposed in 1961. It followed a long lull in United States interest in Latin America, and something of the same sort had been called for repeatedly; as drafted, it reflected a mass of good ideas that had been explored by various writers but were perhaps insufficiently sorted out and clarified. Unfortunately, it came at a time when the Latin American terms of trade had begun to slip. Insufficient preparation in Latin America preceded it, so that the first reaction there was an expectation that the United States would at once start handing out checks. A preliminary meeting of Presidents might have been a way to make it clear that this was, in fact, the start of a new and important multilateral program, with great responsibilities and equally great possibilities on all sides. But such a meeting was not called.

Nevertheless, most of the countries, once they had caught the new tune, came forward with plans and projects. On the technical level, achievement has been large; some forty projects, benefiting twenty million people, have already been approved by the Inter-American Development Bank alone. Meanwhile, administration within governments is being improved, and long-needed reforms are cautiously under way.

This optimistic report inspired criticism, which took three forms:

First, a philosophic complaint that the United States, being by habit a pragmatic country, had never taken the time or the trouble to define its basic aims with regard to Latin America, and that this lack created a breeding ground for suspicions that the Alliance was, in fact, a new and subtle way for the United States to exploit Latin America and to keep it disorganized and impotent in the world power struggle.

Second, a preference that financing be given, not to individual projects—a scheme that creates a kind of fragmentation of effort and effect—but in the form of lump sums, to be applied by governments as they see fit, each national planning board to determine its own priorities and the Inter-American Bank to be the sole disburser of funds.

Third, that the way to save the Alliance is to "Latin-Americanize" it by putting all resources into the Inter-American Bank; persuading the United States to become humble and drop the public relations approach, which is destroying the multilateral image and making it seem bilateral; dispelling false optimism that the Alliance will do all, and stressing the need for sacrifice and work in Latin America; persuading the United States to ally itself with the reformers in each country, even though they are of the nationalist variety. Divergent views were expressed as to the relationship between nationalism and reformism, but the dominant opinion was that reformists exist throughout the political spectrum. Moreover, some internal contradictions in most nationalistic movements may render them, from the operational viewpoint, rather unwieldy instruments for rational reforms or consistent developments.

The conclusion of the discussion was that "rich America and poor America need to get together," although there was no clear agreement on the terms of this coexistence. Little mention was made in this seminar of relative poverty and riches within the individual countries.

The question was raised as to how a "mystique" or inspiration which would enlist popular support for the Alliance could be created. Clearly the cooperation of all groups is essential, but how can it be obtained? This inquiry led first to an interesting statement that any mobilization for the creation of a continental mystique must go to the people before it approaches governments, and that such mobilization might not be too difficult. It then moved on to European precedents for organizing economic structures, such as the OEEC, the European Payments Union, and especially the Common Market, all of which have done their share in helping to create a mystique of unity.

The Free Trade Zone in Latin America was cited as starting a trend toward the creation of a Latin sense of solidarity and continental personality. From that suggestion flowed another and more daring one for the creation of a Western Hemisphere Parliament to bring together members of the different legislatures of South and North America for a discussion of common problems. Such an inter-parliamentary body might be able to come to grips with the need for reform and the ways to achieve it. This suggestion was based on the statement that while governments now talk together in the persons of their executives, the national Congresses do not; in consequence, these latter frequently misunderstand, misconstrue, and defeat the executive aims. It was added that fiscal reforms in particular might prove easier if Congresses got together. Some members favored concentration on such efforts, but only on a Latin American basis, while others looked to the strengthening of institutions that are, or would be, hemisphere-wide.

The suggestion of a Parliament for this hemisphere, while recognized as somewhat Utopian at the moment, sparked a series of suggestions more positive than those in the earlier discussion. At one time, the spirit of Bolívar seemed to hover outside the glass wall, and continental integration to be the object of a sizable desire. This dream was checked by the phrase, "wishful thinking," and the charge that the fear of North American dominance was spread too wide to make possible any broad organization similar to that in Europe.

Nevertheless, the old lure of European patterns reasserted itself; the discussion of the position of Latin America in a pluralistic world, which was the third great subject in hand, became more lively and more enthusiastic as the specter of merely continuing the weary north-south recriminations receded. Descriptions of the present phase and future aims of the European Community were accompanied by vigorous statements that this Community was not ironclad nor exclusive, that it did not banish country nationalisms in order to set up a new regional nationalism, that it did not intend to discriminate against nonmembers but would welcome expansion. These expressions of intent, combined with the assertion that the Community's ends were not selfish, but for the general good, reinforced the charm of the image.

In the course of the discussion, the problem of African-Latin American competition came up. A Nigerian-Brazilian proposal was described as aiming to foster eventual free entry for tropical products into the markets of industrialized countries. As long as discrimination persists in the EEC in favor of African coffee and cocoa, there should be intermediate mechanisms which will compensate those countries that are victims of discrimination, while at the same time giving financial assistance to facilitate the adjustment of African countries to the eventual loss of preference.

Long-run problems creating more serious tensions were foreseen when an Atlantic Community emerges, and it was urged that studies of the effect of such a Community be started well in advance. It was suggested that if the industrialized countries were to accept the principle of free entry for tropical products, and the right of developing countries to maintain higher tariffs during a fixed period of industrialization, Latin America might find advantages in joining such a movement.

As the discussion of broadening the pluralistic base of Latin American relations developed, the continent began to appear with beneficial lines radiating toward Europe and Africa, as well as toward the United States. The Latin American members obviously felt themselves being freed from a disagreeable dialogue and enabled to talk and move in many directions; even the somewhat battered North American image took on a slight glow as good offices of the United States in European organizations were described, wherein the erstwhile ogre was becoming the active pleader that Europe awaken to Latin American needs and problems.

At the same time, members were warned against trying to move too fast, and without adequate preparation. Obviously the value of conversations with Europe is great, but it is unfortunate that they could not have taken place earlier. Again Latin America is confronted with a *post facto* situation and may begin to regret that she had no part in earlier discussions which led to the present European structure. But countries in the process of development need to use caution and must proceed along their own lines without expecting too must help from Europe, which has its own responsibilities.

One European member reverted to the idea of a properly organized Latin American federation. Europe, he said, was traditionally confused by the twenty Latin American countries. If there could be created a single organization of Latin American states, the Latin American image would take on clarity and rationality, and an interest for Europe.

The new hope engendered by these pluralistic suggestions was not quite quenched by the warning that the hour was already late, the Latin American populations increasingly impatient, and a catastrophic clash between rich nations and poor nations by no means impossible. Brazil's inner tensions were very much in the minds of members of this Conference. One member's parting advice was, "We must have strong socialism, strong independence, strong neutralism." And another explained, "What Latin America wants is not love, but respect." Revolution is, of course, one way to try for this, but whether it is the best way was not discussed.

During discussion of the above report of Seminar A in the Plenary Session, some thought that the positive aspects of nationalism had not been sufficiently emphasized. For undeveloped countries, large or small, nationalism may be basic to economic progress, though in developed countries it may be regarded as a passing phase. It may be good or bad, depending on its interpretation. There can be too much of it, as when leaders recognize the need for foreign capital but take steps to preclude its introduction; or too little, as when citizens with ample resources are unwilling to invest in the development of their own countries, but prefer to send their capital abroad. More should be done in each country to encourage the interest and support of private domestic capital for development of the nation's—and its own—prosperity.

Also, what about the effect of United States nationalism which sometimes appears in Congressional circles, in conservative universities, in business and financial circles? This phenomenon is in part a reaction against extreme nationalist attacks from other countries. It may conceivably lead to lack of enthusiasm or support of the Alliance, or to a hardening of the line on foreign aid in general, or, at worst, to an ineffectual or isolationist foreign policy. The nationalist "movements" in the United States are small in magnitude and intensity as compared with nationalism in Latin America, but the public needs more information as to what and why the United States will gain by helping the developing countries to build strength and lessen their internal tensions.

The Alliance for Progress was well covered in the discussion. The opinion was expressed that the beneficial possibilities of greater participation in or cooperation with the Alliance on the part of European countries should be further explored, by all parties concerned, as a means of lessening existent tensions in the Alliance program of aid.

Seminar B—Tensions Within Nations

The presiding Officer of Seminar B was Galo Plaza, former President of Ecuador. Tensions in the following fields were selected for analysis: the social implications of inflation, the new social classes, militarism, the role of the university and the student population, minority problems, rural-urban migrations, the church and its influence, and the role of labor.

Emphasis was given to conscious tensions consequent upon the inhibiting of individual aspirations for which no institutional solution could be found. It was taken for granted that these tensions could well be both healthy and sociologically normal, especially at a time of transition from one stage of development or one kind of society to another. This is exactly what is happening in most Latin American countries where a traditional, hierarchical, agrarian, and paternalistic society is changing into an urban, industrial, individualistic, and democratic society. A distinction was made between tensions and conflict, this last being a costly and extreme position, but, at least in theory, not necessarily undesirable.

The group considered how to determine tension points and sources and how to eradicate them without paying too heavy a toll in terms of social costs to the society. In certain instances, tension is not only desirable, but should be encouraged as a sign of vitality. Tension and release of tension were considered normal when occurring within the over-all social system, without causing any breakdown. Abnormal or pathological tensions would then be those that created situations without any possibility of release within the system in force. The job of the social scientist is not to profer judgment values but to indicate the available solutions and their respective costs to society and to the integration of the human personality.

The group proceeded to deal with the main social tensions involved in inflation and the way it affects a mixed economy. Inflation creates tensions because it awakens desires in the individual that cannot be satisfied within the reigning system of distribution of property and income, and because the rise in prices is, in fact, a confiscation of real wealth. Inflation sometimes leads indirectly to socialism, carried out by illogical mechanisms and for obviously political purposes, because it destroys the differential salary scale and most directly hurts the middle classes. Governments may seek to counteract inflation by rate readjustments that usually come late and are inadequate to the general rise in prices. Private capital therefore loses interest in public utilities and long-term investments, thus creating a situation which obliges the state to enter the investment vacuum.

Inflation adversely affects the money market and the export trade, while benefiting importers and certain recently established industries; it also distorts the credit market. The government becomes the only body in a position to make long-term loans. Short-term loans and investments follow a rising trend. In this way, the government is in the position of redistributing property in favor of certain privileged groups by long-term loans at interest rates that are lower than the rate of inflation. These become subsidies in disguise.

In this process the sectors favored by the state come out the winners: for example, new industrial activities, large agricultural concerns and firms with good political connections. The losers are those that require credit but do not have the right political connections or the means to obtain it because the market is exhausted: such are the traditional industries, small-scale farming, and small and medium-size business firms.

Those who profit from inflation make up a new economic class. Their main distinguishing feature is the accumulation of wealth without the expense of any effort. Neither work, capital, nor technical preparation justifies the huge fortunes that the members of this group have made in a very short time. This New Class is composed of businessmen who get government credit through long-term, low-interest loans; of people who speculate with previous knowledge of the rise in prices; of middlemen who make the most of peak demand to reap the difference between what the consumer is able to pay and the real value of the product.

The New Class corrupts the society directly through its operations and indirectly by its example and conspicuous consumption, thus transmitting to the lower levels of the population opportunistic and avid attitudes of "get rich quick" and profit without labor. It represents a bourgeois form of development in the Marxist sense, and therefore provokes a Marxist reaction and a tension of a revolutionary nature. The irresponsibility of the members of this New Class makes the masses feel that public affairs are completely amoral and that "anything goes."

There is a connection between inflation and industrialization. Attention must be given here to a psychological factor that is strong in underdeveloped countries, namely, the "fascination of industrialization." The feeling is associated with nationalism, as the people seem to be prepared to make considerable sacrifices in goods and services because of it. Nationalistic groups are singularly opposed to undue reliance on expanding exports of primary products, especially minerals, since this smacks of colonialist policy. This is an emotional attitude without basis in economic fact.

In recent years a true middle class has emerged in many Latin American countries, mainly in the towns and cities. This middle class has a keen interest in the consumption of goods and services, but present economic systems can hardly satisfy its aspirations. The only solutions the middle class can find consist of successive salary raises and multiple jobs, which are continuously being erased by rising prices.

Inflation is used, implicitly or explicitly, as a philosophy of government and a way of attenuating or dissipating pressures and conflicts without altering the basic social structure. This is an "easy way out" for the government.

There is no doubt that inflation changes and determines behavior patterns from the top to the bottom of the social pyramid. The businessman and the consumer learn to adapt to an inflationary society, its rhythm and its processes. Everybody tries to get the most out of inflation, the debtors from the creditors, those who take from those who lend, the buyers from the sellers, in a chain that ends with the government and that constantly follows and encourages the inflationary spiral.

Another pernicious source of conflict which is old in Latin America is internal colonialism. Certain regions prevail over others, towns over rural areas, some economic sectors over others. Certain areas of the Latin American countries are subjected to a shrinkage of capital with benefit to other areas which, internally, exercise a magnetic predominance over an underdeveloped surrounding area. This trend can be fought in many ways by regional and urban planning, a more fairly distributed system of taxation, and a program of spreading industry away from densely populated areas.

The part played by intervention of the army in Latin America has much to do with the power structure of Latin American society. The absence or weakness of national parties, the "personalismo" in politics and the "caudillo" tradition—all factors that vary from country to country—make the situation highly complex. Militarism can also be stimulated from outside sources, the fear of Communism, and the subversion of the established order.

Furthermore, the oligarchical right wing of many countries uses the army as a weapon of survival in so-called "preventative coups." On some occasions the army may become an independent force, a kind of "moderating power" against party chaos, united by a sort of *esprit de corps* and ill-defined notions of maintaining the peace and respect for the laws. In other instances, the army has split into mutually hostile factions and has then used the civil power as a moderator. While this Conference was in session, three Latin American countries found themselves under the control or threat of military intervention.

The armaments race in Latin American countries, encouraged by a supposed need for hemisphere defense and unsolved frontier questions, has increased military budgets tremendously at the expense of basic social and economic needs. What is more, something like an international military brotherhood seems to exist which seeks political influence through personal contacts of continental scope. On the other hand, the fact must be recognized that in some countries the army fulfills a social and economic as well as a political function. The army is often an outlet for chronic unemployment, a symbol of the nation's strength, unity, and internal stability. It also constitutes an undeniable historical fact. Starting from the principle that the army should be subject to, and in the service of, the civil authority, and that nowadays military coups are anachronistic, the solution would be to encourage and fortify civil institutions so as to make it impossible for the army to arrogate the functions that by right belong to the civil authority. Militarism must also be fought by measures of basic structural reform.

In Latin America the university is presently an important source of tensions. The university is, in part, a reflection of the society to which it belongs, and is subject to its structure and basic framework. Its cultural function is therefore contaminated by its political and social functions. It is more a source of power and prestige than an educational institution for producing culture. It is not a democratic university because its autonomy is fictitious. The universities are dependent on federal grants; in some countries they are tied to the apron strings of the Minister of Education. The old-fashioned professorship system is a hindrance to technical and scientific progress, prevents the renewal of university staff, and even shuts out people of real value. The unavoidability of part-time attendance on the part of teachers and of students limits the opportunities for democratic association and even the transmission of knowledge. Given the mutual frustration of teachers and students, the radical position of certain student circles in Latin American universities is not surprising.

Much is being done to alter this state of affairs. Some universities are trying to get around the difficulties presented by their rules and regulations by creating autonomous institutes and allowing the student to play a greater part in university life. Universities are attempting to move toward a full-time schedule for professors and for students.

When dealing with tensions between minorities in the Western Hemisphere, the racial conflicts in the United States must not be forgotten. The Brazilian experience in racial harmony should be recognized, although the race question in Brazil is linked to the class question and racial tensions have been transformed into social tensions. The future seems highly optimistic as regards both the Negro and the Indian.

Other tensions, which some consider of greater significance than the racial question, are the tensions between the "élites" and the mass, between urban and rural culture, between an imported "white culture" (European) and an Indian or mestizo culture, between written culture and the oral culture of illiterate or semi-literate people.

Tensions between the Catholic Church and the people can be observed at the points where the church is still accumulating economic or political power. Where the church as an institution absorbs the functions of other groups, grave conflicts tend to arise because the church hierarchy, too, becomes affected by the ideological schism dividing other institutions. The Latin American people are religious, if not formally Catholic. Yet, in spite of the tremendous moral influence of the church and the important part it has played in the civilizing process, particularly in connection with the Indian, its connections with political power, derived from the colonial past, prejudice its spiritual mission and the part it could play in the promotion of basic reforms.

One aspect of development is the emergence of a scientific outlook characterized by objectivity and critical reflection. The religious mind seeks an interpersonal relationship based on faith and trust. Iberian Catholicism is distinguished by the mixing of the two attitudes, or by the projection of the religious outlook into the secular sphere, thus prejudicing both. When divine providence is applied to nature, the result is magic. The solution of the apparent contradiction between the church and science would seem to be a conscious separation of the two worlds. Experience would show that the clergy can play an important part in directing social and economic progress if they recognize this fact and also receive training in secular fields.

Labor unions and organizations play an increasingly important part in economic and social development. Three trends dominate the scene. First, the oligarchies often intentionally confuse the free democratic labor movement with Communism, refuse any discussion with the union leaders, and do all they can to stifle labor organizations. The second trend is the attempt made by Communists to infiltrate and to win commanding positions within the unions so as to exploit them in favor of the party. Union leaders are being systematically trained in increasing numbers in the Soviet world to work in our hemisphere. The third tendency, of which Brazil is a good example, is the control of labor unions by the governments. When this occurs, the unions become even more vulnerable to Communist infiltration. The situation may so deteriorate as to result in a kind of corporative state which is distasteful to democratic thought. The change to development of a democratic type would have to take place on three fronts: by making the labor classes union-conscious and aware of the barriers set up by the oligarchies; by training union leaders; by fighting the obstacles that impede the improvement of working class conditions.

Conclusions

1. Chronic inflation, whatever its causes, creates a high degree of social tension on many fronts. This is a most serious Latin American problem.

2. The growth of a middle class, and the greater material and educational aspirations of all classes, have put serious pressures on the whole productive system of Latin American society. This

results in frustration of the real and acquired needs of several levels of the societies.

3. Universities must, by necessity, reflect the societies of which they are a part. Latin American education is generally not related to Latin American necessities. In universities, neither teachers nor students are now fulfilling their proper roles; teachers are not teaching and students are not studying. A crucial release of tensions would involve a reform of university education.

4. Traditionally, the army has played a stabilizing role in some Latin American nations. It has provided the force for "palace revolutions," but it has also prevented chaos. Militarism, however, has been a barrier to the development of responsible democracy and continues to be so. The United States must understand, and Latin American countries must realize, that to continue to support military development is contrary to each nation's welfare.

5. The church is a traditional Latin American institution with great cultural and philosophical influence over its people. If the church is to have a social role, however, this must be carried out in social terms. The clergy, trained theologically in an authoritarian system of thought, must also be trained to work in an egalitarian and democratic secular world.

6. The development of labor unions and the training of labor leaders have been neglected in Latin America. Governments tend to have too much control over labor movements. Business tends to view all labor movements as Communist inspired. Thus, labor movements are vulnerable to Communist infiltration.

7. Finally, the great majority of tensions within nations in Latin America result from the changes in social and economic structure now in progress throughout the continent—changes from a paternalistic, semi-feudal, agrarian society to an industrial, impersonal, bureaucratic, and even socialized way of life—that are taking place with the speed of the twentieth century.

Comments on the above report in the Plenary Session suggested that Seminar B had devoted disproportionate attention to infla-

tion, and that it dealt primarily with inflationary conditions peculiar to Brazil. The fact is that the degree of inflation ranges from
virtual stability in some Central American countries to a galloping
inflation in Chile, Bolivia, and particularly in Brazil. Nevertheless,
all countries are concerned with its potential dangers.

It was explained that a discussion of inflation *per se*—its complex causes and its remedies—would have deviated from the objectives of the Seminar, which were to deal with it purely as a source
of tensions at various points in the economy. The tensions resulting when inflation becomes a political issue need further emphasis
—the pressure, by those who lose through this process, for government measures to lessen inflation, and the political movement for
inflationary measures on the part of the "beneficiaries." As for the
"New Class," not only inflation but the over-all process of change
may bring a variety of new groups to the surface, and these "New
Classes" may be good or bad in their influence.

It was thought by some that not all the effects of inflation are
necessarily bad. A certain amount of it could be viewed as an aid
to industrialization and an inevitable concomitant of development.
From this point of view, stabilization seems to follow as a consequence of development instead of being a precondition. On the
other hand, attention was called to the record of Europe after
World War II in halting inflation without prejudicing rapid
growth. Some thought the experience of Europe irrelevant, in view
of the heavy investment that was made through the Marshall Plan
and other growth factors present in Europe. Others felt inflation to
be a dangerous tool of policy; heavy industry is most needed in
achieving balanced economic growth, and inflation creates a
treacherous market for calculating the possible role and need for
heavy industry. On balance, inflation was recognized as a disturbing and potentially explosive factor, which in all countries requires
much further study of possible remedies or measures to alleviate
the tensions created.

As for various domestic institutions, it is necessary to go beyond
criticism of their present shortcomings; specific projects and plans

must be devised to involve university students and faculties, the military, and the church in the development of the communities and the nation. Also, more specific measures should be devised to strengthen the position of the labor unions as responsible and respected factors in accelerating development, increasing production, obtaining better distribution of the product, as well as in terms of wages and working and living conditions. This view is accompanied by hopes that labor unions might become a kind of spearhead, with their collective weight brought to bear on a wide variety of political, economic, and social problems, and contributing more to political stability.

SEMINAR C—PRECONDITIONS FOR ECONOMIC AND SOCIAL DEVELOPMENT

The presiding officers were Paul Hoffman, Managing Director of the United Nations Special Fund, and José A. Mayobre, United Nations Commissioner for Industrial Development.

It was agreed to take up the following topics: (1) psychological factors affecting development in Latin America; (2) the role of education; (3) planning for development; (4) the role and characteristics of foreign aid; (5) political organization, and (6) the influence of legal concepts on development and the need for suitable legislation. For each of the topics, the joint Chairmen made suggestions for discussion or called upon a member of the Seminar to open the discussion.

1. *The Psychological Factors*

A positive disposition to development by the leadership and the people of a country is an essential precondition for economic and social development. Without this disposition, external aid and national planning for a more rational allocation of resources can be of only limited effectiveness.

The experience of India was cited as an illustration that these psychological conditions for development can be created by a political leadership committed to development as an overriding political strategy. The utilization of new instruments such as community development programs and democratic leadership training, involving all segments of the society (including rural and urban workers) in the planning and implementation of the program, can create and change attitudes favoring acceptance of the difficult social and economic changes and sacrifices required in the development process. In particular, a "problem solving" attitude needs to be instilled among leaders.

The psychological motivations for full participation in the development program were explored. It was pointed out that the development plan needs to consider the kinds of incentives that will meet the basic human needs of the people within their own cultural setting. Fuller participation and involvement by the rural population of Latin America were especially stressed.

The effectiveness of the "grand plan" idea as an instrument for generating psychological support for a national, regional, or worldwide development effort was cited with particular reference to the Marshall Plan, Brasilia, the Alliance for Progress. A grand plan, however, must be preceded by an appropriate evaluation of problems.

The significance of the "catalytic project" in demonstrating that development means the solution of problems that are immediate, close at hand, and meaningful to the people was noted as of special significance in view of the very long-range aspect of many of the most important parts of the development plan. The need to develop a "sense of motion," a sense of achievement during all stages of the development process, was stressed. In some cases, cultural or scientific achievement may be a most effective way to create this sense of progress. The need for keeping a balance among the economic, social, and cultural phases of a nation's development was pointed out, with special stress on the psychological effect.

The multilateral nature of the Alliance for Progress received particular attention. The Alliance has too frequently been considered a United States instrument for bilateral aid to Latin American countries. It was pointed out that President Kennedy's announcement of the Alliance for Progress was a summary of long-standing and frequently expressed needs of Latin American countries, a restatement of much earlier commitments of Latin American nations to a continental approach to national and regional development. The lack of a clear understanding of the multilateral nature of the Alliance by both the aid-giving and the aid-receiving nations is a significant psychological obstacle to the fulfillment of the objectives of the Alliance as first envisaged in Operation Pan America, the Act of Bogotá, and Punta del Este.

Until each nation of the Alliance includes in the political and economic policies of its government a deliberate consideration of the implication of those policies on other nations in the Alliance, its full force will not be achieved. The Alliance for Progress faces a longer and more difficult road than the Marshall Plan to which it is frequently compared. The difference between the reconstruction of advanced industrial societies after a war and the building of new industrial and modern agricultural societies is marked and will require new methods to maintain enthusiasm and patience, particularly during the early stages of the operations of the Alliance.

Resistance to the social and economic changes agreed to by the signatories of the Alliance is perhaps the primary cause of tension. It was suggested that the continued functioning of the Alliance for Progress as a truly multilateral instrument for continental development is an essential psychological condition for breaking down existing pockets of resistance to the necessary social reforms. The Alliance represents a major test to determine whether large-scale development can be achieved by democratic institutions.

The psychological problems created in the process of aid giving and aid receiving were also discussed. It was agreed that this is a very delicate relationship which requires constant attention by both parties. The attitude of the aid-giving country; the conditions placed on the aid; the quality of persons sent to administer and advise on the programs; the psychological effects of multilateral and bilateral aid; and the need to Latin-Americanize the aid-giving organizations were all discussed. Also, the attitudes, expectations, and responsibilities of the aid-receiving nations were explored.

In general, it was felt that much has to be done to give the aid-giving countries more confidence in the ability of the aid-receiving countries to use this assistance, and to reduce fears that the aid-giving countries will interfere in the domestic affairs of the recipient countries.

Often trade and aid are dealt with separately, and the relationship between them—psychological as well as real—is not sufficiently recognized in practice. It was felt that the Alliance for Progress does not pay enough attention to trade problems, including prices of basic products. However, the progress of the Latin American Free Trade Association was noted as an encouraging movement, which also gives a sense of achievement and may lead to a greater Latin American political conscience on a continental scale.

2. *The Role of Education*

An adequate educational system was accepted as an essential precondition of full economic development. A massive educational effort is called for in Latin America within the next decade. This effort will be a heavy charge on available resources. The suggestion was made that one sector from which such costs might be met would be that portion of national resources now being used for the military, which might be appreciably reduced. It was also suggested that attention be paid to reducing the cost per student through reorganization of the educational system and better use of existing facilities.

Two basic factors are essential in building an adequate educational system: quantity and quality. With very few exceptions, there is no need to stimulate the population's demand for education facilities, since such demand now exists. The problem is rather one of providing the school buildings and the teaching staff. In many instances it would be preferable for national attention to be focused more on the training of teachers, with local resources mobilized through self-help and community development projects for school construction.

On secondary and higher levels, the problem is essentially one of equating supply of and demand for trained people. It is frustrating for industries and other economic enterprises to lack educated and trained personnel and equally so to have well-prepared individuals for whom there is no employment.

Regarding quality in Latin American education, the point was made that the educational system has been traditionally oriented toward forming an aristocratic élite, an objective which conflicts with the current need for educating and training all people for roles in a developing and industrializing society. The present need for vocational education, particularly on the secondary-school level, was emphasized. One speaker noted that in Europe the ratio of vocational and technical school graduates is six for every university graduate, whereas the ratio in Latin America is less than one for one.

Likewise, on the university level, it was noted that the traditional emphasis has been on the classics and humanities, whereas the growing need is for scientific and technical training; the universities of Latin America have generally been slow to adapt themselves to this need. Some apprehension was also expressed concerning the ill effects of exaggerated emphasis upon autonomy and student participation in governing the universities. This has led to a tendency toward excessive political activity in the universities and the turning out of poorly trained graduates.

All of the work of education is not carried out in formal educational institutions. The role of the press, the political parties, the trade unions, and other institutions in broadening the intellectual horizons of large parts of the population was stressed; some worry was expressed about the poor quality of much of the journalism, which tends to emphasize sensationalism.

In this connection, there was discussion of the use of in-service training or on-the-job training for the preparation of the skilled workers, technicians, white collar workers, and even the lower ranks in management and public administration; all these are needed by new industries and by government. It was agreed that such training needs to be greatly expanded, and several cases of successful use of these techniques were noted. Research also requires more emphasis.

Finally, it was pointed out that the very process of education engenders certain kinds of discontent and tensions. It was agreed that this is not all bad, and that the basic question is whether or not such tensions can be directed into constructive channels. There is an urgent need for educational planning, and particularly for a careful weighing of alternatives and a linking together of the different stages of education; the results of educational improvement are not usually obtained until several years have elapsed.

3. *Planning for Development*

In order to achieve the objectives of a higher rate of growth and steady social improvement in Latin America, decisions need to be rationalized. This is the essence of planning under any system, though the extent and depth of planning may vary from country to country, according to its political maturity, its institutions, and its ability to formulate and carry out its development programs.

In spite of the lack of sufficient statistical information and knowledge of natural resources, the basic economic and social problems of Latin America have been defined and the broad lines of solution are known. Increasing attention is being paid to analysis of the facts and to the training of persons as expert in this type of work. The crucial issue is why planning, however narrowly conceived, is not put into practice. In some countries it may not be possible to provide more than a general framework within which government policies can be adopted, while in others specific targets may be set for different sectors of the economy and appropriate policies for the public and the private sectors can be worked out in detail. In either case, it is increasingly recognized that development must be subjected, as time goes on, to rational programming for both planning and execution.

Taking into account the experience of other areas, it was felt that one of the main difficulties is political. Until political decisions are taken regarding objectives, the technical work of the economists may be of mere academic interest. Often the technicians are far ahead of the politicians in their thinking, and often the plans come to nought because the political steps to put them into action are not taken. It is therefore important that at the highest level there should be a conviction that a plan is desirable, and that, once the decisions are made, the general plan should be followed closely by all sectors of government, subject only to the flexibility required to take account of year-to-year changes in circumstances.

In this connection, some attention was given to the organization of planning. Some speakers considered that the planning group should be under the direct authority of the chief executive. It was pointed out, however, that in most countries there is a planning council or a cabinet group at the top level, and a technical group below it, and that this arrangement seems suitable. Some felt that the planning council should be under the Minister of the Treasury, since an investment program, to be realistic, must be matched by a financial program covering taxation, earnings of state enterprises, internal and external borrowing, channeling of domestic private savings into required fields of investment, improvement of financial and banking institutions, and policies designed to avoid inflation or to restrain an existing inflation.

The execution of plans also requires much more attention on the political side. Political pressures may frequently require changes in the investment programs, but they should be kept to a minimum through maintaining authority over the execution of the plan at the highest level. Where different political parties participate in the government, a careful prior agreement on criteria is required to avoid later inaction.

In mixed economies, such as those prevailing in most of Latin America, the process of development requires that policies be adopted to encourage private investment, particularly in industry and agriculture, since failure by the private sector to achieve its goals may result in a general failure of the plan. It is therefore essential that in order to obtain the full cooperation of the private groups, they should at an appropriate stage be enabled to participate in the discussion of the targets and policies relating to their economic sector.

It was also recognized that the increasing need for foreign loans and other aids in the carrying out of Latin America's development, as envisaged under the Alliance for Progress, points to the need for better plans. The efficiency of foreign aid can be increased when there is a clear idea as to the areas where such aid is required and the use of domestic resources in connection with it.

Finally, it is urgent to educate political groups, private sectors, the military, labor organizations, and the community at large on the real nature of economic and social planning, both to erase preconceptions that identify planning with statism and to facilitate the fuller participation of such groups at different stages of the process.

4. *Foreign Aid*

Discussion of this subject centered on bilateral versus multilateral aid, the appropriateness of different sources of aid, and certain financial aspects of the Alliance for Progress. It was agreed that external aid should supplement domestic financing, which should carry the main burden in the process of development in Latin America. It was also accepted that the aid-giving country imparts such aid not only for the benefit of the aid-receiving country but in its own interests. There is, in fact, a growing economic interdependence, based on respect for the political independence and sovereignty of each state.

It was pointed out by a number of participants that the success of foreign aid depends on a clear understanding between the parties as to the purposes of the aid in question. It would be a great mistake to undertake commitments under false assumptions. In such a case, serious tensions may be generated. It was noted that the aid-giving country frequently assumes that its aid program is a means of obtaining the friendship and adherence of another country for its own political or strategic purposes. In general, under-developed countries resent having to accept aid under such conditions.

In the case of the Punta del Este Charter, the purposes of foreign aid are clearly stated: to contribute to a more rapid economic growth and social improvement in the framework of democratic institutions, on the basis of self-help and of structural reforms tending to achieve a better distribution of income and wealth. These purposes were accepted by all the signatories of the Charter, but in the light of the first year of operation of the Alliance for Progress there is doubt as to whether every country has accepted its commitments with the same degree of conviction and with equal determination to fulfill them. Thus, even taking account of differing conditions in Latin American countries, progress has appeared to be slow.

This has a bearing on foreign aid, since in Latin America external financing is still considered to be insufficient, despite new sources of long-term loans. On the one hand, access to more funds is needed in order to increase the operations of such new institutions as the Inter-American Development Bank; considerable importance was attached to the need for the participation of Western Europe in supplying part of the capital needs of Latin American development. On the other hand, aid-giving nations must realize that a structural change of the type foreseen at Punta del Este, and the new type of hemisphere cooperation it involves, cannot be achieved overnight. What has already been done, or begun, should in no way be underestimated.

A preference was expressed for external aid through multilateral rather than bilateral programs. This attitude is due to tensions arising in the past from negotiations between weak and strong countries, with the latter usually exercising a strong political and economic power over the former. The Punta del Este Charter emphasizes multilateral action and assigns to the Organization of American States and the Inter-American Bank important roles in evaluating development programs, in carrying out reforms, and in providing financial resources. The Inter-American Bank has been instrumental in securing a readier acceptance of many of the institutional and administrative changes that are required to make loan operations successful, and has done so with less friction than if the same result had been attempted through bilateral programs.

The advantage of multilateral aid programs was also stressed in connection with surveys of national resources and studies of pre-investment; the impartiality of experts of the United Nations and similar organizations is never questioned. This applies to aid for economic and social planning, as well as to educational programs. Foreign universities and foundations are also utilized for this type of work.

5. *Political Preconditions of Development*

Political instability is one of the fundamental characteristics of the contemporary Latin American environment and has seriously affected development. Attention was drawn to the role of the military as a factor leading to instability. It was suggested that because the defense role of the armed forces has very greatly diminished, due to modern technology and other factors, the military has lost its sense of direction, and become a disturbing factor in the national politics of most Latin American countries. Furthermore, the excessive expenditure on the armed forces which characterizes most of these countries is self-defeating, even in military terms, because it weakens the economy. Since it is utopian to think of the complete abolition of the armies, it was suggested that the next best thing would be to reorient the objectives of the military towards economic development. Some progress in this direction has already been made in some countries.

Considerable discussion centered around the role that political parties could play in contributing to political stability and hence to economic development. A view was expressed that the political parties had generally failed in the traditional role conceived for them as a means of alternating groups in power. As a result, the whole idea of the feasibility of democracy was brought into question; perhaps some alternative to traditionally conceived democracy might be more adapted to the Latin American environment.

Other speakers, however, argued that democracy was not in question, nor was the existence of political parties. Rather, the issue was one of finding institutional forms of political democracy which grow out of the Latin American environment. Furthermore, the mere fact that one party had a large and more or less permanent majority in a country did not necessarily mean that democracy did not exist.

It was pointed out that the emergence of modern political parties during the last generation has contributed to political stability in two ways. First, it offered some challenge to the armed forces as the possessors of the last word in Latin American politics, since on certain occasions, the parties had shown considerable ability to thwart military coups, and to survive persecution at the hands of army dictatorships. Second, the parties also tended to limit the personalism which has always been a destabilizing aspect of Latin American politics.

The role of the organized labor movement in generating greater stability, by using its economic power as a check on military adventurism, was also noted, as well as the role of the United States labor movement in seconding the efforts of the Latin American trade unions in this regard.

Another institutional prerequisite to economic development was said to be agrarian reform. Such a reform not only broadens the market for goods manufactured in the various Latin American countries, but also provides new small landholders with incentive to increase and improve their production. Although redistribution of the land is the basic ingredient of agrarian reform, others are necessary, including adequate credit, technical assistance, and sometimes even the engendering of demand for industrial goods among the peasants as a spur to their greater production. Agrarian reform must be adapted to the conditions of each country. Contributing greatly to achievement of ultimate political stability, it thus also serves to stimulate economic development.

Finally, the question was raised as to whether the institutional development of the Western Hemisphere, in terms of the creation of common markets and free trade areas, and of the Alliance for Progress, was not tending to set up a closed political and economic system in the New World, thus leading to a weakening of traditional ties with Europe. Various speakers argued that such was not the intention of the Latin Americans or the North Americans, that on the contrary there was desire in both parts of the hemisphere for greater European aid in the program of economic development of Latin America. However, it was also pointed out that there was a certain defensive aspect of these new institutional arrangements in America, arising from fear of the negative effects, in this part of the world, of the European Common Market, and particularly of its inclusion of the tropical areas of Africa which are competitive with much of Latin America.

6. *Legal Concepts and Legislation for Development*

A good legal framework is essential for the execution of development programs, since it is a means of securing continuity and predictability, as well as impersonality, and of preventing an arbitrary exercise of power. However, legislation must be adapted to reality. The heritage of colonial legislation and the later incorporation of liberal ideas into the constitutions of most Latin American countries have not always produced a clear basis for the type of legislation that economic development requires today. It is only recently that provisions have been adopted to enable the State to undertake planning, land reform, and, in general, to orient economic activity towards specified objectives. Much legislation is unsuitable, or consists of a maze of regulations of which the purpose has not been properly defined. This is particularly true of fiscal legislation. One of the first tasks should be to review existing economic legislation to determine its suitability.

This review, and the adoption of new legislation, should be elements in planning adequate development policies. If a country is able to adopt such policies, competent legislation should follow.

Some of the areas where it is needed are the organization of the planning process, including relations between central and state governments; incentives for private industrial and agricultural investment; treatment of foreign capital; public utilities rates; banking and financial institutions; land reform; labor and employment; education; social security; taxation; public administration. Several speakers laid special stress on the last area, particularly on the need for assuring greater integrity in the exercise of governmental functions.

In the Plenary Session it was felt that Seminar C had dealt ably with the preconditions for development, although there was again some concern about relative emphasis.

Some believed that, although the increasing role of the public sector in Latin America is generally accepted, more emphasis needs to be given in development to the role of private enterprise, both foreign and domestic. Even in the present mixed economies, the private sector is the largest; it is often the most efficient and cheapest way of getting development. Measures to mobilize more of these resources, and more constructively, deserve fuller attention in connection with the Alliance and other development plans.

Although the meaning of "catalytic" or "impact" projects as a necessary part of planning is thoroughly understood, it might be advisable to spell them out in specific terms as projects for water supply, sanitation, and especially housing, which are critical problem areas and ripe with tensions in all Latin American countries.

Also, it was suggested that excessive concern was shown for planning at the state level, whereas a new trend is needed towards including planning at the regional level as an alternative to statism and as a means of involving more of the people and getting greater results.

Regarding education, there was agreement with the Seminar's conclusion that twentieth century Latin America requires a new approach emphasizing pragmatism and technology, but a warning was voiced that care must be taken, while reorienting higher education, not to lose the cultural values of the humanities.

LATIN AMERICA IN A PLURAL WORLD

One of the topics which excited great interest is the image which Latin America projects and the role it is to play in an expanding and pluralistic world. It is obvious that each country must make strong and carefully considered efforts to overcome its internal divisive elements and to attain a higher degree of unity in its pursuit of economic and social development. At the same time, if these countries are not to be left behind by the forces at work in the world today they must have better intra-regional ties, in order to strengthen their own development and that of the region as a whole.

Looking in upon itself, Latin America sees that the fragmentation of its markets, its politics, and its economic policies impairs its influence in relation to the rest of the world. The people have had their political independence long enough to realize that it means little in terms of world power. Hence the urgency of efforts towards more rapid unification. Latin Americans are impressed by the extent to which Western European nations have overcome some of their old nationalistic barriers and have achieved a degree of unity which, without question, has brought an increasing degree of prosperity to each country and to all of Western Europe. There is some apprehension about the impact of the European Common Market on Latin American economies and on other developing areas. Descriptions of the present phase and future aims of the European Community were accompanied by vigorous statements that it did not banish country nationalisms in order to set up new regional nationalism, that its ends were not selfish but included a generally expanding world economy. In any case, there seemed to be agreement that the tendency towards regional and sub-regional economic groupings in Europe, Southeast Asia, and Africa should receive further study without delay, special attention being given to coordination lest these arrangements create regional barriers impeding the world economy.

In the political context, a new place in the world means for many participants an opportunity for Latin America to pursue an independent foreign policy and to make its own interpretation of the Cold War issues. An independent foreign policy, however, does not necessarily mean "neutralism" in the sense that this is emerging in the Asia-Africa scene. It is expected that the Latin American republics will continue to be associated with the inter-American family, with institutions of representative democracy and that, in the economic sphere, a sizable role will continue to be played by private-enterprise capitalism. Attitudes towards the Cold War will reflect a difference between the developed and the underdeveloped countries. The "industrialized" countries feel that the real threat is external and, to them the Cold War may be defined as a security problem. For Latin America, the threat is internal, directed at their economic development, without which the political and social stability, already achieved in the developed world, will never be realized.

The third dimension in the drive for a new place in the world is cultural. Latin America has aspirations for democracy, freedom and social justice, which it proposes to achieve within the context of its own historical personality. Achieving greater economic and political unity and stature serves to consolidate faith in its own cultural values as an important factor in its impression upon the world.

EVOLUTION OR EXPLOSION?

In conclusion, how did the Conference evaluate the prospects for evolution rather than explosion? According to several participants, the situation is made complex by the diffusion or fragmentation of power which characterizes any period of revolution. The power might be reconcentrated, but this seemed unlikely unless done under extreme left or extreme right positions, a solution rejected by virtually all the participants. The hope of an orderly adjustment rests upon the ability to reach some balance through a coalition of power in which the different sectors may find their appropriate place.

The Latin Americans felt strongly that such a coalition is a prerequisite to continued economic growth. To this end, projects must be devised which will unite the people, attract their loyalty, provide assistance to the liberal groups in their solving of serious problems, and create symbols around which the complex society may order itself. In the view of one participant, Latin America is not yet at the boundary of disaster, and, although it is on that path, there is still time to change its course. The issue will be decided in the field of ideology. Therefore, a strategy needs to be devised by Latin America and based on its own experience.

But a sobering point remains to be noted and underscored. Much was said during the Conference about the approaches to be made—multilateral, people-to-people, self help—but these will come to naught unless they are accompanied by changing attitudes in the élite and power classes. These groups, which hold economic and political power in most countries, must be aroused to the realization that reforms are in their own self interest. Unless their leadership will see the handwriting on the wall and recognize the explosive dangers in a rigid and uncompromising posture vis-à-vis social and economic reforms, these élite groups will, sooner or later, be swept away by the whirlwinds that are already brewing in Latin America. No amount of self help or outside aid will avail to bring about the desired evolution—or avert explosion—unless the leadership groups in Latin America are prepared to accept and promote basic changes in institutional and power arrangements, and to aid in mobilizing domestic wealth and resources.

The basic role of developed nations is to assist Latin American development in a way devoid of any traces of neocolonialism. This implies a continued and intensified multilateral approach, using international organizations, with nations working together as equals, not in a competition between the weak and the strong. Self-help, mutual regional help, and outside help provide the basis for hope that in the individual countries, and in Latin America as a whole, development and integration will go hand in hand to provide the sense of solidarity, maturity, responsibility, and forward motion that will prevent countries from exploding through internal tensions, and keep the continent as an entity from falling apart.

The Conference is finished, but where do we go from here? On several occasions the thought was expressed by participants that a real need exists for a continuing and closer dialogue between business and professional men and political and educational leaders of Latin America and the emerging Atlantic community. The Bahia Conference was a felicitous mixture of public and private interests represented by men of critical and searching minds giving their full attention to common problems in a non-crisis atmosphere; it represented a new and promising vehicle for communication in the Latin American context. In other areas similar devices have been developed which have proven immensely effective in stimulating thinking and action in new directions and in modifying the course of events. In Latin America the need to create more analytical self interest among the élite classes, to associate the liberal elements of both hemispheres, to join forces on problems of mutual interest, and finally to mobilize an effective public opinion is indeed critical. The reopening of the channels established in Bahia at regular intervals would provide a lively vehicle for continued probing into the basic development problems of Latin America.

APPENDIX A

BIOGRAPHICAL NOTES

MILDRED ADAMS, correspondent for *The Economist* of London and American adviser for *La Revista de Occidente* of Madrid, got her training in journalism at *The New York Times*. A graduate in Spanish and Economics, she was for some years Executive Director of a study project concerned with the history of the Federal Reserve System. She is a member of the Board of Directors of the Foreign Policy Association, and a member of the Instituto de las Españas, and the Hispanic Society. Her books include an economics primer and translated volumes by José Ortega y Gasset and Germán Arciniegas. In private life she is Mrs. W. Houston Kenyon, Jr.

GERMÁN ARCINIEGAS, Colombia's Ambassador to Italy, is an author, educator, and diplomat. During his diversified career he was Editor of *El Tiempo* of Bogotá, Vice Consul in London, Chargé d'Affaires in Buenos Aires, Minister of Education, and Visiting Professor at Columbia University, University of Chicago, University of California, and Mills College. His many published works include *Caribbean, Sea of the New World* (1946), *The State of Latin America* (1952), and *Amerigo and the New World* (1955). He is an Honorary Associate of the National Academy of Arts and Letters.

CHESTER BOWLES was sworn in on December 12, 1961 as Special Representative and Adviser to President Kennedy on African, Asian, and Latin American Affairs. Prior to his White House appointment, Mr. Bowles served as Congressman from the second district of Connecticut and was a member of the House Foreign Affairs Committee from 1958 to 1960. His career in public affairs includes a two-year term as Governor of Connecticut, 1949–1951, and Ambassador to India and Nepal, 1951–1953. He has devoted much of his time to speaking and writing on foreign affairs.

ROBERTO DE OLIVEIRA CAMPOS, Brazilian Ambassador to the United States, entered the diplomatic service in 1939. At the 1944 Bretton Woods Conference he was Adviser to the Brazilian Delegation. From 1946 to 1953 Ambassador Campos acted severally as adviser, economic observer, and alternate representative for Brazil at meetings of various organs and agencies of the United Nations. In 1955 he became Managing Director of the National Bank for Economic Development and in 1958 was elected President. Prior to his present appointment, Ambassador Campos was in charge of Brazil's financial negotiations in Western Europe.

REYNOLD E. CARLSON has been The Ford Foundation's Representative in Brazil since 1960. A graduate of Northwestern University, Dr. Carlson received his Ph.D. from Harvard. During his academic career, he was Professor of Economics at Vanderbilt University, directed the Institute of Brazilian Studies, and taught at Johns Hopkins University. He has also been senior economist in Latin America for the World Bank and served as an economist and consultant on Latin America for the United States Government and the United Nations.

DANIEL COSÍO VILLEGAS, Director of El Colegio de México, is widely known as an educator, economist, and author. During his academic career he was Professor of Law at the National University of Mexico and the Central University of Madrid. He served his Government with distinction as Economic Adviser to the Treasury and Foreign Affairs Ministry of Mexico, and as delegate to the XIII United Nations General Assembly. In 1959 he became President of the United Nations Economic and Social Council. Dr. Cosío is the author of numerous books, the most recent being the *Modern History of Mexico* (5 Vols. 1954–60).

JOSÉ FIGUERES, twice President of Costa Rica (1948–9 and 1953–8), is a man of multiple interests: an economist, a political thinker, and an entrepreneur. He led the revolt in 1948 which defeated the communist-dominated Government of Costa Rica. With his followers he organized the National Liberation Party, planned its program of social reform, and continues as its President. A frequent lecturer at United States and Latin American universities, a prolific writer of articles and essays, and an exponent of Inter-American cooperation, Dr. Figueres has been decorated by eighteen European and Latin American countries.

FRANÇOIS FONTAINE is Director of the Information Bureau for the Common Market, the Steel and Coal Community, and Euratom in France. Beginning his career as a journalist, he later served as an attaché to the Ministry of Foreign Affairs, and in 1947 he became head of Mr. Jean Monnet's Cabinet in charge of the French Modernization and Equipment Plan. He has been associated wtih the European Communities in various official capacities since 1952. Mr. Fontaine wrote *Democracy on Vacation* (1959) an essay on France entitled *The Restrained Nation* (1956).

EDUARDO FREI MONTALVA was elected from Santiago to the Senate of Chile in 1957 and represents the Senate before the Council of Social Security Service. He served a previous term in the Senate in 1949 and was also Minister of Public Works, Transportation and Communication. A graduate of the University of Chile, he returned there as a Professor of Law Legislation. Senator Frei's published works include *Chile Desconocido, La Política y el Espíritu,* and *La Verdad Tiene su Hora,* which was awarded the Literary Prize of 1956.

LINCOLN GORDON, United States Ambassador to Brazil, has held many government posts in the field of economics and international relations. Educated at Harvard and Oxford Universities, he returned to Harvard in 1946 as Professor of Business Administration and Government. He served as Chief of the Mutual Security Agency Mission to the United Kingdom, 1952–55, and, at the same time, Minister of Economic Affairs in the United States Embassy in London. Prior to his present appointment, Ambassador Gordon was Professor of International Economic Relations at Harvard University.

FELIPE HERRERA was elected the first President of the Inter-American Development Bank in 1960. From 1952 to 1958 he served his native Chile as Under-Secretary of Economy, General Manager of the Central Bank of Chile, and Minister of Finance. As Executive Director of the International Monetary Fund, Dr. Herrera represented Argentina, Bolivia, Chile, Ecuador, Paraguay, and Uruguay from 1958 to 1960. He has had extensive experience representing Chile in several capacities at international and inter-American meetings and has written many books and articles related to development and monetary and fiscal policy.

MAX KOHNSTAMM has been President of the European Community Institute for University Studies since 1959. A native of Amsterdam, he was Private Secretary to Queen Wilhelmina, and in 1948 he entered the Netherlands Foreign Office and became Director of European Affairs. He has been associated with the European Community since 1952, serving with the Coal and Steel Community, heading the Diplomatic Mission of the High Authority in London, and acting as special adviser to the President of Euratom. Mr. Kohnstamm is Vice President of the Action Committee for the United States of Europe.

LUIS ALBERTO MONGE, newly appointed Ambassador from Costa Rica to Israel, was a member of the Legislative Assembly from 1958 to 1962. A graduate of the University of Costa Rica, Mr. Monge specialized in social reforms and labor relations and has led the Democratic Movement of Trade Unions in Costa Rica. He is also Secretary-General of the Inter-American Regional Organization of Workers (ORIT) and is Director of the publication, *Combate*.

EGIDIO ORTONA has been Director General of Economic Affairs in the Italian Foreign Ministry since June 1961. He was appointed Ambassador to the United Nations in 1958 and the following year was elected President of the Security Council. After graduating from the University of Torino, Dr. Ortona began his career in 1932, serving in diplomatic posts in Cairo, Johannesburg, and London. From 1944 to 1958 he served as First Secretary and later as Minister-Counsellor in the Italian Embassy in Washington.

LESTER B. PEARSON, leader of Canada's Liberal Party, graduated from the University of Toronto and Oxford University. During his distinguished diplomatic and political career he was Canadian Ambassador to the United States, Secretary of State for External Affairs, and President of the UN General Assembly in 1952–53. He was awarded the 1957 Nobel Peace Prize for his leadership in the United Nations effort to end the British-French-Israeli invasion of Suez. From 1951 to 1958 Mr. Pearson was Chancellor of Victoria University, Toronto. He holds honorary degrees from twenty-five universities, including

Toronto, Yale, Princeton, Ceylon, Columbia, and Harvard. He is the author of *Democracy in World Politics* (1955) and *Diplomacy in the Nuclear Age* (1959); and is presently International Executive Chairman of the Council on World Tensions.

GALO PLAZA, well-known diplomat and expert on agriculture, was President of Ecuador from 1948 to 1952. He holds doctorate degrees from the University of Maryland and Columbia University. During his distinguished career, Dr. Plaza served as Minister of National Defense, Ambassador to the United States, and Delegate to the San Francisco Conference at which the UN Charter was drawn up and signed. In 1958 he was Chairman of the UN Observers Group in Lebanon; in 1960, Chairman of the UN "Advisory" Committee on the Congo. He was a member of the Commission of Experts to study the problems of creating a Latin American common market.

LUIS B. PRIETO F., President of the National Congress of Venezuela and Second Vice President of the National Executive Committee, is well-known as an educator. He holds a Doctorate in Political Science from the Central University of Venezuela, was a Professor of Psychology at the Instituto Pedagogico Nacional, and was the founder and first President of the Venezuelan Federation of Teachers. Dr. Prieto served as Minister of Education and was a member of the Revolutionary Committee of the Government, which was in power from 1945 to 1948. He is the founder of the Democratic Action Party of Venezuela.

DAVID ROCKEFELLER, President of the Chase Manhattan Bank since 1961, is Chairman of the Rockefeller Institute and Vice President of Rockefeller Brothers Fund. With his four brothers he participates in many joint enterprises in the fields of philanthropy and economic development. A graduate of Harvard University, he studied at the London School of Economics and received his doctorate degree in economics from the University of Chicago. Mr. Rockefeller joined the Chase Bank in 1946 and from 1950–52 was responsible for the supervision of the bank's business in Latin America.

MARIO HENRIQUE SIMONSEN, Director of the Department of Economics of the National Confederation of Industry, is a rising young Brazilian economist. He is a Professor of an advanced course for economists at the Getulio Vargas Foundation in Rio de Janeiro and serves as a consultant with "Consultec," the Brazilian Institute of Economics of the Vargas Foundation.

VICTOR L. URQUIDI of Mexico is economic consultant on economic development to the Ministry of Finance and the Bank of Mexico. A graduate of the London School of Economics, he has held positions as research economist with the International Bank for Reconstruction and Development and the UN Economic Commission for Latin America. From 1952 to 1958 he was Director of ECLA's Regional Office in Mexico and responsible for the Central American Economic Integration Program. Mr. Urquidi is the author of numerous articles and books on economics, has been a Fellow of El Colegio Nacional since 1960.

APPENDIX B

LIST OF PARTICIPANTS AT THE BAHIA CONFERENCE

FRAGA, Alberico   Brazil
Rector of the University of Bahia
PEARSON, Lester B.   Canada
Leader of the Liberal Party

VICE-CHAIRMEN

CAMPOS, Roberto de Oliveira Brazil
Ambassador to the United States
GORDON, Lincoln   United States
Ambassador to Brazil
HOFFMAN, Paul G.   United States
Managing Director, United Nations
Special Fund
MAYOBRE, José A.   Venezuela
United Nations Commissioner for
Industrial Development
PLAZA, Galo   Ecuador
Former President of Ecuador

ADVISORY COMMITTEE

*CARRILLO-FLORES, Antonio
Ambassador to the   Mexico
United States
DE SMAELE, Albert   Belgium
Chairman, Belgian Economic Council
HERRERA, Felipe   Chile
President, Inter-American
Development Bank
KATZ, Milton   United States
Director, International Legal Studies,
Harvard Law School

NEHRU, B. K.   India
Ambassador to the United States
ORTONA, Egidio   Italy
Director General, Economic Affairs
Ministry of Foreign Affairs
*PREBISCH, Rául   Argentina
Executive Secretary, Economic
Commission for Latin America
*SANTAMARIA, Carlos Sanz de
Ambassador to the   Colombia
United States
*WATSON, Arthur K. United States
President, IBM World Trade
Corporation

COORDINATOR OF
CONFERENCE REPORTS

CARLSON, Reynold E.
Representative   United States
of The Ford Foundation in Brazil

RAPPORTEURS

ADAMS KENYON, Mildred
Writer and Lecturer   United States
RIOS, José Arthur   Brazil
Coordinator, Social Services of
Guanabara State
URQUIDI, Victor L.   Mexico
Economist, Author and Lecturer

PARTICIPANTS

ABDEL-RAHMAN, Ibrahim Helmi
United Arab Republic

* Members of Advisory Committee not present at Salvador.

Director-General, Institute
of National Planning

AHUMADA, Corvalan, Jorge   Chile
Director, Planning and Development
Center, University of Venezuela

ALBORNOZ, Miguel   Ecuador
United Nations Resident Representative for Technical Assistance Board
and Director of Special Fund Programs in Mexico

ALEXANDER, Robert J.   United
Professor of Economics,   States
Rutgers University

AMACHREE, Godfrey K. J.   Nigeria
United Nations Under-
Secretary in charge of Civilian
Operations in the Congo

ANDRADE, Victor   Bolivia
Ambassador to the United States

ATWATER, Verne S.   United States
The Ford Foundation's Representative for Argentina and Chile

BARBOSA, Raul   Brazil
President, Banco Nordeste

BERTHOIN, Georges   France
Deputy of European Coal and Steel
Community's Ambassador to London

BULLIS, Harry A.   United States
Chairman of the Board of Directors,
Council on World Tensions, Inc.

CLARK, William   United Kingdom
Director, Overseas Development
Institute, Ltd.

CLINCHY, Everett R.   United States
President, Council on World
Tensions, Inc.

COLLADO, Emilio   United States
Vice President, Standard Oil Co.
of New Jersey

DI TELLA, Guido   Argentina
Industrialist and Professor of
Economy, University of Buenos Aires

DRUMMOND, Roscoe   United
Columnist, news   States
analyst and lecturer

FIGUERES, José   Costa Rica
former President of Costa Rica

FRAENKEL, Peter   United States
Program Associate, Latin American
Division of The Ford Foundation

GERMANI, Gino   Argentina
Head of Department of Sociology,
University of Buenos Aires

GORDON, Melvin   United States
Member of Board of Directors,
Council on World Tensions, Inc.

GREATHOUSE, Pat   United States
Vice President of United Auto-
mobile Workers of America

HEISKELL, Andrew   United States
Chairman of the Board of Directors,
TIME, Inc.

HOLMES, John W.   Canada
President, Canadian Institute of
International Affairs

IGNACIO-PINTO, M. Louis
Ambassador to   Dahomey
United Nations

JAGUARIBE de Mattos, Hélio
Sociologist and Lecturer   Brazil
on Political Science

KAMBARA, Tomihiko   Japan
First Secretary, Japanese Embassy,
Brazil

KLABIN, Israel   Brazil
Industrialist and economic advisor

LEITE, Cleantho de Paiva   Brazil
Executive Director for Brazil,
Bolivia and Ecuador of Inter-
American Development Bank

LEVESQUE, Rev. Father Georges-
Henri   Canada
Vice-Chairman, Royal Society of
Canada

LOPES, Lucas   Brazil
Industrialist and Minister of
Transportation and Public Works

MAGALHÃES, Juracy   Brazil
Governor of the State of Bahia

MAY, Stacy   United States
Economist, author and consultant
to Rockefeller Office

MEDINA, Echavarría, José   Spain
Consultant, Economic Commission
for Latin America, Santiago

MONGE, Luis Alberto   Costa Rica
Labor Leader, Member Legislative
Assembly

MOSCOSO, Teodoro   Puerto Rico

United States Coordinator, Alliance for Progress
NORIEGA-MORALES, Manuel   Guatemala
Member, Committee of Nine, Alliance for Progress
NUSEIBEH, Hazem   Jordan
Minister of Foreign Affairs
OAKES, John B.   United States
Editor, Editorial Page of
THE NEW YORK TIMES
PAREJA Diezcanseco, Alfredo   Ecuador
Professor, Latin American Studies, University of Florida
PETER, Georges   France
Chairman, International Tin Council
ROCKEFELLER, David   United States
President, The Chase Manhattan Bank
SALOMON, Irving   United States
Chairman, Executive Committee, World Federation of United Nations Associations
SANCHEZ, Luis Alberto   Peru
Rector, University of San Marcos de Lima
SCHEEL, Walter   Federal Republic of Germany
Minister for Economic Cooperation
SIMONSEN, Mario   Brazil
Henrique, Economist
SLATER, Joseph E.   United States
Associate Director, International Affairs Program, The Ford Foundation
SMITH, Carleton Sprague   United States
Chairman, Academic Advisory Committee, Brazilian Institute, New York University

TANNENBAUM, Frank   United States
Latin American Seminar, Columbia University
TEIXEIRA, Anisio   Brazil
President, National Institute of Pedagogic Studies
TRIGUEIROS, Oswaldo   Brazil
A Director of University of Brasilia
VAN EMBDEN, Nicolas de Groot   Netherlands
Head of Secretary-General's Office, O.E.C.D.
VEKEMANS, Father Roger   Chile
Labor Consultant, Head of Department of Sociology, Catholic University of Chile
WAGLEY, Charles   United States
Director of Institute of Latin American Studies, Columbia University

PARTICIPANTS FROM THE UNIVERSITY OF BAHIA

AZEVEDO, Thales de
Director of the Department of Cultural Affairs
CALMON, Jorge
Professor of American History and School of Philosophy
NOGUEIRA, Adalício
Professor of Roman Law, School of Law
PONDE, Lafayette
Professor of Administrative Law, School of Law
MESQUITA, Renato
Professor of Sociology, School of Philosophy
SAMPAIO, Nelson
Professor of General Theory of the State, School of Law

APPENDIX C

COUNCIL ON WORLD TENSIONS
304 East 42nd Street, New York 17, New York

The Council on World Tensions is a private, non-governmental, and non-partisan organization, directed by leaders in national and international affairs. It conducts high-level studies and international conferences on practical steps toward peace based on better economic and social conditions for all peoples. These projects are carried out in cooperation with universities in different parts of the world.

The Council thus affords opportunities for influential public, business, and university leaders from various continents to work together toward policies for improving situations of tension. It helps to inform public opinion by distributing its publications in cooperation with educational, civic, economic, religious, and communications agencies.

Since 1950 the Council has been aiding education for greater understanding of the changing relationships among peoples of different nations, races, religions, and economic and social systems. It cooperates on programs with national organizations such as the National Education Association and the Junior Chamber International.

Studies of problems within South and Southeast Asia and the Pacific and the relationships of these areas with other regions, in progress during 1963, will lead to a major conference on internal and external factors in development to be held in Southeast Asia in 1964. A conference to be held in Africa is also planned.

INTERNATIONAL EXECUTIVE CHAIRMAN
Lester B. Pearson

INTERNATIONAL CO-CHAIRMEN
Konrad Adenauer
Vijaya Lakshmi Pandit
Carlos P. Romulo
Paul-Henri Spaak
Adlai E. Stevenson

DIRECTORS
Harry A. Bullis, *Chairman*
Leo Model, *Treasurer*
Lansdell K. Christie
Everett R. Clinchy, *President*
Andrew Cordier
Samuel Dretzin
Melvin J. Gordon
Margaret Grant, *Executive Director*
Ernest A. Gross
Anna Rosenberg Hoffman
Paul G. Hoffman
Sidney Maestre
Lester B. Pearson
Charles H. Percy
George Romney
Oscar S. Straus
Arthur K. Watson
Walter H. Wheeler, Jr.